AS IF SILENT AND ABSENT

Learning about female slavery
in egypt, and taking last weeks
gender discussion. Does it
surprise you the value of female
slaves in egypt?

EHUD R. TOLEDANO

As If Silent
and Absent

BONDS OF ENSLAVEMENT IN THE ISLAMIC MIDDLE EAST

YALE UNIVERSITY PRESS   NEW HAVEN & LONDON

Set in Scala types by Binghamton Valley Composition.
Printed in the United States of America.

Library of Congress Cataloging-in-Publication Data
Toledano, Ehud R.
As if silent and absent : bonds of enslavement in the Islamic Middle East / Ehud R. Toledano.
p.   cm.
Includes bibliographical references and index.
ISBN 978-0-300-11461-4 (cloth: alk. paper)
ISBN 978-0-300-12618-1 (pbk.: alk. paper)
1. Slavery—Middle East—History.   I. Title.
HT1316.T645 2007
306.3'620956—dc22   2006036927

A catalogue record for this book is available from the British Library.

The paper in this book meets the guidelines for permanence and durability of the Committee on Production Guidelines for Book Longevity of the Council on Library Resources.
10 9 8 7 6 5 4 3 2 1

For Maya and Iddo Toledano,
my beloved children, now lovely young adults,
for whose presence and love I am forever grateful

CONTENTS

ACKNOWLEDGMENTS

THIS BOOK WAS CONCEIVED in a series of three scholarly formative events. I was first made keenly aware of the need to develop a renewed approach to the study of Ottoman enslavement when preparing for, and then participating in, a workshop organized at Emory University in May 2003 to discuss a "roadmap" for the third volume of the *Cambridge World History of Slavery*. I owe a great deal to the editors, Professors Stanley Engerman and David Eltis, and the other participants for a most stimulating exchange of views. Some of the main ideas in the book were then also tried out on the participants of a conference on the history of the eastern Mediterranean, which took place in Antakya, Turkey, in May 2003. My gratitude goes to the organizers and participants for comments on my paper, which after significant elaboration became Chapter 5 of this book. The seeds sown at Emory and Antakya were further cultivated in a conference entitled "Slavery, Islam, and Diaspora," convened in October 2003 at York University, Toronto, by Professor Paul E. Lovejoy. Again, the convener and his team, especially Behnaz A. Mirzai, Ismael Musah Montana, Yacine Daddi Addoun, and the other participants deserve much credit for comments and discussions around the keynote address I was honored to deliver at the conference. A writing spree came while I was a guest of the Maison Mediteranéene at Aix-en-Provence in June 2003. The director, my friend Professor Robert Ilbert, and his colleagues provided an ideal ambiance for scholarly reflection, and I wish to thank them for their kind and generous hospitality.

My graduate students at Tel Aviv University also deserve honorable mention: Michael Nizri located some missing links at the archives in Istanbul and at other libraries, and Dr. Mira Tzoreff and Doron Sakal helped with references to relevant materials they came upon while doing their own research. At Yale University Press, Christopher Rogers, Eleanor Goldberg, and Mary Pasti were involved in the production of this book; they have always been efficient, helpful, encouraging, and a pleasure to work with.

Last but not least, my deep gratitude goes to three colleagues whose invaluable and insightful comments on the manuscript have greatly improved the final product: Professors Joseph C. Miller, Roger Owen, and Jane Hathaway. The flaws that undoubtedly still remain are entirely my own fault.

NOTE ON TRANSLITERATION AND TERMINOLOGY

OTTOMAN TURKISH WORDS have been transliterated according to modern Turkish standards, and Arabic terms follow the style adopted by the *International Journal of Middle East Studies*. I have deliberately tried to minimize the use of terms in foreign languages unfamiliar to readers of English, and essential terms are explained when they occur in the text for the first time. Turkish and Arabic words usually appear in the singular and are italicized on first appearance, then romanized as they recur; when the plural of such words is required, a romanized "s" is added to them. Responsibility for all translations from Ottoman Turkish and Arabic is mine.

I have usually preferred "enslaved," "enslaved person/s," "enslavement," and "slaver/s" to "slave/s," "slavery," and "slaveholder/s" or "slave owner/s." But when the wording felt somewhat awkward, as in certain compounds or adjectival uses, I used "slave trade," "slave dealer/s," "slave experiences," "slave narratives," and at times "slave voices." However, I did keep the more traditional usage when quoting or paraphrasing sources or scholarly literature. When "slave" is used, often after possessive pronouns, it is usually qualified by "legal" or "lawful."

AS IF SILENT AND ABSENT

Introduction

ENSLAVEMENT OF HUMANS BY OTHER HUMANS was a universal phenomenon. It was not peculiar to any culture, nor did it derive from any specific set of shared social values. This book, therefore, is not about exceptionalism, whether Islamic, Ottoman, Arab, Middle Eastern, or Mediterranean. Human bondage in its various forms existed in almost all known historical societies and cultures. Since biblical times, all monotheistic religions have sanctioned slavery, although they did try to mitigate its harsh realities; other belief systems were not free from various forms of enslavement either. That is why this book is neither about assigning blame nor about absolving from guilt. Something in human nature made slavery possible everywhere, and it took major transformations in our thinking to get rid of it; these came barely a century and a half ago, at an admittedly late stage in our history. This book, then, is all about humanity and its failings, about the struggle and survival of the enslaved, about the universal desire to be free. The stories come from the Ottoman-Islamic world of the eastern Mediterranean basin in the long nineteenth century, but the implications reach far beyond these spaces or these moments in time.

Lamentably, enslavement in non-legal, directly proprietary terms still exists today in many parts of the globe, transmuted into a wide variety of phenomena featuring extreme lack of freedom, exploitation of labor, and oppression of body and mind. But even the previous forms of brutal ownership die hard and, worse, keep resurfacing in both new and old regions, demanding our attention and calling for immediate action. The memory, too, keeps coming back, refusing to let go, informing and bedeviling the present, still guiding political agendas. For Benjamin Zephaniah, African-Caribbean-British radical activist and poet—in this order, as he himself would insist—the heritage of enslavement is very much alive, with all its pain and hurt; it is also inextricably intertwined with the notion of empire, the long-gone British one.

When offered knighthood by Queen Elizabeth in November 2003, Zephaniah turned it down angrily, publishing in *The Guardian* the following lines, which caused quite a public stir:

> Me? I thought, OBE me? Up yours, I thought. I get angry when I hear that word "empire"; *it reminds me of slavery,* it reminds of thousands of years of brutality, it reminds me of how my foremothers were raped and my forefathers brutalised. It is because of this concept of empire that my British education led me to believe that *the history of black people started with slavery and that we were born slaves,* and should therefore be grateful that we were given freedom by our caring white masters. It is because of this idea of empire that *black people like myself don't even know our true names or our true historical culture.* I am not one of those who are obsessed with their roots, and I'm certainly not suffering from a crisis of identity; my obsession is *about the future and the political rights of all people.* Benjamin Zephaniah OBE—no way Mr Blair, no way Mrs Queen. I am profoundly anti-empire . . . I have nothing against her [the Queen] or the royal family. It is the institution of the monarchy that I loathe so very much, the monarchy that *still refuses to apologise for sanctioning slavery.*[1]

For Zephaniah, memory, slavery, identity, culture, and politics are woven into one fabric. Although in these lines there is no demand for

1. Benjamin Zephaniah, "Me? I Thought, OBE Me? Up Yours, I Thought," *The Guardian,* 27 November 2003 (Internet edition available at http://www .guardian.co.uk/arts/features/story/0,11710,1094011,00.html); the emphases are mine.

reparations, a formal apology is strongly demanded, and its absence is seen as an active statement in and of itself. In addition, the enslaved ancestors seem to haunt Zephaniah and impose upon him some imagined demands: that he adopt a political agenda that honors their memory and that he perhaps also avenge their humiliation. As Robin Cohen observes, this position is not unique or unusual. "Despite their subsequent liberation, settlement and citizenship in various countries," African-Caribbean people abroad have a strong sense of "their common history of forcible dispersion through the slave trade."[2] In a poem, this time against black poets accepting "smart big awards and prize money," Zephaniah writes:

> The *ancestors* would *turn in graves*
> Those poor black folk that once were *slaves* would *wonder*
> How our souls were sold
> And *check our strategies*.[3]

But because even old-fashioned enslavement continues to exist in parts of Africa, the Middle East, and other afflicted regions, Zephaniah's stance is less "top-down" than it might otherwise seem. Indeed, he does speak for those who are still being oppressed, although from time to time we manage to hear their silenced voices, too. Thus, for example, we are next introduced to another actor in that saga, this time one with first-hand—rather than remembered—experience of enslavement. The story also raises the question of whether there is in fact a disconnect between *lived* and *remembered* experiences of bondage.

At times, simply changing the dates serves to historicize the particular story, as in one that Nicholas D. Kristof published in the *New York Times* in April 2002:

> Abuk Achian was 6 years old when Arab raiders rampaged
> through her village in southern Sudan, carried her off on
> horseback and turned her into a slave. Ms. Achian, now a
> pretty woman of 18 with ebony skin, is one of many thousands
> of Sudanese women and children who have been kidnapped

2. Robin Cohen, *Global Diasporas: An Introduction*, Seattle: University of Washington Press, 1997: 144.
3. Benjamin Zephaniah, "Bought and Sold," in Benjamin Zephaniah, *Too Black, Too Strong*, London: Bloodaxe Books, 2001; the emphases are mine.

and enslaved over the last 20 years . . . [She] was one of about
30 former slaves whom I met in Sudan (despite the efforts of
the government, which did just about everything it could to
limit my reporting here). Her story is typical: She is a member
of the Dinka tribe, black Africans who are Christians or ani-
mists, while the kidnappers are Baggara, or Muslim Arab
herdsmen.[4]

For all we can imagine, based on extrapolations from archival and
narrative evidence dating back a century and a half, what follows in
Kristof's article is an authentic first-person account of the culture shock
experienced by the enslaved: "I was so scared," she recalled of her first
few weeks in captivity. "I couldn't understand the language that they
spoke, and I was crying. But they beat me until I stopped crying and
started to learn their language." What comes next is more typical of rural
areas in the eastern Mediterranean during the Ottoman period (1516–1918)
and less typical of realities in urban households, but it does give a sense of
the cost of running away: "Her duties were to sleep outside with the
camels, milk them, and make sure they did not run off. Her master beat
her regularly and forbade her to ever talk to other Dinka. Ms. Achian
says she tried to escape once. Her master caught her, tied her hands together and hoisted her by her arms from a tree branch so that her feet
did not touch the ground. Then he flogged her into a bloody mess with
a camel whip, cut her with a knife and let her dangle in the air all night."

The rest is certainly representative of the social adjustment required
of the enslaved and of the way Ottoman societies integrated them:

After a few beatings, she also agreed to become a Muslim and
later underwent the genital cutting that is widespread among
Sudanese Muslims [not common in urban areas of the Empire].
When she was 12 her master sold her to be the bride of a young
man. Initially Ms. Achian was afraid of her husband, but soon
came to love him and had a son with him. "He treated me well,"
she said. "He was a very good man."

Well, perhaps not that good a man. He too was a slave-
raider, and he would periodically go off to attack Dinka villages

4. Nicholas D. Kristof, "A Slave's Journey in Sudan," *New York Times*, 23 April 2002.

and return with new slave children. Ms. Achian said she felt
sorry for the new slaves but never dared complain to her husband. Then her husband was killed on one of these raids, and
Ms. Achian found herself a widow, at age 16. Her parents-in-
law seized her son and beat her when she protested, and so
she left her boy behind and ran off to freedom.

Kristof concludes his account with a discussion of the various political approaches to ending these practices, basically reiterating how
relevant the issue still is in the public arena. Benjamin Zephaniah can
speak of the suffering of his long-gone ancestors and honor their
memory. Kristof can speak for the living Abuk Achian out of respect
for her suffering, dignity, and honor. But are Zephaniah and Achian
connected, or do they inhabit worlds that are as far apart as the spaces
they occupy? I will argue in this book that they and the people whose
voices they embody indeed share the same universe of discourse and
emotive experience. I shall attempt to show that both Zephaniah and
Achian inhabit an experiential space that coheres with the historical
oecumene of enslaved Africans and, by a qualified extension, of enslaved
Circassians in the Ottoman Empire. But they also have characteristics
in common with enslaved people and their descendants in other parts
of the globe.

Indeed, as an ongoing, unresolved problem and as a painful, unrelenting heritage, both *historical* and *present-day* enslavement—as well as
their lingering consequences—bedevil social and political agendas in
many countries. Modern technologies in such fields as biological anthropology and forensic DNA testing are being employed to adduce evidence in the public debate about enslavement and to advance legal cases
in court. Thus, for example, in an editorial entitled "Honoring the Slaves
of New York," published on 4 October 2003, the *New York Times* criti-
cizes the "years of delays and missed deadlines" in closing a sad chapter
in the history of enslaved Africans in New York City by "rebury[ing] the
remains of more than 400 Africans whose graves were accidentally uncovered during the building of a federal office tower in Lower Manhattan
in 1991."

The African Burial Ground originally contained ten thousand to
twenty thousand bodies, and its accidental discovery shattered some of

the myths about New York as a free state, one not afflicted by the practices of the antebellum South. We learn that not only was enslavement used to build the Dutch colony of New Amsterdam, founded in the seventeenth century, but a study of the remains opened a whole Pandora's box. A team of biological anthropologists at Howard University, where the remains were removed in 1993, has shown that enslavement in the North was no less harsh than enslavement in the South. "Of the more than 400 skeletons studied in this project," according to the editorial, "about 40 percent are of children under the age of 15—most of whom died of malnutrition and suffered from diseases like rickets, scurvy and anemia. The environment was so hostile that some anguished mothers ended their children's lives." Thus, the open and reopened wounds of enslavement bleed in the present, instigating demands for reparations yet again. One was launched in London in late March 2004.

"Descendants of black American slaves," the BBC reported then, "are to sue Lloyd's of London for insuring ships used in the [slave] trade."[5] The action was being taken on behalf of ten plaintiffs by a high-profile U.S lawyer. A few quotations from the interview with the lawyer reveal how the past still lives in the minds of many descendants of enslaved Africans scattered in various parts of the world. Edward Fagan said that by underwriting slave ships in the eighteenth and nineteenth centuries, the U.K.'s oldest insurance firm played a key role in the enslavement network. "Lloyd's was one of the spokes in a hub-and-spoke conspiracy," and the company "knew that what they were doing led to the destruction of indigenous populations. They took people, put them on board ships and *wiped out their identities*" (on the use of this cultural argument, see Chapter 5). Fagan further rejected the claim that events were too far in the past, saying that there are "ongoing injuries that these people suffer from. Why is it too far-fetched to say blacks should be entitled to compensation for damages and genocide committed against them, when every other group in the world that has been victimized in this way has been?"

In this case, the American plaintiffs have produced DNA evidence linking them, they say, with ancestors on recorded slave ships which

5. *BBC News*, U.K. Edition (Internet), 29 March 2004; the emphasis further down in this paragraph is mine.

sailed between Africa and the United States. One of them referred to insurance documents in his possession dating back to the time when
Lloyd's of London underwrote the ship his ancestors were on. But the
BBC reported another voice on this issue. A reparations campaigner,
Kofi Klu, argued that reparations were more than just a question of
financial compensation. "Racism," he said, "is the direct product of
historical and contemporary enslavement." The same sentiment was
echoed by the barrister Lincoln Crawford, OBE, a member of the Race
Equality Advisory Panel, who also chaired the Home Office working
party on slavery. Crawford said, "There is no doubt that slavery was
a crime against humanity and for a lot of black people the consequences
of slavery still exist today."

Another, more famous case shows the continuing impact of historical enslavement and present-day discrimination.

In 1998, DNA evidence established the fact that Thomas Jefferson,
third president of the United States, had a sexual relationship with an
enslaved woman named Sally Hemings. Their union produced at least
one child, whose descendants now trace themselves to the Jefferson
family and link their history to the family estate at Monticello, in Virginia. A Jefferson family group established the Monticello Association,
which holds annual reunions at the historical site and also owns and
maintains the graveyard at Monticello.[6] After the Hemings' claim was
established, attempts by some Jefferson descendants to bring them into
the family fold, include them in the reunions, and allow them to be
buried in the estate cemetery were foiled by a solid majority within the
Monticello Association. Racial epithets were hurled at the Hemings, and
they were banned from membership and refused rights of burial in the
graveyard. In one of the association debates, a member said that he had
"no interest in associating with the Hemings descendants in this life—
or in death"; a reference to "their kind" drew loud applause from other
members.

Such incidents and the lingering sentiments they represent led
President George W. Bush to address the issue of enslavement and its
impact on African-American history in a speech he delivered in 2003 on

6. The story described in this paragraph is derived from Lucian K. Truscott IV,
"The Reunion Upon a Hill," *New York Times*, 10 July 2003.

Goree Island, Senegal, where slaving ships left for the Americas.[7] The president's speechwriters managed to touch on almost all the thorny points in the current debate over enslavement: the cruelty and suffering, the culture shock and deprivation, the defiance and resistance, the courage and unrelenting desire to achieve freedom, and the validity of judging the moral standards of a bygone age—all these figure in the speech. In and of itself, the comprehensiveness of the list indicates the significance of past enslavement in present-day politics in the United States and former slaving societies. Many of these issues are no less relevant, however, to the debate on enslavement in the Mediterranean world, where Ottomans, Arabs, and others exploited for centuries the labor of enslaved Africans, Europeans, and northwest Asians. Albeit from a somewhat different perspective, these themes will be discussed in the following chapters.

The "cameras" of our historical exploration will be placed, as much as possible, in the hands of the enslaved, rather than in those of the slavers, where they have rested in most standard documentary accounts. To accomplish this switch in point of view we shall have to deploy a different language and search for a new approach. Enslavement, I shall argue, is a form of patronage relationship, formed and often maintained by coercion but requiring a measure of mutuality and exchange that posits a complex web of reciprocity. Including both enslaved and slaver in a web of reciprocity enables us to move away, at least to a plausible degree, from the common grammar of exploitation, oppression, resistance, and struggle used to portray their relationship. Now the slaver becomes less omnipotent, the enslaved less impotent. Both are actors in that relationship, and each works to maximize advantage and minimize damage. Both parties develop expectations and trust, and when these are disappointed or breached, a sense of betrayal sets in that may lead to action. Action is the stuff of the human stories that unfold in these pages.

---

7. http://www.whitehouse.gov/news/releases/2003/07/20030708-1.html, "Remarks by the President on Goree Island, Senegal," 8 July 2003, 11:47 A.M. (Local).

CHAPTER ONE

Understanding Enslavement as a Human Bond

THE OTTOMAN EMPIRE was the last and greatest Islamic power of the modern era. In many ways, the history of the Middle East between 1516/1517 and 1918 is a chapter in Ottoman history, and Ottoman traces have lingered in the eastern Mediterranean many decades after the demise of the Empire.[1] Some major features of political, social, economic, and cultural life born and developed under the sultans survived well into the twentieth century and arguably are detectable even today. While often viewed in the West as a paragon of conservatism and stagnation, the Ottoman Empire was a complex and fascinating entity through many periods of its long history; it was dynamic and adaptable, pragmatic and resilient, tolerant and accommodating, as the past two decades of intensive research have shown. There were periods in which it resembled its negative image, but an overall account of the teeming and diversified social life under its rule certainly defies that image.

The "long nineteenth century," from the last decades of the eighteenth century to the first two decades of the twentieth, was a period

---

1. For a succinct assessment of the Ottoman heritage, see Albert Hourani, "The Ottoman Background of the Modern Middle East," in Albert Hourani, *The Emergence of the Modern Middle East,* London: Macmillan Press in association with St. Antony's College, Oxford, 1981: 1–18.

of great transformation inside the Ottoman Empire and in its international milieu. To cope with growing European expansionism and intervention, the Ottomans adopted their version of self-evolved, self-styled modernization. Some reform measures were tailored to Ottoman needs; others were resisted and rejected. Through all this, however, the increasing European presence in Ottoman societies became an undeniable reality in the Mediterranean and beyond. As I have argued elsewhere, policies to do with enslavement and the slave trade were among the most striking examples of the Ottoman attempt to resolve and contain European, mainly British, pressure: the Empire prohibited the traffic in Africans in 1856 and had gradually suppressed it by the end of the nineteenth century, whereas enslavement remained legal.[2] In this book we shall see how British representatives in the Empire became—in the eyes of the enslaved—part and parcel of the patronage system.

THE EMPIRE AND THE ENSLAVED

Scattered data and reasonable extrapolations regarding the volume of the slave trade from Africa to the Ottoman Empire yield an estimated number of approximately 16,000 to 18,000 men and women who were being forcibly transported into the Empire each year during much of the nineteenth century.[3] The most reliable estimates for the total volume of

2. See Ehud R. Toledano, *The Ottoman Slave Trade and Its Suppression, 1840–1890*, Princeton: Princeton University Press, 1982.
3. The most reliable works on this are by Ralph Austen, and the numbers cited below are his, from "The 19th Century Islamic Slave Trade from East Africa (Swahili and Red Sea Coasts): A Tentative Census," in William Gervase Clarence-Smith (ed.), *The Economics of the Indian Ocean Slave Trade in the Nineteenth Century*, Special issue of *Slavery and Abolition*, 9/3 (1988): 21–44; and "The Mediterranean Islamic Slave Trade Out of Africa: A Tentative Census," *Slavery and Abolition*, 13/1 (1992): 214–248. See also Thomas M. Rick's thorough consideration in "Slaves and Slave Traders in the Persian Gulf, 18th and 19th Centuries: An Assessment," in Clarence-Smith, *Economics*, 60–70. For Paul E. Lovejoy's higher numbers and criticism of Austen's figures, see Lovejoy, "Commercial Sectors in the Economy of the Nineteenth-Century Central Sudan: The Trans-Saharan Trade and the Desert-Side Salt Trade," *African Economic History*, 13 (1984): 87–95; see also Lovejoy (ed.), *Transformations in Slavery: A History of Slavery in Africa*, Cambridge: Cambridge University Press, 2000: Chapter 7.

coerced migration from Africa into Ottoman territories during the long nineteenth century are Ralph Austen's: from Swahili coasts to the Ottoman Middle East and India—313,000; across the Red Sea and the Gulf of Aden—492,000; into Ottoman Egypt—362,000; and into Ottoman North Africa (Algeria, Tunisia, and Libya)—350,000. If we exclude the numbers going to India, a rough estimate of this mass population movement would amount to more than 1.3 million people. During the middle decades of the nineteenth century, the shrinking Atlantic traffic swelled the number of enslaved Africans coerced into domestic African markets, as well as into Ottoman ones. These figures should have resulted in a fairly noticeable African diaspora into both Turkey and the successor Arab states of the Middle East and North Africa and even into the Balkans.

However, if we look for persons of African descent in these regions, we find only scattered traces. In Turkey, there are African agricultural communities in western Anatolia, in such towns and villages as Torbalı, Söke, Ödemiş, Tire, and Akhisar, with a larger concentration in the province of Aydın near Izmir and in the region of Antalya.[4] Even in the city of Izmir itself, where the largest African population in the Ottoman Empire lived at the end of the nineteenth century, an estimate that it had two thousand African residents in the first half of the twentieth century is disputed as possibly too high. Since African Ottomans and African Turks were considered Muslims and Turks, respectively, they are, in the words of one scholar, "virtually statistically nonexistent in the official demographic records" of the Empire and the later Republic.[5] They are absent from standard reference sources such as yearbooks (salnames), directories (rehbers), and statistically compiled indexes. By comparison, persons of African extraction live in greater numbers in the post-Ottoman Levant, in Saudi Arabia, the Gulf states, and North Africa, among the various Bedouin tribes in desert areas, and in settled villages bordering on desert areas. In Egypt, Africans seem to have a larger presence than elsewhere in the Middle East.

4. Günver Güneş, "Kölelikten Özgürlüğe: İzmir'de Zenciler ve Zenci Folkloru," Toplumsal Tarih, 11/62 (February 1999): 4–10 (statistics in this paragraph are from pp. 4–5 and 9).
5. Esma Durugönül, "The Invisibility of Turks of African Origin and the Construction of Turkish Cultural Identity: The Need for a New Historiography," Journal of Black Studies, 33/3 (January 2003): 289 (based on Güneş, "Kölelikten Özgülüğe," 4).

All in all, the impression is that only a small fraction of the descendants of enslaved Africans are still in the post-Ottoman Mediterranean region. Where have they all gone? Several explanations have been offered, including some plausible ones. The most common is that many enslaved persons perished because they were not used to the cold weather and because they suffered from contagious pulmonary diseases. The life expectancy of survivors was also quite low. In addition, Islamic law and Ottoman social norms sanctioned concubinage and subsequent absorption into the host societies. An enslaved woman impregnated by her owner could not be sold, her offspring were considered free, and she herself was freed upon the death of her master. Thus, the passage of several generations ensured not only the social absorption of such free children but also their visible disappearance.

The enslaved Circassians, Georgians, Greeks, Slavs, and other non-Africans who entered Ottoman territory either voluntarily or by force were absorbed in a similar matter. The enslaved Circassians were mostly refugees driven from the Caucasus by the Russians from the mid-1850s to the mid-1860s. In the Caucasus, Circassian society comprised several tribal units sharing related languages, cultural traditions, and social organization.[6] Under Russian rule, the bonded class of agricultural workers (in Adygé Circassian, *pshitl*) was considered enserfed, but in Ottoman law they were accorded the status of "slave" (Turkish, *köle*). In reality, the pshitl were more the clients-protégés (Arabic, *tabi'*) of each landlord-patron (Adygé Circassian, *pshi*; Ottoman Turkish, *bey*). This status was hereditary, and the offspring of free and bonded marriages inherited the status of the enslaved parent.

Other Circassians and Georgians, largely young women, were brought into the Ottoman Empire by slave dealers for service in urban elite harems. A preference for white women prevailed among male members of the Ottoman imperial elite in the long nineteenth century and even before. Accordingly, agents for the imperial harem and agents of leading households

6. For a brief summary, see Seteney Khalid Shami, *Ethnicity and Leadership: The Circassians in Jordan*, Ann Arbor, Mich.: University Microfilms International, 1985: 17–39, 53–57. The bibliography contains major studies and ethnographic works on Circassian and Caucasus peoples. Shami prefers "caste" to "class" in referring to the agricultural workers.

were instructed to recruit young women among the Circassian and Georgian populations of the Caucasus. These women were trained in the recruiting household and socialized into elite household roles.[7] As the nineteenth century drew to a close, recruitment declined under the growing restrictions imposed on the practice by the Ottoman government, but even the imperial harem and some of the top-ranking officeholders continued to recruit.

Another phenomenon that gradually disappeared, although it was still visible in the nineteenth century, was for households to purchase Circassian, Georgian, Slav, and other light-skinned men and train them to be members of the Ottoman military-administrative elite. These men were known as *kul,* in Arabic *mamluk,* and for centuries formed the backbone of the Ottoman imperial elite. In the first half of the seventeenth century, the monopoly held by the imperial household over the recruitment of kuls was broken, and many heads of elite households, mainly in the provinces but in the capital as well, began to recruit enslaved retainers for their own militias. Well into the nineteenth century, these were known as the kuls of the kuls (Turkish, *kulların kulları*); I will call them kul-type slaves.[8] Because kuls and kul-type recruits were linked to the female cognate phenomenon of harem slavery, I refer to them together as kul/harem slaves. This group comprises one more element: the eunuchs, who were the mediators between the women of elite harems and the male world. At the court, the Chief African Eunuch and his corps of African eunuchs had great influence even as late as the early twentieth century.[9]

There are a few remaining types of unfree labor. First, it should be noted that agricultural enslavement also existed in Egypt during the cotton shortage caused by the American Civil War in the early 1860s. Enslaved Sudanese were carried into the Egyptian countryside to work the cotton fields. The most prevalent form of enslavement in the Empire, however, was domestic service in elite households, which was largely performed

7. Ehud R. Toledano, *Slavery and Abolition in the Ottoman Middle East,* Seattle: University of Washington Press, 1998: 29–41.

8. Ibid., 24–29.

9. Ibid., 41–53. On the Chief Black Eunuch and his connection to Cairo in the eighteenth century, see Jane Hathaway, *The Politics of Households in Ottoman Egypt: The Rise of the Qazdaglis,* Cambridge: Cambridge University Press, 1997: Chapter 8.

by African, Circassian, and Georgian women. Enslaved men performed such menial tasks such as diving for pearls, mining, and occasionally constructing public works. The large variety of functions performed by enslaved persons in Ottoman societies, coupled with the equally varied places of origin from which the enslaved were wrenched, are the subject of considerable research. Rather than thinking of all the types of enslavement as unrelated, we will more fruitfully see them on a *continuum* of varying origins, cultures, functions, and statuses.[10]

By the end of the nineteenth century the size of the enslaved population hovered around 5 percent of the total population. As Madeline Zilfi observes, enslavement was "the practice of a small, privileged minority and as such scarcely reflected the experience of the majority."[11] The overwhelming number of families, she adds, were monogamous and did not own slaves nor employ free servants. Nonetheless, the complexity of the practice makes it necessary to look for an approach that can accommodate its internal contradictions and seeming intractability: high and low status are mixed, honor and shame appear intertwined, even to someone trained in non-Ottoman, non-Islamic forms of enslavement. To better understand the phenomenon we may classify the position of enslaved people according to six main criteria that affected their treatment and fortunes:

- the *tasks the enslaved performed*—whether domestic, agricultural, menial, or kul/harem
- the *stratum of the slaver*—whether a member of an urban elite, a rural notable, a smallhold cultivator, an artisan, or a merchant
- *location*—whether in the core or a peripheral area
- *habitat*—whether urban, village, or nomad
- *gender*—whether male, female, or eunuch
- *ethnicity*—whether African or not

10. A model for understanding Ottoman enslavement is suggested in my article "The Concept of Slavery in Ottoman and Other Muslim Societies: Dichotomy or Continuum?" in Miura Toru and John Edward Philips (eds.), *Slave Elites in the Middle East and Africa: A Comparative Study,* London: Kegan Paul International, 2000: 159–176.
11. Madeline C. Zilfi, "Servants, Slaves, and the Domestic Order in the Ottoman Middle East," *Hawwa,* 2/1 (2004): 29.

The following observations emerge from this matrix:

- Enslaved *domestic* workers in *urban elite households* were better treated than enslaved workers in other settings and predicaments.
- The lower the stratum of the slaver and the *farther from the core* and the *less densely populated* the habitat, the *greater the chances the enslaved* had to receive *bad* treatment.
- The lives of enslaved *Africans* and enslaved *women* were more often than not *harder than the lives of enslaved whites and enslaved men.*

Thus, for example, women in urban elite households—where, arguably, enslavement was the mildest—could be, and not infrequently were, exposed to uncomfortable situations that would be seen today as sexual harassment at best and sexual enslavement at worst.

An initial obstacle to an open and honest treatment of enslavement in Ottoman and other Islamic societies is the "attitude hurdle." Writers about Islamic societies in general have been sensitive—some might say, overly so—to any shred of criticism, be it hedged, balanced, or even implied. The Orientalist tradition, or paradigm, in Middle Eastern studies has been seen, often with good reason, as judgmental, patronizing, moralistic, and deprecating toward Arabs and Muslims, their culture, their religion and belief systems, and their political and economic life. All have been seen as reinforcing negative political attitudes toward contemporary causes espoused by Arabs and Muslims, ultimately marginalizing or even excluding them from the international community.

Too often the debate over the history of enslavement has been suppressed by the reluctance of Arab and Muslim writers to engage in an open discussion with their foreign counterparts about human bondage. Excepting modern Turkish scholarship and a few contributions from scholars in Arab countries, the work produced by Arabs and Muslims has been apologetic and polemical; it has taught us very little about the life of enslaved people in Islamic societies.[12] All the while, various aspects of slavery have been hotly debated and thoroughly researched and analyzed in most non-Islamic societies. There are, however, some indications that the defensive indigenous posture about Islamic enslavement is being remolded.

12. For a discussion of the discourses on slavery in Middle Eastern societies, see Toledano, *Slavery and Abolition,* Chapter 5.

Still, we can hardly fault Arab and Muslim writers who feel that their cultures and values are being constantly scrutinized and who perceive their countries as being politically, and at times militarily, under attack from stronger and richer countries. Threatened by the knowns and unknowns of globalization, many find solace and a sense of security in local culture, in Islamic tradition, and, on the margins, in radical, violent activism. While globlization and the reactions to it in Muslim societies are relatively recent, the defensive attitude regarding enslavement in Islamic societies is at least a century and a half old. It dates back to the early attempts by British abolitionists through their powerful government representatives in Islamic countries, especially in the Ottoman Empire, to persuade local and imperial authorities to suppress the slave trade and abolish slavery.[13]

European criticism of Ottoman slavery elicited a defensive—though complex and differentiated—reaction from Ottoman officials, writers, and intellectuals.[14] By and large, it was seen as an interference that targeted the very foundations of the Ottoman social order, because slavery was an integral part of family and culture. Only in the last quarter of the nineteenth century did local opponents articulate their views in published works, which, at the same time, began to reflect the growing number who criticized enslavement on moral grounds.

In an earlier book I put the main argument that constituted the defensive position in the following words:

> The crux of the Ottoman argument was that slavery in the em-
> pire, as in other Muslim societies, was fundamentally different
> from slavery in the Americas. In the main, it was far milder
> because slaves were not employed on plantations, were well
> treated, were frequently manumitted, and could integrate into
> the slave-owning society. Islamic law, it was further maintained,
> encouraged owners to treat their slaves well, and manumission
> was considered a pious act, for which the believer could expect
> remuneration.[15]

13. For a detailed discussion of these issues, see Toledano, *Slave Trade*.
14. For an analysis of Ottoman attitudes, see Toledano, *Slavery and Abolition*, Chapter 4.
15. Toledano, *Slavery and Abolition*, 15. For an interesting parallel in the attitudes of both Filipino nationalists and American politicians regarding slavery in

On the whole, scholars working on Islamic and non-Islamic slavery tended to accept this view. Following the analytical categories that were developed over decades of research on various types of enslavement, Islamic societies were classified as "societies with slaves" rather than "slave societies." Slavery in these societies was believed to have been milder, better integrated, more open to inclusion, hence its abolition occurred late and never constituted a major political issue. However, perceptions have been changing over the past two decades or so, on the whole becoming more critical, less accepting, perhaps less prepared to tolerate the broader implications of what we may call the good-treatment thesis.

But before we tackle the attitude hurdle confronting us, we must reset the conceptual environment in which we wish to operate. Accordingly, it seems to me absolutely essential to establish that I, at least, and arguably most scholars working in this field, view slavery as a universal phenomenon, not peculiar to any culture nor deriving from any specific set of shared social values. Because human bondage in its various forms existed in almost all known historical societies and cultures, no writer may claim the moral high ground vis-à-vis any culture in this regard.

By leveling the moral playing field, we in no way wish to suspend judgment with regard to enslavement, nor do we advocate an abdication of responsibility. As we strive to understand the social, economic, political, and cultural circumstances in which enslavement was widespread and universally acceptable in historic societies, we also do not shy from condemning it as reprehensible regardless of where and by whom it was practiced. Understanding why enslavement was so natural in so many societies does not lead to condoning it.

I wish to take this argument one step further. Here, as we reconstruct the world that the enslaved inhabited, we shall consider all the options available to slavers and other members of society, recognizing that there were at least three: a person could decide not to own slaves; slavers could choose not to mistreat their slaves; and slavers could manumit their slaves after a set period of service—which in Ottoman society was between seven and ten years.

---

the Philippines, see Michael Salman, *The Embarrassment of Slavery: Controversies over Bondage and Nationalism in the American Colonial Philippines,* Manila: Ateneo de Manila University Press, 2001: 257–259.

These options and others were available to free members in most societies, including Ottoman and Islamic ones. We are not talking about situations in which free labor was unavailable, not even about free labor being less efficient or less economically sensible to use.[16] It was a matter of choice to own slaves, to treat them well or badly, and in due course to manumit them after the recommended period, keep them longer than that, or even resell them after many years of service. Obviously, when there is choice, there is also responsibility, but this was so in many societies throughout history, and no special blame is here being allocated to Ottoman, Arab, or Muslim slavers in particular. As we dispose of that distressing obstacle to proper investigation of slave experiences in the Ottoman Middle East, we may reexamine the argument that Islamic enslavement was so much milder than its counterparts that it perhaps cannot be discussed within one and the same analytic framework.

In this regard, there are two separate but related questions: Was the putatively mild form of Ottoman enslavement practiced throughout the Empire, and did it apply to all types of slaves in society? And, given the great variety of slave types in Ottoman society, do we regard persons within all categories as slaves? More specifically, can we classify as enslaved also persons of the kul/harem stratum? Can we include in the same category the following three well-differentiated groups: the privileged members of the Ottoman imperial elite; the many enslaved domestics; and the agricultural laborers?

My own thinking—and that of others—has evolved over the past two decades. In the early 1980s, when my first work on the suppression of the Ottoman slave trade in the nineteenth century was published, I was keenly aware of the sensitivity of the subject and actively sought not to offend any of my readers. I readily acknowledged the significant differences between Ottoman enslavement and that practiced in the Americas but argued that Ottoman enslavement was not a separate social institution requiring another set of analytic tools to understand. The task was made easier because I was dealing with the slave trade rather than with

16. For a recent assessment of the domestic labor market in the Ottoman Empire, see Zilfi, "Servants, Slaves." The author rightly points out that laudable as Islamic-Ottoman manumission practices were, "they helped guarantee a supply of cheap labor in the form of ex-slaves," a practice affecting mostly women (8).

slavery, and similarities there were virtually undisputable.[17] I ended the book with the following credo: "In this book I have tried to avoid the pitfalls of crude cultural value-judgment without, however, hiding my own convictions. Thus, while rejecting the self-righteousness of much of the writing in the West on Ottoman slavery, this book—in organization, emphasis, language, and even metaphor—was written with the belief that the abolition of *legal* bondage, regardless of mildness or severity, was a positive step toward the still distant goal of true human freedom."[18]

In another book, written in the late 1990s, this time treating Ottoman slavery and abolition, I argued for a more differentiated position regarding the "good-treatment debate."[19] There I used studies by Jay Spaulding on the Ottoman-Egyptian Sudan, Mary Karasch on Brazil, and Claire Robertson and Martin Klein on Africa to point out that even in domestic slavery situations, especially when women were concerned, it would be quite inappropriate to describe their experience of enslavement as mild. The intimacy of home, family, or household did not guarantee good treatment of the enslaved, these studies revealed, and concubinage was a far cry from the ideal depicted by contemporary witnesses and later scholars who used their accounts. A methodologically gendered interpretation of enslaved women's experiences and a tendency to privilege "voices from within" and "bottom-up" views have yielded a rather harsh picture of realities under enslavement, which is incommensurate with the mild version proffered by Muslim and non-Muslim observers.

We now must incorporate into the good-treatment debate yet another and relatively new kind of argument. It comes from Africans who see themselves as heirs to the Africans who were forcibly transported into the Ottoman and Arab Middle East and North Africa. Perhaps best and most powerfully summarized in the *Declaration of the Conference on Arab-Led Slavery of Africans* of February 2003, the argument concerns what I would call the denial of choice and agency. Simply put, the powerful (here, Ottomans and Arabs) stand accused of bestowing on the unwilling powerless (here, enslaved Africans) the questionable benefits

17. Toledano, *Slave Trade*, 3–5.
18. Ibid. 284.
19. Toledano, *Slavery and Abolition*, 14–19.

of their "mild slavery," "good treatment," and "high culture." Thus, among other articles we find in the *Declaration* the following statements:

> WE CONDEMN, in the strongest possible terms, the practice of forced concubinage of enslaved women, and the use of enslaved African women for the purpose of breeding children who become and continue to be property held by Arab masters . . .
>
> WE ACCUSE Arab societies, for the historical and continued taking into slavery of young girls to serve as sex slaves to their masters with no right to marriage unless prescribed by their masters . . .
>
> WE CHARGE the responsible Arab societies of ethnocide of African people through forced cultural Arabization processes.[20]

This is clearly a bottom-up rather than a top-down discourse; it seeks to speak for the absent and the silenced, for those deprived of their agency, unable to act in their own lives. The debate is thereby charged and politicized; the historian is urged to reevaluate the assertions about the mild nature of Islamic slavery. But were slaves indeed as deprived of agency as they are here presumed to have been? When we explore this issue in the following chapters, we shall discover how the enslaved themselves experienced their powerlessness, how they acted to resolve the tangle into which they were brutally thrust, and how they found ways to respond to oppression and abuse.

Before we move on, however, we need to return to the second question within the good-treatment debate, that is, whether the kul/harem class should be included in the category of Ottoman enslavement. Leading Ottomanists have suggested alternative terms to describe the predicament of people in that group, feeling that they cannot properly be lumped together with members of the less privileged groups of domestic and agricultural slaves in Ottoman society. Metin Kunt referred to the kuls as "the sultan's servants," whereas Suraiya Faroqui preferred to call them "servitors."[21] As

20. *Declaration of the Conference on Arab-Led Slavery of Africans*, Sunnyside Park Hotel, Johannesburg, 22 February 2003 (the emphases are mine); see also Güneş, "Kölelikten Özgürlüğe."
21. See Metin Kunt, *The Sultan's Servants: The Transformation of Ottoman Provincial Government, 1550–1650*, New York: Columbia University Press, 1983; Suraiya

against that, in her recent book *Morality Tales,* Leslie Peirce firmly asserts that "the privileges of elite slavery were temporary."[22]

Peirce points out that elite slaves were not allowed to bequeath their wealth—nor status, I would add—to their offspring, and their wealth reverted to the sultan's treasury upon their death (a loophole was available to them through the mechanism of charitable endowment known as *vakıf/waqf*). Just as the sultan "controlled his enslaved servants' religious and cultural identity and their material environment," Peirce argues, he also "controlled their right to life, taking it if they were judged to have violated their bond of servitude." She then defines what in her view is "a paradox at the heart of the Ottoman system—that ordinary subjects enjoyed rights denied to those by whom they were governed. One of their rights was immunity from the sultan's direct power of life and death."

Over the centuries of Ottoman imperial rule, certain aspects of kul servitude were gradually mitigated in practice, but Peirce is certainly correct in her observations. As in my previous works, here, too, my view is that all legally bonded subjects of the sultan should be treated as enslaved persons for the purpose of social analysis. This is an integrated, inclusive position—that is, there was no *difference of kind* between kul/harem slaves and other types of Ottoman slaves, although there certainly were *differences of degree* among them *within* the category of Ottoman slavery.

The good-treatment argument is perhaps best summed up in the often made statement that many slaves were better off—that is, better cared for—than many of the sultan's free subjects, especially in material terms. Many slaves, it is further claimed, would not have traded their position for the uncertainties and vulnerabilities of the free poor and other marginals in Ottoman societies. Human beings, however, are not merely economic beings, and as we will see in the dozens of stories of slave experiences in the following pages, for the most part slaves did not wish to remain enslaved. Regardless of the alleged mildness of Ottoman, and other Islamic, slave experiences, bondage was a condition

Faroqhi, "The Ruling Elite between Politics and 'the Economy,'" in Halil Inalcik and Donald Quataert (eds.), *An Economic and Social History of the Ottoman Empire, 1300–1914,* Cambridge: Cambridge University Press, 1994: 564 ff.

22. Leslie Peirce, *Morality Tales: Law and Gender in the Ottoman Court of Aintab,* Berkeley: University of California Press, 2003; all quotations here and below are from 315.

Paradox .

most enslaved people tried to extricate themselves from. Many went to a great deal of trouble, took enormous risks, and fought against heavy odds to achieve freedom. In so doing, enslaved Ottoman subjects were not different from enslaved persons in any other society, and their efforts deserve to be recognized and appreciated.

Not surprisingly, many of the slavers themselves realized that the enslaved did not warmly embrace enslavement. The very language used in Ottoman government documents and official correspondence reveals that the state and its officeholders knew very well that enslaved persons complained about their situation and that many of them demanded— from both the courts and various government agencies—that effective steps be taken to redress their grievances.[23] Documents even include statements to the effect that the enslaved have a *natural desire for freedom* (*memluklerin tabii olan arzu-yı hüriyetleri*) and actively seek to be liberated.[24] It was common to refer to such requests as demands to be *"rescued/saved* from slavery" (*memlukiyetten tahlisi*), as in a telegram from the governor of Trabzon to the grand vezir sent in 1872.[25] Thus, as the century drew to a close, the rhetoric deployed by the Ottoman state in dealing with enslavement was developing similarities to the discourse on abolition that we find in Western societies.

Perhaps the most striking example of similarity to Western rhetoric is the text of official certificates of manumission issued by the Ottoman government during the last decade and a half of the nineteenth century. These documents contain such phrases as "This manumission [literally, "freedom"] certificate is being handed to [name of person] to clarify that s/he is released from the *bond of slavery* and that henceforth the said per-

---

23. An example of such typical, matter-of-fact references to slave complaints reads: "in places where complaints and claims by slaves have been presented" (*üsera tarafından şekayet ve iddia vukubulan mahallerde*). This one is from BOA/Ayniyat defterleri/1136, Mühacirin mazuliyet ve saireye, 4.2.1867. (BOA, used henceforth, refers to Başbakanlık Osmanlı Arşivi [Republic of Turkey]—specifically, the Prime Ministry's Archives.)

24. "The intention of these [people] to get out of the status of slaves" (*bunların memluk sınfından çıkmak kasdıyla*). These examples are taken from BOA/Ayniyat defterleri/1011, #148, Bab-ı Ali to Umur-ı Adliye ve Mezhebiye Nezareti, 26.4.1879.

25. BOA/Ayniyat defterleri/1136/# 265, Bab-ı Ali to the Mühacirin İdaresi, 24.1.1872.

son will be like all other free persons, so that s/he cannot ever be claimed—by any person or by any means—to be a slave."[26] An Istanbul court stated in October 1890 that granting manumission papers to an enslaved woman would thenceforward give her the benefits from the *"pleasure* [sweetness] *of freedom."* "She will be like other free Muslims, *at liberty to do as she chooses and permitted to live where she desires."* In January 1888 another court, this time in Salonika, also stressed the freedom of movement granted to a freed slave, saying that being set free meant that he could "move to where he wished *without anybody interfering* with that."

All this is in sharp contrast to the defensive rhetoric deployed against the criticism leveled at the Empire by the outside world. It was toward Europe that the mildness and good-treatment discourse was projected in order to deflect the moral arguments of abolitionism, which were seen as seeking to embarrass the Ottomans and, essentially, to deprecate Islamic culture as a whole. Despite a modicum of internal reflection and some self-criticism, this Ottoman posture persisted until the demise of the Empire and even afterward.[27]

A NEW APPROACH TO ENSLAVEMENT

Without claiming to break new theoretical ground, let me put forward some new perspectives on the history of enslavement in the Ottoman Empire, which might have some implications for the study and understanding of enslavement in other societies—both Islamic and outside the world of Islam—with realities similar to or resembling those in the Ottoman case. The contribution of this book to the debate over enslavement consists of three elements:

- an attempt to recast the master-slave dyad in the frame of a slaver-enslaved relationship, which is seen as a form of patronage
- a framework for the interpretation of the individual stories of enslaved persons

26. Documents cited in this section are from FO 198/82/X/M 00518: Certificate of Manumission form, n.d.; Istanbul court decision, 9.10.1890; and Salonika court decision, 30.1.1888 (all emphases in this paragraph are mine). (FO, used henceforth, refers to the British Foreign Office.)
27. For more on this, see Toledano, *Slavery and Abolition,* Chapter 4.

- presentation of the removal of enslaved persons from their homes into Ottoman societies as an instance of coerced migration creating forced diasporas

Taking these together as constituent parts of a unified approach, we can, it is hoped, shed some light on an important aspect of Ottoman social history.

Patronage and Attachment: The Master-Slave Paradigm Revisited

In Ottoman societies, as in many other Islamic and non-Islamic societies, enslavement was one of the "modes of belonging" to a social unit. This notion appears in Ottoman sources as *intisap,* for which I prefer here to use *attachment.* Individuals did not exist in a vacuum, and each one was attached to some sort of a social group. For most of the enslaved in the Ottoman Empire, the unit of attachment was the household. Here, by households we mean the more sociopolitically complex elite urban units, not the family units referred to in demographic and population studies. For other enslaved persons the primary attachment was kin based and usually consisted of the nuclear (or simple) and extended (or joint) family, plus the various structures connecting such units to each other, whether clan, tribe, or other kin-related formation.[28]

People also belonged to other, non-kin groups, often according to the kind of community they lived in. Urban communities were usually divided according to quarters and neighborhoods and classified by trade and guild, as by religion, confession, or ethnic group. Village and pastoralist communities were normally less diversified, but they too were often internally differentiated. Other types of groups that overlapped with those mentioned thus far were spiritual-mystical or *Sufi* orders and *Zar*-practicing associations. Gender played an important role in all of these groups, determining the role of women and reflecting their expe-

28. The most useful introduction to the social structure of Middle Eastern societies is Dale F. Eickelman, *The Middle East and Central Asia: An Anthropological Approach,* 3rd ed., Upper Saddle River, N.J.: Prentice-Hall, 1998. For families and households in Istanbul from the 1880s into the years of the Republic, see Alan Duben and Cem Behar, *Istanbul Households: Marriage, Family, and Fertility, 1880–1940,* Cambridge: Cambridge University Press, 1991.

rience of the various *modes d'appartenance*. Individuals could belong to a number of groups, constantly negotiating the various roles and statuses they were assigned in each.

For example, a person could belong to the tribal kin group he or she was born into, the quarter in town he or she resided in, the guild that was formed by members of his or her trade, and the Sufi order of his or her choice. An enslaved person could belong to a nuclear family if he or she managed to form one, to the slaveholding household into which he or she was purchased, and to a Zar-practicing association if one was available in the neighborhood. These multiple attachments did not necessarily entail for the individual a conflict of loyalties, nor did they have to create cognitive dissonance. More often than not, these sets of affiliations complemented and reinforced one another, together constructing the person's identity, indeed, set of identities. Properly socialized and—in the case of the enslaved—resocialized individuals were skillful enough in negotiating these multiple attachments.

Nonetheless, it is important to stress that the enslaved identity constructed by many slaves was not all consuming but rather enabled a view of Self that transcended the confines of enslavement. This was not unique to enslaved Ottomans but was true of slaves in the Viceroyalty of Nueva Granada from the late eighteenth century, as Renée Soulodre-La France points out. She rightly notes that this was manifest in their ability to deploy a broad range of strategies "from outright rebellion, to flight, to self-manumission, to knowledgeable manipulation of the legal system, to accommodation within that system."[29] In one of the court cases she cites, an enslaved person named Pioquinto Contreras struggled to get what he believed he deserved—the right to rest and convenient working conditions at an advanced age. Indeed, his struggle showed that his identity as a human being went beyond the bounds imposed by his enslavement.

During the seventeenth and eighteenth centuries, the household emerged as the basic unit of belonging or attachment throughout Ottoman lands. Although households surely existed before that period, they came to play a distinct role in Ottoman societies as a result of the

29. Renée Soulodre-La France, "Socially Not So Dead! Slave Identities in Bourbon Nueva Granada," *Colonial Latin American Review*, 10/1 (June 2001): 87.

large-scale transformation that took place in the Empire beginning at the end of the sixteenth century. We need not go into the various factors that caused the transformation, as they have been amply discussed in the literature.[30] Suffice it here to note that a two-fold process of *localization* and *Ottomanization* was taking place in the provinces, producing Ottoman-Local elites throughout the Empire.[31] The Ottoman imperial elite was becoming less mobile, with posts being assigned within limited regions, so specialization according to the needs of specific provincial clusters was developing within the military and the bureaucracy. Members of the imperial elite developed strong ties to the local economy, society, and culture and linked their and their children's future to one province, often to one city. At the same time, local elites—urban and rural notables,

30. The main contributors to the debate over the transformation of the Empire's governance in that period are Huri Islamoğlu and Çağlar Keyder, "Agenda for Ottoman History," in Huri Islamoğlu-Inan (ed.), *The Ottoman Empire and the World Economy*, Cambridge: Cambridge University Press, 1987: 42–62; Roger Owen, *The Middle East and the World Economy, 1800–1914*, rev. ed., London: I. B. Tauris, 1993: 1–23; Kunt, *All the Sultan's Servants*; Faroqhi, "Ruling Elite," 545–575 (especially 552–556); Rifaat Ali Abou-El-Haj, *Formation of the Modern State : The Ottoman Empire, Sixteenth to Eighteenth Centuries*, Albany: State University of New York Press, 1991; Hathaway, *Politics of Households:* 1, 14, 24 (and throughout the book); Hathaway, *A Tale of Two Factions: Myth, Memory, and Identity in Ottoman Egypt and Yemen*, Albany: State University of New York, 2003: 4–6; and Oktay Özel, "Population Changes in Ottoman Anatolia during the 16th and 17th Centuries: The 'Demographic Crisis' Reconsidered," *International Journal of Middle East Studies (IJMES)*, 36/2 (May 2004): 183–205, on demographic and economic pressures during the sixteenth and seventeenth centuries. This debate has helped to revise the Decline Paradigm, which is now virtually defunct in Ottomanist discourse, though unfortunately still quite alive outside the field of Middle East studies and even to some extent within sections thereof.

31. The arguments put forth in the following paragraphs are fully developed in my forthcoming book but in part have already been published in two articles: Toledano, "The Emergence of Ottoman-Local Elites (1700–1800): A Framework for Research," in I. Pappé and M. Ma'oz (eds.), *Middle Eastern Politics and Ideas: A History from Within*, London: Tauris Academic Studies, 1997: 145–162; Ehud R. Toledano, "Social and Economic Change in the 'Long Nineteenth Century,'" in Martin Daly (ed.), *The Cambridge History of Egypt*, vol. 2, Cambridge: Cambridge University Press, 1998: 252–284.

ulema,[32] and merchants—were seeking to become part of the imperial administration, trying to attain government offices, and being Ottomanized in the process. The localizing imperial elite and the Ottomanizing local elites gradually merged into Ottoman-Local elites, which better served the interests of both sides.

Of major importance in this process was the household, or, rather more specifically in our case, the Ottoman-Local household, which served as the social, economic, political, and even cultural unit that facilitated and promoted Ottoman-Local integration. In the seventeenth century, households were being created around leading officeholders in the bureaucracy and within the military. While forming initially around the nuclear and extended family of the founder, from the outset they relied on patronage relationships between the head of the household and a broad array of clients. The essential component of any household was the founder's retainers, who were a sort of militia force, often small and armed, who protected the interests of the household. A concomitant component was the producers of the household wealth, the agricultural laborers and manufacturers of marketable goods, who enabled its expansion through recruitment and networking. Marriage among the various households was another essential element for forming inter-household alliances to promote common causes and take over income-producing economic assets. Conjugal arrangements provided the sociopolitical cement that bonded household coalitions, or factions, as they were often called, and made networking possible. Though essentially a constructed notion, households also had a physical dimension, being located in estates, often one or several complexes that housed dozens of individuals, hundreds in the larger ones, who performed a wide variety of functions including command and control, enforcement, financial management, service, and trade.

32. *Ulema* is used in this book to describe the various groups of men who were trained in the Islamic school system (*medreses*) to perform government jobs in the judiciary, the lower-education system, the medrese (quasi-academic) world, the administration of vakıf endowments, and the mosques (as prayer leaders and preachers). The ulema have too often been depicted as a homogeneous group acting in concert and sharing common interests, but they were in fact a quite diversified group with often conflicting links to the state and other groups in society.

Household heads vied for resources and coalesced locally, usually in a provincial town where the local governor resided, but they soon realized that it was essential to build a network that would transcend subdistrict, district, and even provincial bounds. Truly successful household coalitions had to be connected to the imperial capital, where officeholders were consolidating their patronage networks through the new-type household. In the seventeenth century, the crucial stepping-stone toward household consolidation—that is, its social reproduction—was the ability to survive the founder's demise, to entrench a multigenerational structure. Until the latter part of the century, many households disintegrated when the founder died, leaving the provincial scene to new households and new factions. Gradually some households and some factions proved more resilient, better adapted to the changing circumstances at the center and in the provinces, and more capable of sustaining the incessant competition over resources. By the end of the first quarter of the eighteenth century, in provinces throughout the Empire, a faction of households emerged as hegemonic, securing for its leader and his lieutenants nearly full control of the body politic and the economy. The main offices of state, hence also access to and appropriation of the main income-generating assets, fell into the hands of members of that household.

All this occurred in a world of intense political struggles that were led and directed—through active networking and by skillful deployment of balancing acts—by members of the imperial and Ottoman-Local elites: men and women, kul/harem and freeborn, in Istanbul and in the provinces. Among the most famous of these households let me mention the Kazdağlıs of Egypt, the Eyübizades of Iraq (mainly in Baghdad and Basra), the Azms of Syria, the Husaynis of Tunis, and the Karamanlıs of Libya. In some cases, hegemonic households turned into local dynasties in the nineteenth century (Egypt, Tunisia); in other cases, the *Tanzimat*-state—the Ottoman state during the Tanzimat reforms (1830s–1880s)—removed them and took their place (Syria, Iraq).[33] Ottoman political culture was heavily influenced by patterns that evolved during the last two and a half centuries of imperial rule and left their mark on political interaction in the successor states of the

33. The nature of the Tanzimat-state will be further defined in Chapter 3.

Middle East for decades after the Empire's demise. The strong link between political and economic interaction, the belief in diversification
through placement of family members in competing networks to minimize risk and increase security, the overwhelming impact of patronage
politics, the lingering effect of "grandee families," and the presence of
both formal and informal dynastic orders are some of the salient features that the Ottoman system bequeathed to modern Middle Eastern
and North African societies.

For our purposes here, it is important to examine the ways in which
households recruited and socialized new members. The purchase of enslaved persons for various roles was one of the four most important
channels of recruitment to imperial-center and Ottoman-Local households. The other three modes of recruitment-cum-bonding to a household were biological-kin relationships, marriage, and the voluntary offer
of loyalty and services in return for patronage. Less prevalent were adoption and suckling relationships (made by attaching wet nurses and their
families to the household), but the sources occasionally do mention
them, too. Bonding ensured that loyalty and patronage would flow from
top to bottom and from the bottom up in households across Ottoman societies, linking people from various elites to non-elite groups and individuals. Society was cohesively undergirded both vertically (within a
household) and horizontally (alliances among households). Not infrequently, individuals were bonded to a household through more than one
of these ties, as, for example, when the purchased kul-type retainer of
the household head was also married to his daughter. Attachment to a
household gave an individual protection, employment, and social status.
Not less significantly, it gave household members (*kapı halkı*) a sense
of belonging and an identity, both social and political.

Unattached subjects of the sultan were marginalized in Ottoman societies. Marginalization meant exposure to danger, both physical and
economic. People who did not belong to a household, nor had any
other form of affiliation—residential, guild, communal (religious, Sufi,
ethnic)—were in a way cut loose from society. They were identity-less,
anonymous to the rest of society, that is, to those who were blissfully attached to a household or another social unit. When moving in a village
or town somewhere in the vast domains of the sultan, unattached persons were conspicuous to the rest of the people, who recognized each

other by face and name or by clothes and appearance.[34] The anonymity of unattached persons marked them out as "strangers" (Turkish singular, *garip;* Arabic, *gharib*) and raised suspicion and mistrust.[35] They had to fend for themselves and their dependents, often banding together to help each other.

Ottoman law, like most other legal systems, criminalized the behavior of unattached individuals and the groups they formed on the margins of society. Loitering, prostitution, disturbing the neat urban order by their very presence, seeking shelter in public spaces, and trespassing were some of the things such people were forced to do, for which they constantly ran the risk of attracting the attention of law-enforcement agents. The state's failure to successfully socialize, integrate, or care for the down-and-out produced the kind of actions that any official authority dreads: from pilfering to armed robbery in cities and towns, from produce stealing to brigandry by roaming bands of highway outlaws in the country. While recognizing that it needed to address the problem, the Ottoman state was usually reluctant to use bare force, but when pushed, it moved vigorously to suppress insubordination.

For the enslaved population in the Empire, social attachment was crucial, perhaps more so than to any other group. This was because enslaved persons were essentially kinless.[36] Except for enserfed Circassians who lived with their families on their landlord's estate, all other types of bonded persons lost their kin ties with enslavement. Kul/harem slavery even made kin loss into a major feature in the ideology of the institution. The young men—and, by extension, the young women—who were recruited into the sultan's elite military-administrative corps were sup-

34. On recognition of this sort, see Nora Şeni, "Ville Ottomane et représentation du corps féminin," *Les temps modernes,* July–August 1984: 66–95; and Şeni, "Fashion and Women's Clothing in the Satirical Press of Istanbul at the End of the 19th Century," in S. Tekeli (ed.), *Women in Modern Turkish Society,* London: Zed Books, 1994: 25–45.
35. On anonymity and strangers in Ottoman Cairo in the nineteenth century, see Ehud R. Toledano, *State and Society in Mid-Nineteenth-Century Egypt,* Cambridge: Cambridge University Press, 1990: 200–205.
36. On kinlessness, see Orlando Patterson, *Slavery and Social Death,* Cambridge: Harvard University Press, 1982: 334–342 My comments on this debate are in Toledano, *Slavery and Abolition,* 155–168.

posed to substitute their loyalty to the sovereign for loyalty to their parents. But sometime in the seventeenth century, the monopoly of the imperial kapı (household) was broken, and high officeholders, themselves kuls, were allowed to recruit kul-type retainers, the kuls of the kuls.

First the sultan and later also his senior kuls possessed the loyalty and affection of the enslaved recruits—kuls, harem women, and eunuchs. In theory, severed from their original kin group, these enslaved members of the imperial elite were to acquire new kin—sometimes erroneously called fictive kin—through bonding with their new patrons, high officeholders at the center and in the provinces, whose household folk they became. In fact, research has shown that it was not unusual for kul/harem slaves to maintain their kin ties back home, although the idea and practice of these newly acquired kin relationships remained a major component of the Ottoman system of government.[37] However, with the entry of non-kuls into the army and bureaucracy early on, the pool of recruits was greatly diluted and compromised vis-à-vis the ideal type. Dilution increased during the first decades of the seventeenth century, after the demise of the state-run, periodic recruitment campaigns known as the *devşirme*.

But *reattachment* was no less important to enslaved Africans, who were brutally detached from their kin groups on the continent and transplanted into an alien milieu, socially and culturally so different from the environment they had grown up in. Bonding with slavers was never easy, but it was smoother for those who served as domestics in urban households, more difficult for menial workers in mines and quarries, pearl dhows, and crop fields. When successfully achieved, attachment to a household partially compensated the enslaved for the loss of kin back home, and not infrequently these men and women were accepted into the slaver's family. We have already noted the significance of naming, which was part of a process of recreating the enslaved person's new identity, often with the intention of wiping out the older identity. Past identities of the enslaved were invariably considered uncivilized, seriously deficient

37. See, for example, the interesting case of Ottoman-Egyptian kuls of Georgian origin in the eighteenth century in Daniel Crecelius and Gotcha Djaparidze, "Relations of the Georgian Mamluks of Egypt with Their Homeland in the Last Decades of the Eighteenth Century," *Journal of the Economic and Social History of the Orient*, 45/3 (2002): 320–341.

in religious terms (because non-Islamic), and generally "primitive." Since Chapter 5 will deal extensively with the implications of such attitudes to the cultural integration of enslaved Africans and Circassians, suffice it here to note that in light of such views, reattachment was a complex process, fraught with many hurdles and pitfalls.

Manumission was not a straightforward, smooth process either. Whereas emancipation was what many of the enslaved yearned for, and freedom was certainly a much coveted status, the passage from enslavement to freedom also meant severance of the hard-earned bond that the enslaved had managed to forge with slavers and other household members. By losing their acquired attachment, freed persons risked social marginalization, which entailed exposure to the kinds of hazards mentioned above. Manumission, like resale, also threatened to detach the enslaved from their newly formed attachments, although resale at least offered a chance of another reattachment and effectively barred the option of renewed kinlessness. Things were better for enslaved persons who were permitted to form families while still in bondage. This was not very common for domestic slaves, but it did occur. Manumitted concubines (ümmüveleds) were in a different position, having had at least one child with the deceased slaver and to some extent enjoying the chance of a continued relationship with his extended family, despite the ever-present competition and jealousy in the harem. Among the enserfed Circassians, however, families were more the norm than otherwise, and kinlessness was not a serious threat, if the family could prevent being split up by sale outside the landlord's (bey's) estate.

Regarding the master-slave dyad, which I shall hereafter refer to as the *slaver-enslaved relationship*, a few comments are in order. Enslavement is rightly considered to be the most extreme form of domination. From time to time we shall revisit the question of other, occasionally harsh forms of coerced denial of freedom, like that imposed on incarcerated individuals or indentured workers. However, even in its mild forms, enslavement seems to remain such a stark instance of deprivation and coercion that it stands apart from other phenomena of "unfreedom." What is perhaps sometimes hard to grasp, or even simply to realize, is that even with enslavement, the slaver's capacity to extract labor is not unlimited, nor is the enslaved person's powerlessness total and absolute.

A better understanding of enslavement can be gained only if we conceive of it as *an involuntary relationship of mutual dependence between two quite unequal partners*. Within this broad definition, applied to Ottoman enslavement, there were certainly cases in which enslaved persons had little impact on their lives, just as there were other situations in which they had a great deal of influence on slavers. In all cases, enslaved persons' ability to stand their ground in the relationship depended on the extent to which they could withhold their labor to achieve what they saw as minimal requirements. In other words, their agency depended on denial of services, whether in the fields, the mines, or the household—the last including sexual services and rearing and nurturing children, in addition to the rest of the domestic package.

We might go somewhat further in defining the slaver-enslaved relationship as containing a component of an unwritten pact, which was personal, protective, remunerative, and emotional. In both household and field, fishery and quarry, but to varying degrees, the *bond* formed between the two was akin to a family bond, implicit to which was trust. It is therefore appropriate to introduce the notion of betrayal by one partner or the other when the relationship failed or broke down. When the line was breached by the slaver's abuse, enslaved persons resorted to absconding or, in more extreme cases, to acts of revenge and desperation that were criminalized by the state. When the state itself, or a foreign agent, assumed the role of patron in a relationship with the enslaved, the same sense of betrayal occurred when expectations were not met. At the same time, enslaved persons tried to compensate for what the slaver-enslaved relationship could not provide; they coped with the sense of isolation, at times of alienation, by resorting to *Zar-Bori* healing and other culture-mediated devices.

These responses to the failure of the slaver-enslaved relationship were mostly, though not exclusively, the domain of non-kul/harem slaves. The enslaved elite officeholders could leverage their position vis-à-vis the sultan and his administration in other ways, too. They had no incentive to opt out of the system, that is, abscond, but instead tried to improve their lot by showing efficiency and loyalty. At the same time, they often worked to increase their own personal and household wealth in order to reduce the risks that came with the privilege of holding high office in the sultan's service. Good performance increased their value to the sovereign and within his administration, which reduced substantially the hazards they ran. At times, and under various circumstances, the system, or sections thereof, did not always function rationally, allowing arbitrary decisions to sometimes bring down diligent, talented, and loyal kuls. But the vagaries of Ottoman power politics lie outside the scope of this book.

Another Way to Read the Sources

The main sources for studying Ottoman enslavement are Ottoman state and private records, especially Şeriat and Nizami (new administrative) courts. Relevant records of state correspondence are deposited at both central and local-provincial government archives. Unfortunately, there are only a few slave narratives, which increases the difficulty in recovering voices of the enslaved in Ottoman and post-Ottoman societies. European diplomatic records, mainly consular reports, have been extensively used to fill the gaps, but they can provide only some missing links given their removed nature. In all these, I focused on locating the personal stories of individuals strewn in a variety of records, especially any that provided the most promising ethnographic "thick description." An ongoing dialogue with the stories soon made it necessary to devise a method for assessing their significance and studying them as historical evidence.

A straightforward approach to the available sources is likely to yield the following observation: Whereas slaves appear often enough in various kinds of state and court records, both Ottoman and European, their statements are fragmented, distanced by "layers of mediation" that separate the actual testimony from the record, and insufficient for compiling a satisfactory narrative.[38] Rather than resign ourselves to that pessimistic outlook, I suggest that we adopt a more flexible approach to the interpretation of the available sources. The evidence we actually possess, I argue, can and should form the basis of a viable and credible reconstruction of tentative realities.[39] I shall refer to the patchwork required by

38. I borrowed the quoted phrase from Kathryn Joy McKnight, whose approach bears some resemblance to mine (" 'En su tierra lo aprendió': An African Curandero's Defense before the Cartagena Inquisition," Colonial Latin American Review, 12/1 [June 2003]: 63–85). Similarities in approach are also apparent in the work of Soulodre-La France, for example, in her "Socially Not So Dead!"

39. Though differently framed and formulated here, this approach has common properties with recent studies that are based on similar source materials: Madeline C. Zilfi, "Goods in the Mahalle: Distributional Encounters in

this approach alternatively as "voice recovery" and "experience recon-struction." The historian's craft in this case means filling holes by re-sorting to the *knowable* and *verifiable* social and cultural context, bridging gaps by carefully allowing a *measured* use of the *educated imagination* that, for the historian, brings to life people and communities long gone. For this to work, both the historian and the readers must be comfortable with a reasonable amount of speculation.

We first need to modify our sense of the term "voice." To create a working space for our project, we must extend the notion of voice beyond mere utterances, verbal statements, and speech. Given the paucity of first-person accounts by enslaved Ottomans, we shall try to gauge voice from action. "Actions speak louder than words" will be an essential motto and concept in our working space. Whereas the evidence is limited with regard to what slaves said, it is abundant with regard to what they did and how they acted in various situations. In our process of experience recon-struction, action and intention are almost inseparable. We shall first try to establish what enslaved individuals did, but immediately ask the ques-tions What did they intend by so acting? What did they want to achieve by their deeds? Since actions are not always intended and intentions are not always followed by corresponding actions, we shall try to weigh all the op-tions available to a specific enslaved person at the time of his or her ac-tion, look at the choices made, and attempt to assess the motives. When several options are reasonable, we shall try to rank them by likelihood and point to the implications of each likely option.

In our approach, action will include both commission and omis-sion—that is, not only what the enslaved did but also what they did not do, whether by choice or because of various constraints. Thus, we ask questions that enable us to map the range of expectations an enslaved

Eighteenth-Century Istanbul," in Donald Quataert (ed.), *Consumption Studies and the History of the Ottoman Empire, 1550–1922: An Introduction,* Albany: State University of New York Press, 2000: 289–311; Peirce, *Morality Tales;* and Iris Agmon, *Family and Court: Legal Culture and Modernity in Late Ottoman Pales-tine,* Syracuse: Syracuse University Press, 2005. Paul Lovejoy also senses that this type of microhistorical work is a promising venture: "The innovative direc-tion of the research and analysis is towards *following individual Muslims along their itineraries of slavery*" (Paul E. Lovejoy [ed.], *Slavery on the Frontiers of Islam,* Princeton, N.J.: Markus Wiener, 2004: Chapter 1); the emphases are mine.

person could have constructed in specific circumstances, build a bank of available options, and consider the options of which the person could have been aware or unaware at the time of action or non-action. To be able to offer credible scenarios—both on the basis of the available evidence and by filling the existing gaps—we need to reconstruct the social and cultural environment in which these life stories were unfolding. Although quantitative and statistically acceptable studies in this area are relatively rare, qualitative, in-depth, thick-description-type work is fairly common. We now possess significant contributions by Ottomanists that help most of us feel comfortable with the economic, social, and cultural environment of our research. The excellent studies of the physical surroundings, material culture, social conditions, and economic and political realities make it possible to embed most of the enslaved life-stories in their appropriate urban, rural, or pastoral settings.

For example, we shall examine various stories about enslaved persons who ran away from slavers, we shall glean the circumstances from the evidence, and then we shall weigh the options and ask: Why did that particular enslaved person choose to abscond? What were his or her motives? What were the risks taken? Did running away constitute a social statement? Did it demonstrate agency? When we later discuss criminal cases in which enslaved people were implicated, we shall ask: Why did the offender choose to commit arson, theft, or murder? Who were the intended or unintended victims of the crime? Did the crime make sense—that is, were cause and effect factored in, or was it an act of whim, committed in a rage or out of despair, or was it committed to make a statement rather than to achieve a concrete goal? These and other considerations will be woven into the story to fill the gaps in the records and enable us to assess how slaves in Ottoman societies experienced their predicament and coped with it.

For this kind of puzzle work, social historians will always need to use their imagination, albeit with due circumspection, to travel the distance between their own time and space and those inhabited by the people they study—in our case, the enslaved persons who lived in the Ottoman Empire during the long nineteenth century. We need constantly to move between carefully reading the texts, which we need to do with wide-open and critical eyes, and imagining the actual lives of the women and men with whom we deal, for which we often need to close our eyes.

Constructing the Other requires doing both simultaneously, especially when the Other is removed from our world in many respects: not just time and space (for those who do not live in the Middle East) but also class, culture, ethnicity (for those not African or coming from the Caucasus), and often gender. But my own feeling is that human empathy can cross all these boundaries given the willingness to engage any Other and see him or her first and foremost as human, with all that this entails emotionally, psychologically, and materially.

Finally in this brief methodological introduction, let me say that the nature of this inquiry and the desire to fully engage the reader in it have required me to deploy a somewhat mixed array of narrative techniques. In drawing attention to this aspect, I found Richard Price's address to the Opening Plenary of the American Historical Association meeting in January 2001 both helpful and instructive.[40] With the growing conversion of history and anthropology in recent years, Price's observations, appropriately addressed to a professional gathering of historians, examine the symbiosis of content and form, of historical research and style of writing, of the story and the devices deployed to represent it. Surveying the changes that took place in the presentation of ethnographic research over the past several decades, he traces the move from what Jim Boon described as the "stylistic taboo on authorial viewpoint" and a rather structured narrative form, through the declaration that "anthropology had not only a politics but also a poetics," to Price's own need to match "theoretical concerns about the politics of representation with practical solutions involving the poetics of representation."

For Richard Price, the need to mix theory, practice, and poetics yields the argument that "different historical or ethnographic situations lend themselves to different literary forms (and vice-versa), and that the ethnographer or historian should now face each society or period—or for that matter each potential book—in a new and newly problematic way, searching out or even inventing a literary form that does not come pre-selected or ready-made, in order to effectively evoke that particular society, or that particular historical moment." Far from presumptuously claiming

40. The address, delivered in Boston on 4 January 2001, is reproduced in Richard Price, "Invitation to Historians: Practices of Historical Narrative," *Rethinking History*, 5:3 (2001): 357–365.

that innovative narrative strategies are being deployed in this book, I think that the need to recover slave experiences requires bending—within reason—some of the conventions of historical narrative. Ethnographers, one of Price's reviewers argues, are faced with the challenge of reconciling the "complicated relationship of fact to fiction, truth to fantasy, past to present, and fieldwork to memory."[41] Historians confront the same task as they strive at once to recover the past and ruminate on it, to use the words of the same reviewer.

While adhering, *grosso modo,* to the classical structures of voice and time, I shall stress the different narrative perspectives and occasionally digress from the time axis of conventional historical narratives. I may occasionally allow myself a modicum of poetic license as we try, author and reader, to enter the minds of enslaved people and slavers in nineteenth-century Ottoman societies. To be effective, Clifford Geertz argued, ethnography "would seem to involve owning up to the fact that, like quantum mechanics or the Italian opera, it is a work of the imagination."[42] Although historians have been less willing to acknowledge their use of imagination, it does not seem less applicable to their work, especially when it involves recovering human experience, which requires the ability to empathize beyond the constraints of time, space, and social categories. We, too, need to imagine ourselves in someone else's predicament, and that includes imagining their living conditions, personal interactions, pains, joys, and aspirations. Far from suppressing the historian's authorial voice, we here acknowledge, legitimate, and welcome its presence.

The Slave Trade as "Coerced Migration"

Let us briefly return to the speech President Bush delivered on Goree Island, Senegal, at the departure point of slaving ships, on 8 July 2003.[43] "At this place," he said, "liberty and life were stolen and sold." He then made the point, which accords with one of the main arguments of our book, that the forced movement of enslaved persons was "one of the

41. Ibid., 359.
42. Clifford Geertz, *Works and Lives: The Anthropologist as Author,* Stanford: Stanford University Press, 1988: 149.
43. http://www.whitehouse.gov/news/releases/2003/07/20030708-1.html, "Remarks by the President on Goree Island, Senegal," 8 July 2003, 11:47 A.M. (Local).

largest *migrations* of history" and also one of its "greatest crimes." Indeed, a number of important social and cultural insights concerning enslaved Africans and Circassians in the Ottoman Empire can be gained by examining their forced transportation as a type of migration. Even more can be learned by linking that to the study of diasporas, a study that has come into vogue during the past decade or so.

Immigration and emigration in the Ottoman Middle East and North Africa have not been unusual. In a region still supporting large nomadic-pastoralist communities of various ethnicities—Turcoman and Bedouins immediately come to mind—inbound and outbound movements of people have been a common feature of history. People moved in and out both as groups and as individuals. Conquering, retreating, or passing armies; tribal migrations across the deserts, plains, and plateaus; pilgrims and traders coming alone or with their families, staying or going back; missionaries, roaming dervishes, aspiring *santons*—all brought with them their languages, religions, cultures, interacted with the already diversified populations in the Empire, left their mark, contributed their share, enriching and being enriched by the traditions that spread across these lands, littorals, river basins, and mountains. Out of this wealth of human experiences, I wish to concentrate here on one phenomenon—the trade in Africans and Circassians coerced to come to the Ottoman Empire and enslaved during the long nineteenth century. But I would like to look at it not as an economic or political phenomenon but as a question of cultural inflow, interaction, and fusion.

In the past twenty years or so, a number of studies on slavery and the slave trade have created a framework for interpreting the history of enslaved people in the Ottoman Empire.[44] Scholars have covered the traffic from Africa and the Caucasus, described the main routes, determined the types of slaves, their prices, the customs duties levied on them, the jobs they performed, the social roles they played. They have explained the project of reform, the impact of foreign pressure, the mechanisms of home-grown manumission, the attitudes toward the institution, and the problems of suppression and abolition. However, although some of us have managed to bring out the stories of individual

---

44. For a survey of the literature, see the introduction in Toledano, *Slavery and Abolition.*

slaves, the absence of slave narratives has squelched to a degree the voices of the enslaved, especially the Africans, who occupied the lower rungs of Ottoman society.

Looking at the slave trade as a form of coerced migration not only shifts the emphasis to a culture-oriented, socially driven interpretation of it but also focuses attention on the enslaved person and the process of *passing into* Ottoman societies. The notion of passing-into—not unrelated to *rites de passage*—carries with it the insights enabled by diaspora and migration language, along with the proverbial sense of an individual and collective journey. The enslaved person was wrenched from one set of socioculturally coded attachments, embedded in a local patronage system, and injected into a much different attachment and patronage network. And then, within the new Ottoman environment, diasporic-migratory forces shaped and reshaped the enslaved person's negotiation of matters such as resale, absconding, and manumission. The real potential for a new understanding of the predicament of enslavement in Ottoman societies lies in trying to frame the stories culled from the sources in terms of coerced detachment and reattachment, severance and survival.

Although stories of individual slave experiences abound in archives and libraries, they are often obscured. The delicate process of uncovering the stories has greatly benefited from methodological developments in ethnolinguistics and social anthropology, inspired by works of scholars like Richard Price.[45] Price writes about linguistic and cultural creolization among enslaved African-Americans in a way that appears to me applicable to the case of enslaved African-Ottomans (and perhaps also to that of Circassian-Ottomans). Although the use that is made in Chapter 5 of the notion of "cultural creolization" entails some important conceptual reservations, many insights can still be gained by deploying an Ottoman-tuned, Mediterranean-adjusted version of such an approach.

45. For his recent contributions to this debate, see Richard Price, "The Miracle of Creolization: A Retrospective," *New West Indian Guide*, 75 (2001): 35–64; Price, "Invitation to Historians: Practices of Historical Narrative," *Rethinking History*, 5/3 (2001): 357–365; Price, "Paramaribo, 1710: Violence and Hope in a Space of Death," *Common-Place: The Interactive Journal of Early American Life*, 3/4 (July 2003): http://common-place.dreamhost.com//vol-03/no-04/paramaribo/index.shtml.

Perhaps before we delve into that, however, it might be useful to briefly survey the main points on the road map of migration and diaspora thinking.

Recent years have seen a plethora of studies on migration and diaspora, stimulated by the currently growing transnational and cross-cultural movement of people, a major component of contemporary globalization. These migration waves have caused concern in many receiving societies, whose inhabitants are worried about integration but also increasingly alarmed by the threats of international terrorism. Despite the proliferation of works on these and related topics, very few studies have addressed the phenomenon of coerced migrations such as the slave trade and the involuntary diasporas created by them, which will constitute our main concern in this book.

Broadly speaking, until the 1990s studies of migration theory most often yielded demographic or socioeconomic models.[46] Systematic writing about migration theory began with E. G. Ravenstein's 1885 and 1889 articles, which suggested basic "laws of migration" and discussed among other issues the relationship between distance and movement, stages of migration, and urban-rural differences in the propensity to migrate. These contributions charted the road for future studies by stressing the dominance of the economic motive for an individual's decision to relocate. Already then, Ravenstein included the slave trade as a form of migration caused by compulsion, although he, and those who followed in his footsteps, stressed the element of personal choice and the desire to improve one's standard of living as the driving forces behind migration. Until the 1960s, no new theories of migration were advanced, and the dichotomy between free and coerced migration was maintained, with the latter now including refugee movements and ethnic cleansing in addition to the slave trade and indentured labor movements.

In 1960, Samuel A. Stouffer published a reworked version of his 1940 paper, elaborating a mathematical model that linked migration to what he called intervening opportunities.[47] These were defined as the

46. For a good survey of the main models, see Everett S. Lee, "A Theory of Migration," *Demography*, 3/1 (1966): 47–57.

47. Samuel A. Stouffer, "Intervening Opportunities and Competing Migrants," *Journal of Regional Studies*, 2 (1960): 1–26.

type and number of possible alternative destinations available to potential migrants between *origin* and *destination*. Stouffer maintained that such competing opportunities, rather than the distance itself, as Ravenstein had argued, affect the choice of destination. Accordingly, the number of migrants moving from any origin over a given distance depends on the number of opportunities—real or perceived—at the destination and is adversely affected by the number of alternatives that exist along that distance. Everett S. Lee took this notion one step further, establishing in 1966 the model that became the standard for migration theory until what may be termed the postmodernist challenge of the early 1990s.[48] Lee cast his net very broadly. He defined migration as "a permanent or semipermanent change of residence" and argued that "no matter how short or how long, how easy or how difficult, every act of migration involves an origin, a destination, and an intervening set of obstacles."[49]

Lee's model deals with three main categories: the volume of migration, outbound and inbound movement between the same origin and destination (stream and counterstream), and characteristics of migrants. Within each category, he establishes connections, stressing the relationship between "push" and "pull" factors in both origin and destination, but significantly adding what he calls "personal factors"—namely, human perception of realities and the different reactions by individuals to the same stimuli, both positive and negative. Lee's model was the first to accommodate coerced migration in some form of general migration theory. Although this was done neither explicitly nor deliberately, it is possible to use some of his insights to better explicate aspects of the forced movement of enslaved persons from Africa and the Caucasus into the Ottoman Empire in the nineteenth century. Still, Lee's argument about forced migration addresses mainly the *involuntary* movement of children and often of wives, who were obliged to leave their country when the men migrated *voluntarily*.[50]

Nonetheless, Lee's discussion of migration "streams" has a broader applicability that can accommodate the traffic in enslaved persons. He writes that as migration "tends to take place largely within well defined streams," so does the slave trade, "because migrants must usually follow

48. See Durugönül, "Invisibility of Turks."
49. Ibid., 49.
50. Ibid., 51.

established routes of transportation."[51] It is also true for coerced migration of enslaved people that "in many cases, large movements take on the form of streams which are highly specific both in origin and destination." The routes of the slave trade from Africa and the Caucasus were well established by the second third of the nineteenth century, and the streams were well defined in terms of origins, modes of transportation, entrepôts, and destinations. Arguably, too, the low rate of return to the places of origin—that is, Lee's high migration stream efficiency—was to some extent at least due to the fact that, as he puts it, the "intervening obstacles [horrors of the journey] are great."

But it is from the cultural perspective that Lee's model is most relevant to the Ottoman slave trade, as he notes that migration tends to occur at certain junctions in the life-cycle, thus becoming "a part of the *rites de passage*." Whereas his argument is based on migration by choice, not by force, it does hold true for many of the enslaved who were taken to the Ottoman Empire. The overwhelming majority of these, whether African, Circassian, Georgian, or other, were very young, often in their early to mid teens. Their coerced recruitment into the Ottoman unfree labor market occurred, in many cases, just as they were passing into puberty, entering the workforce, and—for the young females—becoming sexually active. While they would also have gone through these passages in their origin-societies, their enslavement meant that all this took place amid the heightened stresses of resocialization and reacculturation in unfamiliar surroundings, without the support of family and friends, deprived of the comforting and soothing effects that a home culture would normally provide.

An effort to integrate past and present concerns into a coherent migration theory was attempted by Wilbur Zelinsky in several articles published in the late 1970s and early 1980s.[52] However, his five-phase

51. Ibid., 54–55.
52. Wilbur Zelinsky, "Coping with the Migration Turnaround: The Theoretical Challenge," *International Regional Science Review*, 2/2: 175–178, 1977; Zelinsky, "The Demographic Transition: Changing Patterns of Migration," in *Population Science in the Service of Mankind*, Liège: International Union for the Scientific Study of Population, 1979: 165–188; Zelinsky, "The Impasse in Migration Theory: A Sketch Map for Potential Escapees," in Peter A. Morrison (ed.), *Population Movements: Their Forms and Functions in Urbanization and Development*, Brussels: Ordina, 1983: 21–49.

transitional model for describing migration from premodern to modern times is less useful for dealing with phenomena such as the movement of enslaved persons into the Ottoman Empire. A real conceptual transformation in this regard took place about a decade later, with the advent of postmodernist writing (including subaltern and postcolonial ideas) and the rise of cultural studies. Here, migration is inextricably linked to the study of diasporas, which significantly develops the cultural dimension to the point of making it the main axis of analysis. So, too, in our book, is the cultural aspect a key element, though not the only one, in our attempt to delve into the predicament of the enslaved and explore their experiences as members of various Ottoman societies. The important ingredients in our interpretation are therefore the construction of individual and collective identity, the redefinition of notions such as origin/home and destination/host cultures and their interrelationship, and the reevaluation of the concepts of struggle, conflict, choice, and agency with regard to the enslaved.

Within the essential shift in the concepts of migration and diaspora, Robin Cohen contributed the notion of "cultural diasporas," which attempts to bring together the "many migration experiences in the late modern world."[53] This notion is akin in many respects to what I shall call in this book "creolization," namely the mix-and-match braiding of cultural components from various origins into a variety of diaspora cultures, a melange that has sometimes been called "hybrid" culture. I will try to show that the process did not happen pell-mell but had a certain logic to it. It was in the interface between the cultures of the enslaved and the slavers that "aesthetic styles, identifications and affinities, dispositions and behaviours, musical genres, linguistic patterns, moralities, religious practices, and other cultural phenomena" came into play and were transformed into creolized forms (also variously referred to as "syncretic," "translated," "crossover," "cut 'n' mix," "hybrid," or "alternate" forms).[54] In the sense used by Steven Vertovec, we here mean diaspora *as* "mode of cultural production," to

53. Robin Cohen, *Global Diasporas: An Introduction,* Seattle: University of Washington Press, 1997: 128. The following observations are based on his survey; see pp. 127–134.

54. Ibid., 128 (quoting a 1996 personal communication with Steven Vertovec).

be distinguished from diaspora *as* "social form" and diaspora *as* "type of consciousness."[55]

For Cohen and Iain Chambers, identities are formed in open-ended, constantly ongoing processes, and there is no final product. This predicament of the migrant is gauged and further elaborated from the experience of the enslaved, since "to be lost, to be a stranger in a strange land is typical of the human condition, not just typical of those who suffered the forced migration of slavery and indentureship."[56] Thus, we are disabused of the naive notion that creolization produces well-defined, easily catalogued cultural forms. Rather, diasporic communities are, in relation to host societies, "imperfectly conjoined groups," constantly shifting, or, as some would say, they are "traveling cultures."

As we now proceed to examine the long-nineteenth-century coerced migration of enslaved people into the Ottoman Empire, we shift our focus to the individuals who were victimized in this process, but no less to the way they handled their passage and integration into Ottoman societies. An early, fascinating, and so far unmatched study was published in 1958 by Alexander Lopashich on the African community in Ulcinj, a small market town near the Montenegrin-Albanian border, then still part of Yugoslavia.[57] A fine example of a work in social anthropology based on oral history, it surveys the small community of Africans, originating probably in Bagirmi and the central Sudan, who had been enslaved and carried off to North African ports, mainly Tripoli.

Lopashich managed to identify three to four generations within three such families and was able to piece together their life histories and sketch some of the main features of the predicament of enslaved Africans in that seafaring and trading town, with its otherwise Muslim, ethnically Albanian population. What in the middle of the nineteenth century appeared to be a community of a hundred families with several hundred people dwindled gradually to about fifty families in the last quarter of the century and

55. Steven Vertovec, "Three Meanings of 'Diaspora,' Exemplified among South Asian Religions," *Diaspora*, 6/3 (Winter 1997): 277–299.

56. Cohen, *Global Diasporas*, 133 (agreeing with and paraphrasing Iain Chambers, *Migrancy, Culture, Identity*, London: Routledge, 1994).

57. Alexander Lopashich, "A Negro Community in Yugoslavia," *Man*, 58 (1958): 169–173.

to about thirty families in the 1950s. High mortality earlier on, a low birth rate, movement to other towns in the region and beyond (Scutari, Zagreb, Istanbul), and even limited return to Africa are cited by Lopashich as reasons for the decline. Exogamy was discouraged, Lopashich says, but when it occurred, children lost their parents' African features.

More recent and still ongoing attempts to address the issue of the African diaspora have focused on Turkey, Iran, and some Arab states, mostly those in North Africa.[58] John Hunwick has opened up the new discussion on the African diaspora in the Mediterranean in two highly interesting articles which cover mainly North Africa but also bring useful material on several Ottoman cases. For Turkey and Iran we have two recent studies by Esma Durugönül on Turkey and Behnaz A. Mirzai on Iran, both stressing questions of identity and culture. However, much of the work on African diasporas treats North African societies. In fact, these studies were motivated by a keen interest in possession-healing cults (Zar and Bori) and treat other aspects of diaspora life only in passing. Still, their contribution to our understanding of African community life in Ottoman societies is significant, mainly because so many of the social and cultural aspects revolved around these practices. Here, the collection of papers edited by I. M. Lewis, Ahmed Al-Safi, and Sayyid Hurreiz moved the discussion to a new and promising plane.

Esma Durugönül's interest in exploring the African communities in Antalya is primarily concerned with introducing notions of multiculturalism into Turkish contemporary thinking in hopes of better integrating culturally diverse groups such as African-Turks. The questions asked in this context are what "the extent of their knowledge of their past [is], how they self-identify, what emotional ties they feel toward Africa, and whether

58. The following brief survey refers to John Hunwick, "Black Africans in the Mediterranean World: Introduction to a Neglected Aspect of the African Diaspora," in Elizabeth Savage (ed.), *The Human Commodity: Perspectives on the Trans-Saharan Slave Trade*, London: Frank Cass, 1992: 5–38; Savage, "The Religious Practices of Black Slaves in the Mediterranean Islamic World," in Lovejoy, *Slavery on the Frontiers of Islam*, 149–172; and I. M. Lewis, Ahmed Al-Safi and Sayyid Hurreiz (eds.), *Women's Medicine: The Zar-Bori Cult in Africa and Beyond*, Edinburgh: Edinburgh University Press, 1991, especially the more historical articles by Pamela Constantinides, Richard Natvig, Suheir A. Morsy, and Sophie Ferchiou.

the fact that their ancestors came to Turkey as enslaved persons during the Ottoman period (1516–1918) has an effect on their sense of identity."[59] Behnaz A. Mirzai finds that African-Iranians manifest a tendency to stress discontinuities with their places of origin.[60] Rather than identify themselves as Africans, they stress instead their Muslim Iranian identity. This conclusion is hardly surprising, as many other studies show that multiculturalism and the creolized cultural forms of diaspora meet their fiercest resistance from nationalism and nation-states, which are all about welding together nations and integrating minorities by suppressing their separate ethnic identities.[61]

HISTORIOGRAPHY AND THE NEW RESEARCH ENVIRONMENT

The study of world slavery has been traditionally dominated by interest in New World enslavement. Beyond a classic preoccupation with slavery in Antiquity, and scattered studies on slavery in Southeast Asia, Africa, and Muslim societies, most works written over the past century have dealt with the Atlantic slave trade and with plantation slavery in the United States, Brazil, and the Caribbean islands. Owing to the over-whelming concern with the economic aspect of slavery, the role played by American economic historians has been a leading one. Because in other societies, notably Islamic ones, slavery had less economic importance, more sociocultural significance, studies devoted to it have generally been seen as "softer" than the work done by economic historians on the "hard" quantitative data collected about enslavement in the Americas. Even comparative studies on world slavery have tended, until recently, to give little or no weight to work done on "marginal" types of enslavement.[62]

In the past few years we have seen yet another cyclical surge in academic and public interest in enslavement. Perhaps not since the debates

---

59. Durugönül, "Invisibility of Turks," 281. Her forthcoming book will contain information from extensive interviews conducted in the Antalya region.
60. Behnaz A. Mirzai, "African Presence in Iran: Identity and Its Reconstruction in the 19th and 20th Centuries," *Revue française d'histoire d'outre-mer* (*RFHOM*), 89/336–337 (2002), 240 ff.
61. Cohen, *Global Diasporas*, 135. See also Robin Cohen, "Diasporas and the Nation-State: From Victims to Challengers," *International Affairs*, 72 (1996): 507–520.
62. Toledano, *Slavery and Abolition*, 155–158.

of the 1970s has this interest been both as intense and as pluralistic in orientation. The 2001 *American Historical Review Forum* entitled "Crossing Slavery's Boundaries" and the current *Cambridge World History of Slavery* project may serve to illustrate these trends.[63] The *AHR* discussion was led by David Brion Davis, who called for globally comparative work on enslavement and pointed out the hitherto untapped potential in bringing together scholars working on slavery and those interested in abolition.[64] Davis feels that now is perhaps a promising time for a renewed agenda for slavery studies because of a global concern with the following issues: power and exploitation; outsiders and insiders; the construction of race; the expansion of the Euro-American West; the early stages of consumer-driven economies; and the promise and limitations of social reform.

Still, Davis is heavily grounded in New World slavery, at the core of which he identifies "the most extreme and systematic form of personal domination, dishonor, dehumanization, and economic exploitation, a form of exploitation and domination that became a model, in the eyes of successive generations of liberationists, for all Western and white male imperialism." And, even though he himself is not an economic historian, he, too, accepts the leading role of labor economics in explaining New World slavery. The Mediterranean-Atlantic and the Ottoman-Indian connections of the fifteenth century were driven by the labor and consumer goods markets, Davis agrees, but he does puzzle over an unexplained paradox. "In the aftermath of 'the Cliometric Revolution,' historians have not yet found a convincing way to reconcile slavery's productivity and economic growth with evidence of paternalism, slave resistance, or social imbalance and decay. How could workers who were relatively free from market forces produce so much or drive such economic growth, especially when historians claim they were engaged in subtle forms of day-to-day resistance?"

63. See the AHR Forum's Crossing Slavery's Boundaries session entitled "Looking at Slavery from Broader Perspectives," *American Historical Review*, 105/2 (2001): 452–484 (contributions by David Brion Davis, Peter Kolchin, Stanley L. Engerman); the *Cambridge World History of Slavery* project is a four-volume work, the first of which is being edited by Keith Hopkins and Paul Cartledge, and volumes 2–4 by David Eltis and Stanley Engerman.
64. The following quotations from Davis are in *AHR*, 105/2 (2001): 452, 454, 456, 457, 460, and 465.

When offering a possible area of research where answers to that question might be explored, Davis in fact aims precisely at the main concern of our book—the intricacies of the slaver-enslaved relationship. Davis believes that "more attention needs to be given to the psychology and dynamics of nearly absolute power," since his intuition correctly leads him to expect that informal, personal arrangements were negotiated in the "real world" that aided productivity. Indeed, my own assumption is that no amount of coercion can be economically efficient in the long run and that a certain give-and-take even between a slaver and an enslaved person is unavoidable. For productivity to grow and yield a prosperous economy, incentives have to be provided, and the harshness of absolute power must be mitigated. Here I accept Michael Salman's more generalized argument, namely, that "wherever slavery has existed as a social relationship, its practice and its meaning have been shaped by the specific socio-cultural setting, the cognitive bases for the enslavement of some and not others, and locally determined struggles between the *will of masters* and *willfulness of slaves*."[65]

It seems, however, that for those sharing an essentially American orientation in the study of enslavement—be it in North, Central, or South America—work will continue to be driven by economic history, with social and cultural concerns taking a back seat. While recognizing the benefits of a global, comparative perspective, such people will find little satisfaction in comparing a rich prototype to phenomena that have naturally less to contribute to the comparison. Even when employing a global perspective, they will tend to privilege the role of shifting trade routes and the impact of international finance and commerce. In this emerging scholarly division of labor, comparative studies that are not mainly based on economic factors will be left to the social and cultural historians, who are able to deploy readily available frameworks for comparison across continents and cultures. Such frameworks are increasingly derived from work done by social anthropologists and scholars of cultural studies, who almost by definition are interested in transnational phenomena such as migration and diasporas. It is only fortunate that in recent years the research environment is expanding to include the field of Ottoman and Middle Eastern slavery studies.

65. Salman, *Embarrassment of Slavery*, 7; the emphases are mine.

In May 1977, the following footnote appeared in the opening paragraph of a paper submitted by Alan Fisher to a conference held at Princeton University: "To my knowledge, no book or article has appeared in any
language which deals with the institution of chattel slavery in the Ottoman
Empire." The conference was organized by John Ralph Willis and addressed the topic of slavery in Muslim societies, with special emphasis on
Africa. It was predicated on Willis's adaptation of H. J. Fisher's statement
that "Islamic Slavery in Africa has been a fascinating subject to which
many scholars have referred, but of which no detailed modern study has
been made." Alan Fisher asserted then that the statement "is doubly accurate for the Ottoman Empire," adding that "scholars have not only not
studied chattel slavery there, they have not admitted its existence."[66]

Exactly a quarter of a century later, in May 2002, Eve Troutt Powell
dedicated an entire Istanbul conference paper to a survey-cum-critique
of the literature on African slavery in the Islamic societies of the Middle
East, most notably the Ottoman Empire.[67] The paper not only shows the
significant amount of work being done to understand the history of slavery and the slave trade in Middle Eastern societies but also demands a
change of research agenda. Troutt Powell calls for an effort to recover the
voices of the enslaved and puts forth a partially new set of questions per-
taining to the life the slaves made in these societies, their manumission,
and the attitude of society toward freed slaves. This call to break the silence of slaves and bring them back into history is both timely and relevant. It is made so by the achievements of two and a half decades of
scholarly endeavor that have managed in large measure to lay down the
groundwork and provide the basic tools for the next stage of research.

What may be called the research environment is also of vital importance for the development of any field of study. As I have previously argued, the study of slavery in the Ottoman Empire has suffered from the

66. Alan Fisher, "Chattel Slavery in the Ottoman Empire: Some Preliminary Con-
   siderations," in John Ralph Willis (ed.), *Slaves and Slavery in Muslim Africa*,
   London: Frank Cass, 1985.
67. Eve M. Troutt Powell, "Will That Subaltern Ever Speak? Finding African
   Slaves in the Historiography of the Middle East," in Israel Gershoni, Amy
   Singer, and Y. Hakan Erdem (eds.), *Middle East Historiographies Narrating the
   Twentieth Century*, Seattle: University of Washington Press, 2006.

lack of an interested, engaged constituency, more specifically, the fact that there are no *active, self-conscious* descendant communities of African or Caucasian slaves in Turkey or the successor Arab states.[68] This absence meant that no group saw Ottoman enslavement as part of its own history, and no group demanded to have its past properly investigated. But, owing to two recent developments in Turkey and the United States, this seems to be changing now. To me, the first development was truly moving: early in 2005, an (auto)biographical book by Mustafa Olpak, a Turkish descendant of enslaved Africans, was published in Istanbul.[69] The book describes the forcible removal of Olpak's ancestors from Kenya and their transport, via Crete, to the Ottoman imperial capital. Aptly, the author begins his book with the following words:

The first generation lives,
the second reacts,
the third [re]searches . . .

I am Mustafa Olpak. In my family, I am third generation.[70]

The book generated much public interest in Turkey, including several reviews and feature articles in the press.[71] A television documentary is currently being prepared about the history of Ottoman enslavement, to be aired on TRT2 in January 2007, and a grassroots association, created by Olpak, has been working to raise awareness in Turkey of the history and social conditions of African-Turks. A meeting planned by the association for 15 November 2006 and intended for two hundred persons was inundated with more than two thousand responses; it was expected to

68. Toledano, *Slavery and Abolition,* Chapter 5 and p. 158.
69. Mustafa Olpak, *Kenya-Girit-İstanbul, Köle Kıyısından İnsan Biyografileri,* Istanbul: Ozan Yayıncılık, 2005.
70. Ibid., 7. For the historical background, the author draws on the Turkish translation of my first book (Toledano, *Slave Trade*) and on Y. Hakan Erdem's work (*Slavery in the Ottoman Empire and Its Demise, 1800–1909,* Basingstoke, England: Macmillan in association with St. Antony's College, Oxford,1996). For me, this has been a unique opportunity to observe firsthand how historical research and writing can affect, perhaps even motivate, current events.
71. See, for example, Celal Başlangiç, "Osmanlı'nın son köleleri," *Radikal,* 21 March 2005.

have media coverage and to further resonate in Turkey.[72] It seems that, as expected, the rise of a "community of interest" in Turkey might now lead to a heightened focus on the enslaved heritage of African-Turks. This ties in with Eve Troutt Powell's call, mentioned above, for the recovery of slave voices in past Middle Eastern societies, which may signal a willingness on the part of African-Americans to take an active part in consciousness-raising among the silent and as-if-absent communities of Africans in the former Ottoman Empire. Not surprisingly, Olpak mentions Alex Haley's *Roots* as another third-generation product of African enslavement, a clear link and source of inspiration.[73]

Troutt Powell makes two important points that are both relevant and useful to our discussion here.[74] The first is her use of Gayatri Chakravorty Spivak's work on India under the British Raj, in which the author puts the onus for the "subaltern's" silence on the historian. The historian, it is argued, is too often resigned to the seeming absence of direct "voice evidence," instead of working harder and in innovative ways to recover missing voices. Troutt Powell takes Spivak's observations about Hindu women who committed *sati* and applies them to the situation of slaves in the Ottoman Middle East, suggesting that historians should not resign themselves to the apparent absence of slave voices. The other point she makes is in reference to the supposedly daunting comparison of this silence with the abundance of slave narratives in the United States. Following recent studies of that literature, which includes some six thousand such narratives, she observes that these were not direct, authentic expressions of individual slave voices but filtered, constrained, and formulaic texts intended to promote the noble cause of abolition. Thus, even in the richly documented environment of U.S. slavery studies, an adequate treatment of the enslaved person's experience still leaves a great deal to be desired.

Perhaps as significant is the recent demand of an African group, gathered in a conference in Johannesburg on 22 February 2003, that Arab countries own up to what the group called the "Arab-led slavery of Africans," apologize for it, and pay reparations. While certainly as controversial as the similar demand raised by African-American leaders

---

72. Niambi Walker, personal communication by E-mail, 20 October 2006.
73. Olpak, *Kenya-Girit-İstanbul*, 7.
74. Troutt Powell, "Will That Subaltern Ever Speak?"

vis-à-vis the United States, this is a first step in developing another constituency, in Africa itself, to represent the absent voices of former African slaves in the Middle East. "We the people, Africans and African descendants, herein referred to as Africans, striving for the unity of the African Nation," the conference participants declare, "intend to *reclaim our voice,* and to speak for ourselves on the above and related issues, after centuries of *silence* and non-self-expression" (emphases are mine).[75] Their declaration rightly links African inaction on this issue to the "collective amnesia about Arab enslavement of Africans" and calls for "more research . . . on the Arab and Ottoman slave trade of Africans" and the establishment of "relations between continental Africans and the African Diaspora in the Arab world."

There is as yet no parallel development with regard to Caucasian slavery in the Ottoman Empire. Circassians (including Abkhazians) and Georgians, both in the lands formerly governed by the Ottoman Empire and in various diasporas, have been actively interested in their political-historical and cultural heritage but have been less inclined to explore the history of their ancestors' enslavement. This may change, however, since the forced migration from, or ethnic cleansing in, the Caucasus has already been labeled a national tragedy by various Circassian groups in Turkey and Russia, most recently in a joint public declaration in May 2005.[76] At the same time, Georgian academics and intellectuals, such as the historian Gocha Japaridze, are defining as a "Georgian national tragedy" the constant drain of Georgians recruited as kuls by the Ottoman and Safavid empires.[77] An awareness of this kind is a precondition for challenging the accepted view

75. *Declaration of the Conference on Arab-Led Slavery of Africans.*
76. The statement was published following a conference held in Istanbul on 21 May 2005 and can be seen on one of the leading sites maintained by Circassians in Turkey and the diaspora: www.kafkas.org.tr (the tragedy of 1864 is described in Turkish as *Kafkasların trajedisi*).
77. See a brief reference to the drain in Crecelius and Djaparidze, "Relations of the Georgian Mamluks," 321–322. I owe this observation about Georgian sentiments to Professor Jane Hathaway. Dr. Gocha Japaridze [Gotcha Djaparidze] points to other Georgian scholars who wrote works devoted to the enslavement of Georgians by the Ottomans—for example, G. Bey Mamikonian, B. Silagadze, D. Janelidze, and V. Macharadze (personal communication by E-mail, 11 September 2005). He adds that the interest in that chapter in Georgian history continues with such studies as the ones by his former student K. Peradze:

that enslaved persons from the Caucasus region were happily integrated into elite and non-elite Ottoman families, erasing within one generation the "embarrassment of slavery," to borrow Michael Salman's phrase.[78]

The harsher, agricultural slavery endured by the Circassians after their forced migration into the Empire in the 1850s and 1860s was in most aspects akin to serfdom, its cognate institution in contemporary eastern Europe and Russia. Descendants of those enslaved people still live in village communities across Turkey, the Balkans, and even the Middle East—for instance, in Israel and Jordan—but we may doubt how aware they are of issues raised by the enserfment-enslavement of their ancestors. Scholars from the community, like the Jordanian anthropologists Amjad Jaimoukha and Seteney Shami, have studied the ethnic heritage of Circassians and have referred to the enslaved class.[79] Diaspora communities remain keenly interested in their parent culture, and new ties have been re-forming with their homelands, with all that this entails in terms of identity-formation and consciousness-raising.

The changing research environment with regard to enslavement in the Ottoman Empire and the generally growing interest in the study of enslavement in Middle Eastern and other Muslim societies have convinced me that a fresh examination of the available evidence is both timely and necessary. A serious attempt to provide effective tools for such a

---

"Georgian Mamluks in Tunisia in the 18th–19th Centuries," in *Papers Dedicated to the 80th Birthday of Professor Archil Chkheidze*, Tbilisi, 2002: 200–212; "Marital Ties of Tunisian Mamluks [of Georgian origin]," *The East and the Caucasus*, 2 (2004): 119–126; and "On the Solidarity among Ottoman Statesmen during the Late 18th–Early 19th Centuries," *The Near East and Georgia*, Tbilisi, 2005: 82–88 (all three are in Georgian with English summaries).

78. Salman, *Embarrassment of Slavery*, 14. Salman here builds on Orlando Patterson's observation that slavery was the "embarrassing institution" rather than the "peculiar institution."

79. See, for example, Amjad Jaimoukha, *The Chechens: A Handbook*, London: Routledge Curzon, 2005; Jaimoukha, *The Circassians: A Handbook*, Richmond, England: Curzon, 2001; Jaimoukha (ed.), *Circassian Cuisine*, Amman, Jordan: Sanjalay Press, 2003; Jaimoukha (ed.), *The Cycles of the Circassian Nart Epic: The Fountain-Head of Circassian Mythology*, Amman, Jordan: Sanjalay Press, 2000; Ziramikw Qardenghwsch', *Circassian Proverbs and Sayings* (trans. Amjad Jaimoukha), Amman, Jordan: Sanjalay Press, 2003; Shami, *Ethnicity and Leadership;* and recent edited collections.

reevaluation may yield a better account of the voices and experiences of the enslaved in Ottoman societies than has been hitherto achieved. In the current book I shall go back to the evidence that has been uncovered thus far, bring out a sample of the many stories of slave experiences, and devise a method for gleaning from them some insights into the lives of enslaved Africans and Caucasians—people from the Caucasus—in the Empire. The stories themselves, rich and fascinating, will form the core of this work.

A FEW WORDS ABOUT THE SOURCES

The most important sources for studying enslavement in the Ottoman Empire are Ottoman records, whether state-produced or private.[80] For the nineteenth century, state archives include court records, from both Şeriat and Nizami courts, established by the Tanzimat-state and often referred to as the new administrative courts.[81] Enslaved persons appear in these records as absconders or alleged offenders, rendering court files an excellent source for the social and cultural history of enslavement. So far, very few studies of Ottoman enslavement have been based on Şeriat court records, the use of which has been a subject of some controversy in the field in recent years.[82] These few works have dealt with sixteenth-century Üsküdar, sixteenth- and seventeenth-century Cyprus, Ottoman

---

80. For details, see the bibliographic sections in Toledano, *Slave Trade;* Toledano, *Slavery and Abolition;* and Erdem, *Slavery.*

81. Work on Şeriat court records has been conducted for some time, but it has intensified in recent years. Some of the latest works to be published in a long list are Mahmoud Yazbak, *Haifa in the Late Ottoman Period, 1864–1914: A Muslim Town in Transition,* Leiden: E. J. Brill, 1998; Peirce, *Morality Tales;* articles by Beshara Doumani and Iris Agmon, in Beshara Doumani (ed.), *Family History in the Middle East: Household, Property, and Gender,* Albany: State University of New York Press, 2003; Zilfi, "Servants, Slaves"; and Agmon, *Family and Court.* For a recent account of the court system in the Ottoman Empire, see Ruth Austin Miller, *From Fikh to Fascism: The Turkish Republican Adoption of Mussolini's Criminal Code in the Context of Late Ottoman Legal Reform,* Ph.D. diss., Princeton University, June 2003.

82. See, for example, Dror Ze'evi, "The Use of Ottoman Shariʿa Court Records as a Source for Middle Eastern Social History: A Reappraisal," *Islamic Law and Society,* 5/1 (1998): 35–56 (the author's work relies heavily on the Şeriat court records of Jerusalem—see his *Ottoman Century: The District of Jerusalem in the 1600s,* Albany: State University of New York Press, 1996); Zouhair Ghazzal, "Discursive Formations and the Gap between Theory and Practice in Ottoman

Jerusalem, fifteenth- to eighteenth-century Bursa, and eighteenth- to twentieth-century Egypt.[83] However, there can hardly be a doubt that future scholars interested in the history of Ottoman enslavement will turn their attention to şeriat court records as an important source. As for the Nizami court records, a highly promising series of the imperial High Court rulings on murder and theft cases (some committed by slaves), is patiently awaiting interested scholars at the Istanbul Prime Ministry Archives.[84]

Tanzimat-state correspondence regarding matters of enslavement can be found in the archives of both the central government and provincial administrations. The Ottoman archives also contain correspondence between slave dealers, between slavers, and between slavers and slave dealers, all scattered in various files that deal with government attempts to suppress the slave trade in Africans. There are records relating to registration of freed slaves at the police hostel in Istanbul (*Polis Misafirhanesi*) in the province of Aydın and the city of Izmir, where a government-sponsored program of resettlement was in effect.[85] The province of Bengazi in present-day Libya also had a post-emancipation

Shari'a Law," Paper submitted to the Second Joseph Schacht Conference on Theory and Practice in Islamic Law, Granada, Spain, December 1997: 1–44.

83. This list is not exhaustive, but it does give a general idea of the state of the literature: Ronald Jennings, "Black Slaves and Free Slaves in Ottoman Cyprus, 1590–1640," *Journal of the Economic and Social History of the Orient* (*JESHO*), 30/3 (1987): 286–302; Yvonne Seng, "A Liminal State: Slavery in Sixteenth-Century Istanbul," in Shaun E. Marmon (ed.), *Slavery in the Islamic Middle East*, Princeton, N.J.: Markus Wiener, 1999: 25–42; Ovadia Salama, "Avadim be-va'alutam shel Yehudim ve Notsrim bi-Yerushalayim ha-Othmanit" (Slaves held by Jews and Christians in Ottoman Jerusalem), *Katedra*, 49 (September 1988): 64–75 (in Hebrew); Erol Ayyıldız and Osman Çetin, "Slavery and Islamization of Slaves in Ottoman Society according to Canonical Registers of Bursa between the Fifteenth and Eighteenth Centuries," 1996 (unpublished report on work in progress); and Ron Shaham, "Masters, Their Freed Slaves, and the *Waqf* in Egypt (Eighteenth–Twentieth Centuries), *Journal of the Economic and Social History of the Orient* (*JESHO*), 43/2 (2000): 162–188.

84. BOA/Ayniyat defterleri/Meclis-i Vala'dan katl ve sirkate dair, vols. 470–502 (covering the years 1847–1866).

85. For a study based on these records, see Abdullah Martal, "Afrika'dan İzmir'e: İzmir'de Bir Köle Misafirhanesi," *Kebikeç*, 10 (2000): 171–186.

program, the records of which should be in Libyan archives, and similar records might exist for other provinces.[86] Thus far, such records have been only partially used by scholars, and their potential for the study of manumission and post-manumission conditions is very promising.

It is commonly accepted that there are no Ottoman slave narratives. Although this statement may now be slightly revised to include some accounts that have come to light in recent years, the absence of this kind of source has hampered the study of enslavement in Ottoman and post-Ottoman societies. As I already mentioned, the use of slave narratives available for the United States has recently come under scrutiny because it overburdened the sources with significance and with unreasonable expectations that they would reflect realities.[87] These narratives were almost always recorded by abolitionists, not directly by the enslaved themselves, and are therefore seen as formulaic and propagandistic. Even when such voices are present in Ottoman records, they come to us through the handwritten texts of court scribes, or the narrations of travelers, or the reports of foreign consuls, agents, missionaries, and traders. All these texts are linguistically and culturally filtered, which forces us to develop new ways of making them speak for the silent men and women behind them.

A recently published account by an Ottoman palace eunuch, as told to a local official who wrote it down, only emphasizes the research potential inherent in even such filtered accounts.[88] Other stories were told by enslaved persons to their holders and recorded in the memoirs that slavers later published. Again, though filtered, these accounts also provide valuable insights into the lives of the enslaved, for example, their lives in Africa and their capture.[89] Another source is biographical compilations, like the recently published eighteenth-century work by a senior

86. A document in the BOA describes in detail the kind of registration that was conducted in Bengazi by the *kolbaşıs*, or heads of lodges assisting freed slaves (BOA/İrade/Dahiliye/62927/ Şura-yı Devlet, Dahiliye Dairesi, *Mazbata*, 3.9.1884).

87. See Troutt Powell, "Will That Subaltern Ever Speak?"

88. Hasan Ferit Ertuğ, "Musahib-i Sani-i Hazret-i Şehr-Yari Nadir Ağa'nın Hatıratı-I," *Toplumsal Tarih*, 49 (October 1998): 7–15.

89. See, for example, the story of Ebru Ana as told to the author, whom she reared: Ahmed Emin Yalman, *Yakın tarihte gördüklerim ve geçirdiklerim*, vol. 1: *1888–1918*, Istanbul: Yenilik Basımevi, 1970: 13–14.

Ottoman officeholder, Ahmet Resmi Efendi, on the biographies of African eunuchs in the imperial harem.[90] This work, though more detailed, completes a later register of imperial eunuchs' biographies that covers the nineteenth century and the years to 1906. We could certainly learn from it something about this interesting corps of palace officeholders, although direct and indirect narrative accounts are required in order to flesh it out.[91]

European diplomatic records, mainly consular reports, have proven to be a very useful source for the study of the slave trade and slavery in the Ottoman Empire. Given the intense British interest in the abolition of slavery and a milder concern on the part of the French and a handful of other European nations, consuls were as keen to report to London about the traffic in enslaved persons as they were to report about the conditions of enslavement in the various parts of the Empire where they were serving. It was to foreign, mainly British, consulates that enslaved persons went when they ran away from slavers to seek refuge and freedom, which caused consuls to compile and dispatch reports about these cases. But such records have been extensively used by scholars, and it appears that much of what they have to offer has already been exploited to a large extent. Perhaps with the exception of records from the Egyptian consulates regarding the program of manumission instituted by the British authorities from 1882 onward, European sources must now be considered secondary for the study of Ottoman enslavement.

Nonetheless, researchers can still stumble on interesting items in European archives, especially files containing collections of Ottoman private papers. In one such case, a story was found in the Hekekyan Papers at the British Library. Hekekyan Bey was a senior Armenian-Ottoman officeholder in Egypt who was educated in Britain and served in various positions under the governors-general of Egypt during the middle decades of the nineteenth century. In his diary and correspondence, dating to the second half of 1846, Hekekyan describes the absconding, twice, of his eunuch Surur and the illness and subsequent miscarriage it caused to the bey's shocked wife. Then comes the cruel punishment he imposed

90. Ahmet Resmi Ifendi, *Hamîletü'l-Küberâ* (ed. Ahmet Nezihi Turan), Istanbul: Kitabevi, 2000.
91. See my work on this register in Toledano, *Slavery and Abolition,* 41–53.

on the eunuch: he had him sent for a number of months to do hard labor in a mine, where Surur's health deteriorated almost to the point of death. Hekekyan had asked a colleague to make sure that the eunuch performed only lenient tasks at the mine, but that was not done. The frail young man accepted his fate "philosophically," it was reported to Hekekyan.[92] The research emphasis is currently shifting to stories of this and other types, which now begin to form the basis for the history of enslavement in the Ottoman Empire.

92. British Library/Add MSS/Hekekyan Papers/37450/335, Diary entry, ca. mid-1846; 37462/78–80, Aimé Bey to Hekekyan, two letters of August 1846 and September 1846.

CHAPTER TWO

Leaving a Violated Bond

AT THE END of a coerced migration, the enslaved found themselves in an unfamiliar physical and social environment, entering into new relationships and trying to bond with new slavers. The patterns of interaction within the involuntary relationship of mutual dependence between two unequal partners were being set from the first encounter of a particular slaver and with a particular enslaved person. The dyad was dynamic, tested and renegotiated daily by both sides as the content and the nature of the exchange were being determined or dictated and the boundaries drawn. In the context of unquestionable exploitation, however, there had to exist a certain level of trust, which depended on the quality of the bond achieved between the parties. As the ingredients of the "deal" and the "rules of the game" were defined, expectations were also set and the level of abuse calibrated. Accumulated breaches of the rules could result in the enslaved person feeling betrayed, sensing that the relationship was breaking down.

At such breaking points, the option of leaving the relationship, of absconding and seeking an attachment to a new slaver-patron, would become realistic. A gamut of situations and human conditions could and did lead to absconding, from unrelenting abuse to the fear of being resold or the fear that the enslaved family would be split up. In other cases, the desire to opt out of enslavement and replace it with a free bond of patronage was in and of itself sufficient motive for absconding. All these attempts to leave the slaver-enslaved relationship entailed a search for a new patron, whether another slaver, the state, or a foreign consul serving as mediator for placement with a new non-slaver patron.

CHOOSING TO LEAVE: THE PREDICAMENT

The Ottoman law governing slavery followed, for the most part, the path of the Hanafi School of Islamic law, or Şeriat, which was one of the main sources of state law in the Empire.[1] Accordingly, runaway slaves had to be pursued and, if captured, returned to their holders. Only ill-treatment, usually entailing severe physical abuse, evidence for which had to be sustained in court, could form the basis for a court-imposed, involuntary manumission of an enslaved person. That procedure could also be resorted to by slaves not within the context of absconding, al-though captured runaway slaves often charged ill-treatment to mitigate their predicament in the hope of inducing the court to set them free. To counter such potential and actual charges, slavers often accused their runaway slaves of petty theft.[2] Whereas absconding occurred throughout Ottoman history, it perceptibly increased in the last quarter of the nine-teenth century, for the British allowed runaway slaves to be harbored in their consulates throughout the Empire and in their naval vessels.[3] Al-though the Ottoman government officially cooperated with the British and other European powers on the suppression of the slave trade, indi-vidual governors, especially in the remote slave-importing provinces, often developed their own approach to the problem.

In 1869, for example, the British consul in Tripoli, in present-day Libya, reported that slaves were being threatened with being drafted into the army or navy or being prosecuted for theft if they sought

1. For Islamic law on slavery, see R. Brunschvig, "ʿAbd," *Encyclopaedia of Islam*, 2nd ed., vol. 1, Leiden: E. J. Brill, 1960: 24 ff.
2. On this and other aspects of runaway slaves in the Ottoman Empire, see Y. Hakan Erdem, *Slavery in the Ottoman Empire and Its Demise, 1800–1909*, Basingstoke, England: Macmillan in association with St. Antony's College, Oxford,1996: 160–173 (he prefers "fugitive" to "runaway").
3. For details on British efforts to suppress the traffic in Africans into the Ot-toman Empire, see Ehud R. Toledano, *The Ottoman Slave Trade and Its Suppres-sion, 1840–1890*, Princeton: Princeton University Press, 1982: 91–123, 192–278.

manumission through foreign consulates. Being prosecuted for theft, he added, was a common practice regarding runaway slaves. In 1873, the French vice-consul at Massawa, on the western coast of the Red Sea, observed that when a male slave ran away and sought manumission at the French consulate, he was required to prove at the *Shari'a* (Arabic Seriat) court that he had been treated cruelly. If he managed to do that—and, as noted, the burden of proof in the Empire was quite heavy—he was freed and then drafted into the Ottoman-Egyptian army. Matters were no different across the Red Sea in the port town of Jidda, as an Anti-Slavery Society correspondent reported in 1874. He complained that slaves used to run away and seek refuge at the houses of Europeans, but they had stopped recently because the government began to hunt them down, and they were being accused of theft, "which could consist of as little as their clothes." The slavers themselves knew that these were frivolous, trumped-up charges. In at least one case, a female friend of the holder even admitted as much. When she requested that the British consul in Skopje, Macedonia, return to her friend two young, neglected, and abused female slaves, she was asked by the consul's wife about the theft charge that had been brought against them. To that the woman laughingly replied in Ottoman Turkish: "O boş şeydir" (It's nothing).[4]

If on the Ottoman side there was lack of consistency in applying existing agreements with the British, London was cautious and, at times, hesitant when it came to runaway slaves. The British government explicitly distanced itself from a policy of encouraging legally held slaves to seek refuge and manumission in British consulates across the Ottoman Empire. Instructions to agents were very clear in demanding that only in cases of a humanitarian nature, when ill-treatment was patently evident,

---

4. Information in this paragraph is derived from the following sources, listed in order of appearance in the text: FO/84/1305/499–506, Cons. Hay (Tripoli) to Amb. Elliot (Istanbul), 16.12.1869; E. A. De Cosson, *The Cradle of the Blue Nile: A Visit to the Court of King John of Ethiopia*, London: J. Murray, 1877: vol. 2, p. 303; ASS/S18/C43/16–16a, ASS correspondent in Jidda, 12.8.1874 (ASS, used henceforth, refers to the Anti-Slavery Society and its papers in Rhodes House Library, Oxford, U.K.); FO/84/1090/73–8, Cons. Brunt (Skopje, Üsküp in Turkish) to Cons. Longworth (Monastir), 15.3.1859. See also, in this context, FO/84/1570/259–62, Cons. Fawcett to Amb. Goschen (Istanbul), 11.10.1880.

should shelter and good offices be offered to runaway slaves.[5] Still, in practice, because of the distance from London, much was left to the discretion of representatives on the ground. Those who preached abolitionism took a more active approach, allowing even borderline cases to receive support. Slaves were aware of what they could expect of the British consulate in their area; word spread rather fast among them when a lenient and sympathetic agent was present in a certain town, and they would flock to that town in growing numbers, with the consulate often drawing the ire of local slavers. Where there were no real results for slaves seeking manumission, the number approaching those consulates quickly declined.

Adding to that the difference in approach of various local Ottoman governors gives the usual diverse matrix. In the districts where a lenient governor met a zealous consul, slaves could expect to gain their freedom more easily, but if the number manumitted was too large, protest would come from slavers, and the governor was likely to become less cooperative or face a reprimand from Istanbul. Where both governor and consul lacked interest, runaway slaves had to fend for themselves, unable to count on outside official help. When the consul was enthusiastic and the governor hostile, absconding slaves would have some chance, at least until Ottoman complaints met with British reluctance to appear too encouraging, and the resulting reprimand to the consul arrived from London in a diplomatic pouch.

As an example, let me cite an 1873 case from Syria, in which a sixteen-year-old African eunuch was purchased in Damascus for resale in Tripoli.[6] Although quite young, the man had been in service for a few years already, since castration had to be performed before puberty, usually around the

---

5. FO/84/1290/23–7, Wylde (London), FO consultation, 14.8.1868; FO/84/1290/5–7, Foreign Sec. Stanley to Cons. Reade (Cairo), 28.8.68; FO/84/1305/79–80, Amb. Elliot (Istanbul) to Foreign Sec. Clarendon, 2.9.1869; FO/84/1354/163–4, Foreign Sec. Granville to V. Cons. Green (Damascus), 7.8.1872; FO/84/1482/238, Wylde (FO, London) to Foreign Sec. Derby, internal correspondence, 10.1877; FO/84/1544/100–2, Wylde (FO, London) to Cons. Zohrab (Jidda), 11.4.1879.

6. FO/84/1370/137 ff., Cons. Eldridge (Beirut) to Amb. Elliot (Istanbul), 18.9.1873. For more on African eunuchs in the Ottoman Empire, see Ehud R. Toledano, *Slavery and Abolition in the Ottoman Middle East,* Seattle: University of Washington Press, 1998: 41–53.

age of ten.[7] Because only the larger, wealthier elite households could afford to hold eunuchs, our youth had probably served in the harem of one of the high officeholders in a Syrian province, possibly that of a governor-general, of a district governor, or of a top military or administrative officer. Eunuchs absconded very rarely and, like the rest of the kul/harem slaves, preferred to manipulate the system from within rather than seek their fortunes outside. More than other enslaved persons in that class, eunuchs had less to expect from the world outside the harem, since they were handicapped, often unfit to engage in a demanding menial job, and unable to form families and integrate into society. At the same time, within the system, they were prized and much coveted property, often enjoying the comforts of wealth and the high influence of a go-between.

Our young eunuch was sold in Damascus, probably to a slave dealer, who intended to sell him to a buyer in Tripoli. The lad undoubtedly was aware of the possible implications of the deal. Clearly he was determined not to be taken to North Africa, either because he did not like the information he possessed about conditions there or because he did not like what he had heard about the intended slaver, who had to be the governor-general of the province or one of the few other top men in the city of Tripoli. Since information traveled among elite harem members fairly regularly, the eunuch could have heard rumors about the top harem woman (the *paşa's* mother) or women (his favorite wife or concubine). Such information could have come from enslaved women who had served there, from letters exchanged between harem ladies, or via a eunuch network. In any event, because he was determined not to cooperate with the impending deal, his options of remaining within the system were virtually nil, and he had to take his chances outside the harem world.

Our eunuch's information must have indicated to him that he had better chances of getting support at the more distant Beirut consulate than at the closer Damascus one. This could have been either because Consul Eldridge had a better reputation for protecting runaway slaves or because the Damascus government was seen to be more vigorously

7. For a fascinating analysis of the economic aspects of the supply of eunuchs, see Jan S. Hogendorn, "The Location of the 'Manufacture' of Eunuchs," in Miura Toru and John Edward Philips (eds.), *Slave Elites in the Middle East: A Comparative Study*, London: Kegan Paul International, 2000: 41–68.

siding with the slavers. His information proved to have been reliable, and his consequent gamble eventually paid off. The young man escaped to Beirut and was well received at the British consulate. After three months in the consul's custody, he was ordered by the government to return to Damascus to stand trial for theft, the usual ploy of state-backed slavers. Consul Eldridge refused to comply and passed the matter to the embassy in Istanbul, requesting that the eunuch be set free. Ambassador Elliot petitioned the grand vezir, and finally, the eunuch was officially manumitted by state order.

Information traveled among slaves also from Beirut to Yemen, as the following story from 1873 illustrates.[8] Ya'qub ibn 'Abdallah al-Habashi, an Ethiopian man, had been captured as a child, enslaved, and carried away from his country to Jidda. In Jidda he was sold to an Ottoman officer, who proceeded to Yemen, where he was stationed. Ya'qub served there in his master's household for seven years. Later, the officer took him to Beirut, where Ya'qub absconded and approached the British consulate. Interestingly, he stated to consular staff that he was still a Christian, and asked to be freed. Explaining why he had waited so long to do so, Ya'qub said that he knew he had no chance of gaining manumission before reaching Beirut. In the Arabian Peninsula provinces, slavers insisted on their entitlement to hang on to their slaves, at times resorting to violence, and the Ottoman authorities tended to humor them. Presumably, then, it became well known among slaves that it was exceedingly difficult to gain freedom by absconding in those provinces. In our case, Ya'qub's patience paid off, and he was freed by the Mütesarrıf of Beirut, Raif Efendi.

Despite this difficult situation for slaves in the Hijaz and other Arabian regions, matters changed according to circumstances and according to the persons holding office in the provincial administration. Hence, it was important for aspiring absconders to follow the news closely and gather intelligence that could assist them in their planned escape. Targeted, useful information spread quickly even within the Red Sea basin, as the following story reveals.[9] In March 1879, the British consul in Jidda reported that in January, within ten days, about seventeen enslaved

8. FO/84/1482/164–5, Cons. Eldrige (Beirut) to Foreign Sec. Derby, 13.12.1877.
9. FO/84/1544/96–9, Cons. Zohrab (Jidda) to Foreign Sec. Salisbury, 15.3.1879.

African males had escaped to the HMS *Ready* from their Bedouin slave-holders in the villages around Jidda. This appears to be more than coincidence, and it is quite probable that word had circulated rapidly among the tribespeople and their slaves that the British naval vessel was not only not turning absconders away but harboring them on board. In addition, this episode might indicate that this was an organized escape scheme, possibly coordinated among the enslaved African men in question under some sort of spontaneous leadership. It seems less likely that the individuals involved here simply drifted away one by one toward the British man-of-war anchoring offshore.

A good example of how the presence of an Ottoman official who was sympathetic to the slaves and assisted them could, at times, improve matters even in the Hijaz is that of Arifi Bey. This official served as deputy governor-general of Jidda between 1887 and 1890 and strongly supported the anti-slavery measures implemented by the Ottomans and the British in the region. He even suggested that an asylum for runaway slaves be established, as in Istanbul and some other Ottoman cities, so that such persons would not have to be returned to the slaveholders. The case of Tursun, an enslaved African woman, will here serve to show how Arifi Bey acted on her behalf, but will also demonstrate how complex many of these human stories are.[10]

Tursun, captured and enslaved somewhere on the east African coast, or perhaps in the interior, was brought by a small rowboat from the Sudanese port of Sawakin to a village near the Arabian port of Jidda, where she was sold to an unnamed man whom we shall call First Holder. On 17 July 1888, she escaped to the Jidda authorities and asked to be liberated. According to Ottoman policy, based on treaties with Great Britain, Tursun was manumitted and placed, with monthly pay, as a domestic servant at the house of Harun Bey, the health service director. After a while, however, she absconded again and, when searched for, was found hiding in some unspecified location. She was taken into custody and detained at the house of the Jidda mufti, Mehmet Efendi. First Holder then petitioned the emir of Mecca to have her returned to him,

10. İstanbul Üniversitesi Kütüphanesi/Mss # T1072, Arifi Beyin Cidde Vali Kay-
    makamlığında bulunduğu zamana ait muhaberat-i resmiye mecmuası,
    9.1887–2.1890/p 39, # 408, Arifi Bey to the Vilayet of the Hijaz, 7.10.1888.

presumably after the emir revoked the act of her manumission. Our record in this case is the letter which Arifi Bey wrote to the office of the governor-general of the Hijaz in Mecca to inquire whether any decision had been made on the petition sent from Jidda by First Holder. We do not know what answer Arifi Bey received from Mecca, but we do know that he strongly rejected the possibility that Tursun be restored to First Holder, because she had already been legally manumitted by the governor-general of Jidda, and he possibly feared that a precedent might be set to impede runaway slaves.

However, Tursun's case also demonstrates the determination of an African woman to seek freedom and, later, to assert her right not to work for an employer she did not like. First Holder was apparently attached to her, even pointing to the fact that it was he who had named her Tursun when she was still in the possession of the slave dealer who had carried her to Jidda. Naming was a strongly symbolic act; a mere utterance was intended to wipe out the enslaved person's identity and replace it with a new one. Too often observers and scholars have glossed over this brutal act, mentioning only the type of names slaves received in various societies, not delving into the deeper meaning that the act inevitably carried with it. Names chosen and given by parents, often having great significance in their own lives, were replaced by names in Turkish, Persian, or Arabic of flowers, fruits, jewelry, or other ornamental objects, names that the enslaved themselves daily mispronounced in their pidgin Turkish. In fact, naming was a dual act of detaching the enslaved persons from their previous world and reattaching them to a new and strange culture, so different in language, customs, and beliefs from their native one. That this could only partially be accomplished should be self-evident.

The significance of naming was clearly not lost on First Holder, who saw his undertaking of the act as an indication of special bonding and affinity with his new female slave. But he also demonstrated his attachment to Tursun by pursuing the case all the way to the highest religious and moral authority in the Hijaz, the emir of Mecca. Still, and for whatever reason, Tursun was unmoved by his affection and chose not to remain his slave, or anybody else's. Instead, she applied to the governor-general of Jidda and demanded to be liberated. The second time, she asserted her right as an already free woman to deny her labor—again for unknown reasons—to Harun Bey, an important Ottoman official in the province. We do not know whether she had been harassed in that household or whether she simply had higher aspirations, which should not be surprising for a woman who had already twice demonstrated strong will and determination. Unfortunately, we have no information about what happened to Tursun in the end. Theoretically, her manumission could have been revoked, since it was not granted by the slaveholder but imposed by an administrative authority. Still, although Şeriat courts were not enthusiastic about such procedures, it would be quite unlikely that the emir of Mecca, an Ottoman official himself, would annul manumission papers issued by the governor-general of Jidda. If indeed Tursun's manumission remained valid, she was probably released in due course, to be placed at another household or to find employment of her choice on her own.

In general, we should note that Ottoman leniency was often forthcoming on humanitarian grounds. It was not uncommon for the sultan to grant freedom—upon the recommendation of his grand vezir or another top official—to suffering, criminally neglected, physically abused, and destitute slaves. Money was taken from the imperial fisc to purchase slaves' freedom from slaveholders who refused to liberate their slaves. These acts of imperial benevolence were not infrequently prompted by British consular requests on behalf of runaway slaves who had sought refuge at their consulates across the Ottoman Empire. Both the Ottoman and the British archives are peppered with stories of this kind. One such example, contained at the Republic of Turkey archives in Istanbul, comes from Bursa, not very far from the capital, where in late 1852 an enslaved African woman ran away from her master to the house of the British consul.[11] She alleged that the man had beaten and abused her, and refused to go back to him. The consul would not turn her in, it was explained in the Ottoman government report on the case, which was submitted to the grand vezir. The vezir recommended that, because the slaveholder was very poor, the government should buy the woman from him and set her free. Wasting no time, the sultan approved the decision on the following day.

11. BOA/İrade/Hariciye/4530, the Grand Vezir to the Sultan, 8.12.1852, and the Sultan's response, 9.12.1852.

Years later, in the imperial capital Istanbul, Ambassador Elliot drew attention to the fact that absconding was also an issue of gender and ethnicity. Elliot maintained that African runaway slaves were relatively easy to free if abuse by slavers was demonstrable, adding that attempts to tamper with their manumission papers were not common, at least in the center of the Empire. At the same time, the Ottomans showed great reluctance to allow any interference with runaway female Circassian slaves, and the ambassador opined that "any direct interference in it on our part would excite the susceptibilities of the whole Turkish people."[12] This memo is in itself a clear indication that despite the difference between the situation of white harem slaves and that of African domestic ones, a certain number of harem slaves also ran away to British consulates, including even a few eunuchs.[13] Few though harem slaves may have been, it is nonetheless significant that even those most protected, most comfortable, best integrated of slaves still preferred freedom to enslavement and took action to achieve it, despite the risks and obvious British reluctance to support their claims. Their situation was, to a certain degree, like that of their male cognates, the kuls, in that they had options and leeway within the system and in that absconding reflected individual stress and failure to manipulate Ottoman elite culture to serve their needs.

Before we proceed to examine the mind-set of the runaway slave, I should point out that we are still a considerable distance from possessing a reliable database to confidently offer any statistically valid observations. For the moment, I can speak only about impressions formed by extensive reading of the available evidence about absconding slaves in the Ottoman Middle East and North Africa during the long nineteenth century. Although I expect to be able to say—qualitatively—a great deal about slave experiences in the Empire, I am less comfortable about providing quantitative breakdowns of the runaway population by gender, age, ethnicity, or type of enslavement. The data are simply too fragmented, too scattered, and too anecdotal to allow for more than impressionistic observations.

12. FO/84/1570/128, Elliot to Foreign Sec. Salisbury, 15.2.1880.
13. See, for example, FO/84/1543/279–80, memo by Dragoman Hugo Marinich (in charge of slave issues, Istanbul consulate), 8.10.1879.

On the basis of the corpus population, which consists of dozens of cases studied in-depth, it is possible to say that most of the runaway slaves were African and female, but then they were also the majority of Ottoman slaves and, correspondingly, the majority group within our sample. But this impression comes up against another, contemporary impression, that of a consular reporter from 1880 Damascus. That observer maintains that "African male slaves invariably assert their freedom when they reach a man's estate, and that owners can do little to prevent that. These boys melt into society and marry freed African women."[14] We can, however, reconcile the next observation if we take into account the fact that there were many more enslaved African females than enslaved African males in the Ottoman Empire at the time— except among the enslaved agricultural laborers who were being employed in Egypt after the cotton boom of the 1860s—but again, we do not have good numbers.

There can hardly be much doubt that, given the legal injunction against absconding and the determination to enforce it, runaway slaves took great risks when deciding to leave their holders. Some of these slaves did not fully calculate these risks and were not fully aware of the possible consequences of their action. However, most slaves were in touch with the realities of urban life in the Ottoman Empire. They lived within households, were in contact with other slaves, interacted with people outside the household while running errands for their holders, and could communicate fairly effectively with the society around them. In none of the sources I consulted are slaves depicted as disconnected, living apart from their environment, isolated, or cast away. It is therefore safe to assume that they must have heard stories about runaway slaves. Those episodes that ended with capture and retribution were probably amplified and related by slavers to discourage similar ideas among their own slaves. The cases that ended well for the enslaved were probably whispered in their ears by other enslaved people, perhaps by those who were contemplating a similar action.

But slaves knew more than that. They knew that since success was not guaranteed, careful planning, preparation, and cautionary measures were necessary in order to maximize chances of success. The first thing

14. FO/84/1571/218–21, 10.2.1880.

they needed to determine was their final goal: Did they wish to be liberated locally and remain in the community as free laborers, or did they
want to get as far away as possible and melt into a large urban environment, where they would be able to start a new life as free persons? At
times, this was determined by the prevailing circumstances in their origin community and in the target one. Most enslaved persons realized
that to gain their freedom, they needed to rely on outside help. Broadly
speaking, help could come either from official sources or from private
persons. In the first instance, runaway slaves could expect assistance either from Ottoman state officials or from representatives of foreign powers in the Empire. Not only were slaves informed by word of mouth
about British and other consuls who were prepared to harbor them, as
well as about those who would turn them in upon the demand of the local governor, but they also knew where Ottoman authorities were more
committed to hunting down and punishing runaway slaves and where,
conversely, leniency had the upper hand.

Before the British moved vigorously to induce the Ottoman government to suppress the trade in enslaved Africans, the courts were the
main hope that enslaved persons had. Until the establishment of the
new administrative tribunals beginning in the 1840s, the Şeriat courts
were the main organ of the Ottoman justice system. Although recourse
could be had by ordinary subjects to the sultan's Imperial Council (Di-
van-ı Hümayun), this was a quantitatively marginal element within the
system. With the Tanzimat reforms (roughly 1830s–1880s), administrative (Nizami) courts took over major areas of adjudication from the
Şeriat system, including criminal law. Thus, while slaves continue to
appear in the kadi court records (the sicill) in various cases, they appear
in growing numbers also in the new Nizami courts, mostly in criminal
matters.

Şeriat court records from various parts of the Empire contain
numerous cases involving slaves. Many of these concern runaway incidents, which were brought to the courts' attention either after the enslaved person had been captured or when the absconding slave approached the court demanding freedom, usually on the ground of
ill-treatment. Although judges were generally reluctant to impose
manumission on an unwilling slaveholder, if abuse was patently evident, this was one of the few situations in which they took this course

of action. The courts also dealt with violations of manumission contracts between slaver and enslaved, whether after death (*tedbir*) or self-financed (*mükatebe*), and with illegal enslavement or reenslavement of freed slaves. Although the state, through its legal corps officials (ulema), clearly upheld ownership rights over the enslaved, from time to time and from place to place individual kadis ruled in favor of the enslaved, giving precedence to humanitarian considerations over class interests. All in all, and despite their limited success at court, enslaved persons continued to approach the courts in an effort to obtain freedom and justice.

If enslaved individuals contemplating absconding had reason to believe that state officials, Ottoman or foreign, were unlikely to provide them with the support they needed to obtain their freedom, they looked elsewhere for help. In such instances, recourse was had to private individuals, whom the enslaved person came to know and trust in the course of working as a household domestic. These could be relatives or friends of the slaveholder's family, whom the enslaved person had an opportunity to meet on visits or outings. Assistance could also be expected from slaves in other households, with whom interaction was easier than with members of the slaveholding class. But the help that other slaves could offer was limited, since their lives, too, were controlled by their holders' families. An enslaved person could hardly offer temporary shelter to a runaway friend without the knowledge and consent of household members. Food might be smuggled out somehow, but a runaway slave—especially if black, hence more easily detectable—had to prepare a safe hideout ahead of time for the initial few days at least.

Given that until the 1870s, the Ottoman government sided with the slavers, except in humanitarian cases, the risks of absconding were great. Although the Ottoman state did not run a tightly controlled society for much of its history, the technological advances of the Tanzimat period increased the state's capacity to impose central authority. As the century wore on, two contradictory processes took hold in Ottoman society. The first worked in favor of slaves who wished to be freed, as the sultan's government moved to suppress the traffic in Africans and to reduce the size of the enslaved population. This they did partly under foreign, mainly British, pressure and partly out of their own desire to cope with problems posed by Circassian agricultural slavery.[15] The other process was the increasing capacity to track down and recapture runaway slaves, afforded by an improved communications systems (the telegraph), an improved transport system (trains and steam ships), and an improved system of registration and licensing (travel documents, border controls).

As the nineteenth century drew to a close, however, the ideas that followed the technologies won the day, and runaway slaves, as well as illegally captured, enslaved, and transported persons, could expect to be liberated from bondage in all the core areas and in most of the peripheral regions of the sultan's domains. The growing numbers of runaway slaves who managed to regain their freedom began to have a perceptible impact also in economic terms. With risks of losing slaves to absconding and to government-sponsored manumission, slavers gradually came to prefer hiring free labor to buying slaves. As the number of slaves decreased, the number of free servants increased.[16] But the shift was not easy, as domestic slavery was such an acquired habit—I am almost tempted to say a social addiction—that many elite households, which had thrived on it for centuries, found it hard to carry on without it. Substitute arrangements evolved for the transitory period, and as late as the first decades of the twentieth century such households used to adopt unofficially children from poor families and raise and educate them in the house while also using them as domestic servants. In this variant mechanism of patronage, which is akin to *atalık* among the Circassians, the children (known in Turkish as *besleme* or *çırak*) were later married off and set up in life by the patron's family. This was the end of enslavement in the Ottoman Empire.

15. For the Ottoman treatment of Circassian slavery, see Toledano, *Slavery and Abolition*, Chapter 3. For the suppression of the traffic in Africans, see Toledano, *Slave Trade*, 91–123, 192–278.
16. See, for example, observations from Jidda in FO/541/25 (Confidential 4914)/81, Cons. Moncrieff's report (Jidda) on runaway slaves for 1882 (dated 12.1.1883). Gabriel Baer observed that for Egypt "the most important change affecting slavery was the emergence of a free labor market in the late 1880's and 1890's," in his "Slavery and Its Abolition," in Baer, *Studies in the Social History of Modern Egypt*, Chicago: University of Chicago Press, 1969: 161–189 (the quotation is from p. 186).

SEVERANCE STORIES—REASONS, MOTIVES, CIRCUMSTANCES

Broadly speaking, in the Ottoman Empire there were several types of en-slaved persons who decided to sever their relationship with the slavers; the sources refer to these individuals as runaway slaves. There were those who absconded with the intention of registering a momentary protest against their holders. Such enslaved persons expected to be caught soon after running away, a priori intending to be reconciled with their holders for somewhat improved conditions. This was the less glorified, weaker majority, and although they are not the focus of this book, a brief com-ment about their predicament still seems in order.

Here is a quick illustration. The British consul in Jidda, who in the 1880s regularly compiled reports of runaway slaves who sought refuge at his consulate, reported in 1883 that of the twenty-four runaway African slaves—seventeen male and seven female—sixteen were reconciled with their holders.[17] Since thirteen of the twenty-four had complained of ill-treatment, we may assume that at least some of those who were voluntar-ily returned to the slaveholders had been previously ill-treated by them. So we may wonder what those abused slaves could hope for when they agreed to go back to their holders in exchange for promises that might never be fulfilled. But apparently, this was part of the "game," an unwrit-ten understanding by both the enslaved and the slavers that if things got bad for a moment, the enslaved person could escape, and the slaver would not make too much of it if the enslaved person returned within a reasonable amount of time and without too much fuss.

This group of temporary absconders, if I may call them so, still de-serves consideration because even their limited actions did constitute a statement we need to analyze and better understand. To be sure, the majority of slaves in Ottoman society did not run away at any time dur-ing their long periods of servitude. They accepted their predicament, more often than not because they had no alternative; the overwhelming power of slavers and the backing they received from the state clearly reg-istered with the enslaved population. So for most slaves, the risks of try-ing to effect any change in their situation ran higher than they dared to take. Such people tried to work within the system, rather than to break

17. FO/541/25 (Confidential 4914)/79–80, Cons. Moncrieff's report (Jidda) on runaway slaves for 1882 (dated 12.1.1883).

away from it. And, in a system that did not merely wave a big stick but also offered some carrots, this was not an unbearable option for most slaves.

By winning the appreciation and trust of slaveholders, capable slaves could receive better jobs within the household or even be allowed to work outside and keep some of the money they earned. They could also try to convince their holders to enable them, through a self-purchase contract (mükatebe), to buy their freedom over a period of several years, if they had managed to acquire some sort of gainful employment outside the household. Alternatively, enslaved persons could ingratiate themselves with slaveholders in the hope that the latter would be inclined to stipulate in their wills that the slaves be manumitted after the slaveholders' death (tedbir).

But these options could be negotiated only from a position of weakness, entailing both the explicit and implicit acceptance of the legitimacy of enslavement. Any challenge to that notion—by either temporary or serious absconding—would undoubtedly have jeopardized or greatly diminished any chance of realizing such mitigated forms of servitude. Hence, temporary absconders had no prospect of generating long-term, goal-oriented arrangements with their holders to mitigate the terms of bondage. Another possibility is that when they ran away owing to some provocation, momentary rage, or fatigue, they were not fully aware of the probable implications of their actions. In either case, most of the temporary absconders were likely short-term thinkers, triggered to act by accumulated frustration and seeking to redress an immediate grievance. Likely, too, these were not people who believed they could remove or ameliorate the basic impediments in enslavement, nor could they contemplate and plan a process that would, in due course, extricate them from servitude altogether.

Now let me somewhat broaden this category of "temporary absconders" to accommodate yet another group of enslaved persons. These were not temporary absconders per se, because they did not wish to return to their holders under slightly improved terms. Nor, however, were they seeking to fundamentally change their predicament, regain their freedom, and live as free men and women in society. Rather, individuals belonging to this group were somewhere between the two "intention" categories designated here as "temporary" and "permanent." This group was, it seems, relatively small and was composed of people absconding to gain specific pecuniary benefits but not freedom. They appear in an assessment provided by the Ottoman minister of police to Mr. Marinich, the dragoman of the British Embassy in Istanbul in charge of dealing with runaway slaves. The minister told the dragoman in 1880 that quite a few runaway African female slaves, when set free by the government, turned themselves over to slave dealers to be resold, pocketing half the money in the process.[18]

From the perspective adopted in the current work, such actions are not perfunctory or insignificant, but rather in need of contextualization and serious evaluation. The African women who resorted to such action had a clear view of the world around them and of their place in it. Arguably, their view was cynical, too, and we may perhaps reconstruct its properties as follows:

- Although slavery is an exploitive labor practice, it has a few loopholes that we can use to our benefit.
- The options offered to freed African women in this society are not attractive, perhaps even less attractive than what we ourselves have experienced as enslaved Ottoman subjects.
- The main problem with enslavement is that it does not adequately reward enslaved persons for their hard work.
- If by escaping to the police, gaining our freedom, and then submitting to a slave dealer for resale, we can gain some cash—why not?

Freedom in and of itself had no special value for these slaves. In fact, their action made a mockery of it and of its value to other enslaved persons. To those who risked a great deal to gain their freedom by absconding, these individuals sent a clear message, namely, that freedom was not worth fighting for; it was instead a tool to be manipulated to improve one's lot in bondage. Among the enslaved population in Istanbul, as probably in other Ottoman core cities, stories about absconding for pecuniary reasons were circulated and debated. As the minister of police—the senior official dealing with runaway slaves—reported, it was a fairly common phenomenon in the capital, which indicates that the make-believe

18. FO/84/1570/240–50, Amb. Goschen (Istanbul) to Foreign Sec. Granville, 25.10.1880.

absconders contributed a new option to those available to the enslaved population. It is ironic that this was made possible by the softening of the Ottoman government's policy on runaway slaves during the late 1870s and early 1880s, which made such abuses of the system possible. To reduce the occurrence of such faked abscondings, the police detained freed runaway slaves at an uncongenial hostel for several months before letting them return to society.

One last comment on ploys to defraud the Tanzimat-state by abusing its emancipation and rehabilitation policy comes from a report sent from Bengazi, in present-day Libya, to the Interior Ministry in Istanbul, as late in the history of Ottoman suppression as the year 1890.[19] The report claimed that freed African slaves who could not find employment in the province, or who perhaps did not wish to be integrated into society, became vagabonds. At some point, such men would present themselves to the authorities as slaves and ask to be manumitted. This entitled them to receive government support, meager though that was, as we know from earlier requests to increase the amount the Ottoman treasury allocated to Bengazi for such purposes, which, incidentally, was endorsed by Sultan Abdülhamit II, who granted the province even more than initially requested.[20]

If we combine the two deceptive methods employed by freed slaves—African women in Istanbul and African men in Bengazi—we can see how quickly and efficiently the enslaved adapted to the changing economic and social circumstances that affected their lives. As Ottoman slavery lost ground, and as it became easier to be freed from enslavement, former slaves realized that they could exploit the loopholes in the evolving system, which was still in a state of transition. Since it became so easy to be liberated by the authorities, they figured that they could voluntarily go in and out of slavery by flaunting state-issued manumission papers, which changed their status to free persons—and pocket some money in the process.

We should perhaps approach this phenomenon from the perspective of the enslaved and freed, rather than from that of the Ottoman

---

19. BOA/İrade/Dahiliye/62927/Şura-yı Devlet, Dahiliye Dairesi, *Mazbata* and other documents, 11.11.1890–10.1.1891.
20. On this subject, see Toledano, *Slave Trade*, 241–242; and Erdem, *Slavery*, 178–179.

state, its officeholding elite, or even free Ottomans of other strata, as most observers do. From our bottom-up view, these people, street-smart survivors all, virtually turned the Anglo-Ottoman emancipation system into a money-making revolving door, which was their answer to years of deprivation and harsh post-manumission economic realities. Moreover, they skillfully exploited a racial bias that usually worked against them, namely, the collapsing of the categories "African" and "enslaved." Only because they were black could these men and women pass for slaves, although in fact they were not.[21] From the top-down perspective of the Tanzimat-state and the British, these persons were working to defeat a system designed specifically to save them from the injustices and misfortunes of enslavement.

Let us now return to the main group at the focus of this study, the real absconders, those who sought to extricate themselves from enslavement and were willing to take great risks to realize their ambition. Having so far explored the mechanisms of absconding and the intentions entertained by several types of absconders, let us look more carefully into what motivated the serious, committed absconders. Here, again, a number of reasons ultimately impelled the enslaved person to take action and run away. Sometimes there would be an accumulation of reasons, but often there was one major cause, one main grievance. In most of our cases, the main reason for absconding was the need to stop an injurious action by the slaveholder, not to gain some benefit in the free world outside. The enslaved person could have desired to stop without delay one of the following acts of aggression by the slaveholder:

- physical attack in progress or looming
- attempt to abort the fetus of an enslaved pregnant woman
- imminent rape or sexual harassment
- resale after years of service
- impending splitting of an enslaved family by selling one or more of its members outside the household

21. On a similar phenomenon in Sharifian Morocco, where free and freed Africans were rounded up by the state for military service because they were considered slave, see John Hunwick, "Islamic Law and Polemics over Race and Slavery in North and West Africa (16th–19th Century)," in Shaun E. Marmon (ed.), *Slavery in the Islamic Middle East*, Princeton, N.J.: Markus Wiener, 1999: 43–68.

Cases in which the motivation of the absconder was to get a better-paying job as a free person are not as frequent. However, in certain circumstances this was indeed so, as reported by the British consul in Jidda in 1883 in one case.[22] Detecting a diminishing number of absconding incidents, only twenty-four in the latest quarter, the consul observed that the motivation now seemed to be low pay. He added that the men often carried limestone, flour, or water, were employed as pearl divers, bakers, coffeehouse servants, or held other menial jobs and had to turn over their pay to their masters at the end of the day. The men must have figured out, the consul suggested, that they could keep their pay or get higher wages as free persons, which led them to abscond and seek freedom. The situation described here was probably the result of the labor market already reacting to the Anglo-Ottoman measures being applied in the region to suppress the slave trade in Africans. That is, the risks to slavers of losing their investment had tilted the balance in favor of free labor, and jobs were available to manumitted absconders. However, this was a phenomenon of the 1880s, when Ottoman slavery was nearing demise.

On the whole, few Ottoman slaves absconded simply for the purpose of liberation from bondage. Enslaved persons in our population—again, not necessarily a statistically representative sample—ran away mostly to address an immediate threat to their physical and emotional well-being. They were not ideologically motivated freedom seekers per se, but survivors, which in no way diminishes the significance and value of their action. They were brave men and women, who tried, often against considerable odds, to change the course of their lives, and the following stories of their diverse experiences—selected out of the larger pool for reasons of merit, interest, and narrative advantage—deserve our deep respect.

Leaving to End Abuse

Enslaved persons who absconded because of ill-treatment usually acted either to put an *immediate* end to an ongoing act of aggression or to quickly remove themselves from the home of a violent slaver, who had

---

22. FO/84/1642/107–24, Cons. Moncrieff's report (Jidda) on runaway slaves for 1.1–30.6.1883.

just perpetrated a cruel attack on their person. The distinction here is a fine but telling one, between absconding as a reaction to a harsh incident that was either still in progress or just over and reacting to the latest in a series of violent incidents in a long-term physically abusive relationship with the slaveholder. The main difference is that in an accumulated injury situation, the enslaved person usually had been contemplating absconding and therefore could have planned the escape and perhaps found a hiding place or accomplices on the outside. Such escapes were less likely to result from temporary anger or fear than were those made in reaction to a first or widely separated second violent attack. This type of absconding was usually not fully thought out, hence also ill planned, which meant that such runaway slaves were more likely to be captured and returned to their abusive holders.

In most recorded reports of cases involving the abuse of an enslaved person by the slaver, the accusation was stated without details. So, for example, an 1869 British consular report from the port city of Izmir recorded that Selim, aged twenty-two, an enslaved African male, fled to the British consulate from Manisa, a town in western Anatolia, because his master ill-treated him.[23] This type of reporting suggests that a certain tacit hierarchy of abuse toward slaves was acceptable as normative by both the slaver and the enslaved and was generally shared by the Ottoman authorities—usually law enforcement personnel, officeholders, and the different courts—to whom complaints were addressed regarding conduct toward slaves. According to that unwritten, socially sanctioned code of conduct, the use of a certain degree of force was considered acceptable, without being classified as abuse. However, the notion of physical abuse did exist in this context. Excessive use of force was considered to have occurred, it seems to me, if the enslaved person sustained minor injuries, that is, wounds that neither left lasting scars nor permanently crippled the victim. Following the categories of "normative," or "acceptable," and "minor" was the third and most serious category, which consisted of "severe injuries," such as loss of a limb or an organ, or serious bodily harm that left the enslaved person handicapped for life.

23. FO/84/1305/402–5, Cons. Cumberbatch (Izmir) to Foreign Sec. Clarendon, 28.8.1869.

The lower the injury on the scale, the more widespread it appears to have been, with the underlying assumption being that it was contrary to the slavers' economic interest to harm the enslaved and thereby degrade their working capacity. Minor injuries were considered an occupational hazard for slaves, and the sources ignore them. Excessive use of force was classified as ill-treatment, and the records usually mention such cases without providing any details. Then there are those cases in which the slaves were subjected to cruel, if not sadistic, treatment. Some of the stories that fall into the unfortunate category of most severe abuse are told below.

The first set of brief examples comes, yet again, from 1869 Izmir, where the British consul was a committed abolitionist and made a point of reporting such cases to London.[24] In one of these, Cuma (Arabic, Jumʿa), an enslaved African male, ran away from his master and sought refuge at the consulate. He had a "deformed body," in the consul's language, and reported that he had been cruelly treated by his holder. The reason for the slaveholder's aggressive behavior toward Cuma was apparently because he could not find any buyers when he offered him for resale, supposedly owing to his physical handicap. The man reached the consulate with head wounds and a broken finger, which he allegedly sustained from his master. The same consulate also received an African runaway named Mehmet, whose holder was Hasan Ağa of Aydın, a military officer serving in the nearby province. Hasan Ağa had a peculiar way of punishing his slaves—he liked to cut off their ears. He had already done that to two of his slaves when he tried to impose the same cruel punishment upon Mehmet. As Mehmet resisted, Hasan shot him in the leg, at which point the slave took off, determined never to return to his master.

In mid-1858, in Istanbul, an enslaved African woman named Servnaz ran away from her holders and sought refuge with the Ottoman authorities, probably at some law-enforcement facility.[25] Her former mistress had been highly placed—Zeynep Hanım, daughter of Esat Paşa. When Zeynep died, Servnaz was passed on to the custody of Zeynep's legal heirs.

24. FO/84/1305/402–5, Cons. Cumberbatch (Izmir) to Foreign Sec. Clarendon, 28.8.1869.
25. BOA/İrade/Dahiliye/27039/the Grand Vezir to the Sultan, 28.7.1858, the Sultan's response, 29.7.1858, and enclosures.

We do not know why Zeynep had not stipulated in her will that Servnaz be posthumously manumitted—she might have died suddenly, or been too young to take care of such things, or wished to leave her heirs a larger inheritance. Nor do we know who the heirs were, although normally we could expect them to be the deceased person's children, grandchildren, or other relations. In any event, Zeynep's death brought sheer disaster upon Servnaz, for the report compiled by the authorities in this case states that when she approached them, Servnaz was in a dreadful condition, which the report described as "unacceptable." This, we may safely assume, was probably due to neglect and severe abuse by the new holders. Consequently, the treasury agreed—on humanitarian grounds—to pay Zeynep's heirs an amount of money equal to Servnaz's estimated market value and then set her free. The grand vezir endorsed this recommendation, and the sultan promptly gave his consent.

Not very far from the imperial capital, in Skopje, Macedonia, two young, probably African, female slaves, named Fikriye and Rengi Sefa, escaped from their holder's household to the British consul's house.[26] The year was 1859, well before the Ottoman authorities were willing to cooperate with the British to protect and liberate runaway slaves. So it was up to Consul Brunt and his wife to deal with this sensitive matter in the best way they could. The two girls had worked in the harem of an important officeholder with the rank of paşa. Still, the two slaves had clearly been neglected and severely abused. When they reached the consulate, they had poor and dirty clothing on and were covered with vermin. The girls told the consul and his wife that they had been allowed to go to the public bath only once in the past ten months of service at the harem. However, neglect alone would not have impelled them to abscond, and only an incident of severe abuse finally drove them to escape. When they were on kitchen duty, the two reported, they had asked for a piece of cloth to remove the hot pans off the fire, but their mistress refused, forcing them by beating them to remove the pans with naked hands. Despite attempts by intermediaries to have the two returned to the paşa's household, the consul persisted in his commitment to protect them.

26. FO/84/1090/73–8, Cons. Brunt (Skopje) to Cons. Longworth (Monastir), 15.3.1859.

Severe neglect, in itself bordering on ill-treatment, often accompanied physical abuse, as indeed happened in this case. But sometimes neglect alone, on a continuous basis, brought upon the slaves various afflictions, such as the vermin carried in this story or the malnutrition in the next. Enslaved Africans in particular were vulnerable to infection by illnesses to which they could not have built up immunity in their countries of origin, with their different climatic conditions, bacteria, and viruses. Adding to that neglect poor hygiene, deficient diet, and abuse-related stress is a sure recipe for diminished labor capacity and significantly reduced life expectancy, which was not long among Africans anyway. Most slavers were surely aware that they had to take good care of their slaves in order to extract more labor from them and prevent the depreciation of their value in case they wished to resell them. But at times, especially in regions with difficult economic conditions or a harsh environment, the weaker members of society—the enslaved—had to get by with less. And sometimes less was not enough, producing unfortunate realities.

Severe and continuous neglect was revealed to the commander of the British naval ship HMS *Seagull*, cruising in the Red Sea at the end of 1880.[27] Since word must have spread among the enslaved on the coasts around Jidda that the British ship was not turning away runaways, slaves flocked to it, and the captain soon reported that he had taken in eight African male slaves. He then described their condition, which he stated to have been "poor due to ill-treatment and starvation." Some of them, he added, were in need of medical treatment for malnutrition. Several of the absconders told the crew that they had worked as pearl divers; others said they were masons. This report makes me wonder how, in their poor condition they could have performed such physically demanding tasks, and—to set aside for a moment the humanitarian aspect—what the economic logic was that guided the slaveholders, who were often Bedouin tribespeople, when they neglected and starved them.

Leaving to Avoid Forced Abortion
Another kind of physical abuse, with medical implications, was specific to enslaved pregnant women. Enslaved persons were vulnerable to sexual

27. FO/84/1579/266–81, Hall (Admiralty) to Under Sec. of State (FO), including five letters from Commander Byles (HMS *Seagull*), 31.12.1880.

abuse of various types. As the legal property of another person, they were sexually accessible to their holder—or, in unfortunate cases, several holders—and had no protection under the law if they did not wish to make themselves available to him or, more rarely, her.[28] To avoid committing an anachronism, we should remember that married women faced the same situation, since marriage was prearranged, and little choice was involved in the matter, sex included. In many Western countries, among them Britain, marital rape was not criminalized until recently, so the plight of enslaved women in Ottoman households should be put in the context of the generally sorry state of women in almost all premodern societies. Indeed, enslaved women in male-dominated Ottoman households were vulnerable, and their vulnerability should not be lightly dismissed simply because it was common and widely accepted. Sexual harassment within the house was not a rare phenomenon, and forced sex is likely to have been fairly common, partly because the issue of consent was so elusive in that environment. It is true that enslaved men were also vulnerable in this regard, but the impression from the evidence is that they were much less exposed to it than the women were, and more capable of resisting, but also perhaps less likely to report abusive incidents that did occur.

Elsewhere, I have already discussed extensively the question of rape and unwanted pregnancy in the case of Şemsigül, an enslaved Circassian woman in mid-nineteenth-century Cairo. Şemsigül, in her early teens then, was taken from Istanbul to Egypt by boat together with a dozen other enslaved females. The slave dealer who brought them for sale in Cairo forced himself upon her during the trip, and she consequently became pregnant. Since this made it illegal to resell her, the slave dealer had to conceal the fact that she was pregnant in order to sell her into the harem of the Ottoman-Egyptian governor-general. When her pregnancy was discovered, Şemsigül was sent back to the slave dealer's house, where his wife, in an attempt to safeguard her own position and that of her children, attempted to forcibly induce an abortion. However, Şemsigül was saved by a compassionate neighbor, in whose house she later was able to give birth. Subsequently, as the slave dealer

28. On several holders, see Jay Spaulding, "Slavery, Land Tenure, and Social Class in the Northern Turkish Sudan," *International Journal of African Historical Studies*, 15/1 (1982): 1–20.

was trying to resell her, she complained to the slave dealers' guild and was as a result extricated from the vicious circle of bondage and forced concubinage.[29] The whole saga, here recounted only in brief, certainly serves to illustrate that concubinage was not the positive nor even the benign social mechanism that many observers have presented it to be.

On this I tend to follow Claire Robertson and Martin Klein's portrayal of African concubinage, which, as they assert, reinforced women's inferior standing vis-à-vis men in society.[30] However, according to Islamic law as practiced in the Ottoman Empire, if a concubine became pregnant, she could not be resold, and if she gave birth, her child was considered free and the mother was to be manumitted upon the death of the father. The status that such a woman enjoyed—known as ümmüveled (*umm walad* in Arabic), literally "mother to a child"—provided concubines with consider-able protection, which did not exist in the regions of non-Islamic Africa discussed by Robertson and Klein. But again, not all Ottoman concubines became pregnant and not all pregnancies ended in birth. So the group covered by the law was already quite reduced in relation to the broader population of concubines who had no benefit at all. To reiterate what is perhaps obvious, these women were not only involuntarily enslaved but also forced—sometimes brutally and at a very young age—into sexual relations, often with much older men, where consent was not an issue.

The pregnancy of a concubine was not always desirable. Many slavers did not intend the relationship to be legally institutionalized in a legally binding manner. They were in it for sexual purposes only, and the responsibilities they incurred as a result of impregnating a concubine were something they wished to avoid. In addition, a legal wife or wives would likely oppose adding potential heirs to their husband's estate, as would, with the same logic, the other children, if they were already grown up—which often was the case when the father-husband-slaver was middle-aged or old. The concubine herself was often the only person interested in getting pregnant and having a child, especially a boy, which would

29. For the fullest account of this intricate story, see Toledano, *Slavery and Aboli-tion*, 59–80.
30. See Claire C. Robertson and Martin A. Klein (eds.), *Women and Medicine in Africa*, Madison: University of Wisconsin Press, 1983: 6, 8–9. The debate is summarized in Toledano, *Slavery and Abolition*, 16–19.

significantly enhance her position within the household and ultimately enable her to safely pass from enslaved to freed status. It should not come as a surprise, then, that in such circumstances, attempts to forcibly terminate a concubine's pregnancy would occur. Concubines could try to keep their condition a secret in order to pass the point after which abortion was neither legally permissible nor medically possible. But few of them could be as knowledgeable as to realize that abortion was allowed only within four months from conception; in any event, it was hard to determine precisely when the child had been conceived.

With little medical knowledge as to how abortions were performed, women in harems would usually defer to a midwife's expertise or court the advice of an experienced, older woman. In Şemsigül's case, the wife of the would-be father—a slave dealer named Deli Mehmet—gave her some unspecified medication; and when that failed to produce the desired effect, beating with a stick was tried. Şemsigül was finally rescued by a compassionate lady, the wife of a senior officeholder and a friend of the family. This lady took her into her own home, and in that sheltered environment, safe from harassment by the slaveholder and his family, she gave birth to a child. Her story then becomes more complicated, for Deli Mehmet—literally, Mehmet the madman, called that probably because of his capricious nature—tried to put her again on the market. This was contrary to the law, as already mentioned, since Şemsigül was an ümmüveled. Since she did not keep quiet about that flagrant violation of her rights, the matter came to the attention of the head of the slave dealers' guild, who reprimanded Deli Mehmet. Although I have not found the document finalizing the case, it is probable that Şemsigül was ultimately set free either by the guild's head, the police, or the court.[31]

In another case, this time coming from a British consular report compiled in Damascus in July 1863, an enslaved African woman in an advanced stage of pregnancy fled to the consulate.[32] Both her holder and his brother had repeatedly had intercourse with her. When it became known that she was pregnant, the two men quarreled over who had impregnated

31. For further details on this case and some observations, see Toledano, *Slavery and Abolition*, Chapter 2.
32. FO/84/1204/230–1, Cons. Rogers (Damascus) to Foreign Sec. Russell, 17.7.1863.

her: neither wanted the long-term responsibility. We can safely deduce
this from the fact that they both began to beat her in order to induce an
abortion. Consul Rogers referred the case to the Ottoman governor-
general of Damascus, who had the matter investigated, including holding
several interviews with the concerned parties. Apparently, this case was
recognized as a straightforward instance of severe abuse, and the woman
was set free by government order. She remained for a while longer at the
consul's house, probably to allow her to recover and give birth in a safe and
congenial environment. We do not know whether the child was healthy or
damaged by the beating, nor do we know what happened to both of them
later, but this does look like a story with the happiest ending that could be
expected in the circumstances.

Leaving to Stop Unrelenting Abuse

Some of the abuse cases did not end so fast—that is, the abuser continued to pursue the enslaved person, at times for years. Unless the slaves
in such situations could muster equal resilience, they could not possibly
hope to end the abuse and rid themselves of the abuser. The following
two cases will illustrate this point, as they take us to Istanbul, Alexandria, and Izmir during the 1860s. In the imperial capital, the new sultan
Abdülaziz (1861–1876) continued to carry out reforms under the Tanzimat project. In Egypt, which again comes into one of our stories, the
new governor-general Khedive Ismail (1863–1879) launched ambitious
reforms, which outpaced those of his sovereign, Abdülaziz. During
those years, too, the British government increased its pressure on the
Ottomans to apply more rigorously the measures they had agreed to take
against the slave trade in Africans. By that time the British had also
come to realize that they were unable to induce the Sublime Porte, as the
Ottoman government was referred to by Europeans, to suppress the traffic in enslaved Circassians. London's efforts were now focused on restricting the supply end of the slavery equation, rather than on the total
abolition of slavery itself, which by then was deemed to be an unattain-
able goal.[33]

33. For a detailed account of these and other developments in the struggle for the
   suppression of the slave trade in the Ottoman Empire, see Toledano, *Slave
   Trade*, 168–172, 192–223.

In January 1862, an enslaved African woman named Ferah (Joy in English) escaped to the police hostel (misafirhane) for runaway slaves.[34] When she reached the asylum, she had a bad eye injury, the result of a severe beating she sustained at the hands of her holder, a slave dealer ironically named Rahmetüllah (God's Mercy). The matter was investigated by the Istanbul police authorities, and following court procedures, the abuser was sentenced to three years' imprisonment with hard labor. Such a heavy penalty for this type of crime was quite rare, which indicates how seriously the court regarded the injury and the circumstances surrounding it. However, owing to an imperial pardon issued by Sultan Abdülaziz, our perpetrator was released from prison a short while after he had been incarcerated. Following Rahmetüllah's release, he made known his wish to regain possession of Ferah, but she adamantly refused to go back to him. She also refused to be resold to another slave dealer, arguing that Rahmetüllah would use all sorts of deception and trickery to regain control over her.

The impression from reading the Ottoman documents in this file is that Ferah knew with whom she was dealing and felt that Rahmetüllah was almost obsessed with her, totally resolved to have her restored to him by any means. He appears to have been a violent, determined, and vindictive person, who would not stop until he managed to even the score with Ferah, an enslaved woman who had refused to take his abuse and had dared to humiliate him in public. Police and other government investigators who were involved in this case came to the view that Ferah's concern was reasonable and well founded. To protect her from being further pursued and harassed by Rahmetüllah, the authorities recommended that the treasury purchase her freedom from him and that she be duly manumitted. The grand vezir presented the recommendation to the sultan, who approved it within one day and set Ferah free. We have no further information as to what happened later, but it is reasonable to assume that given her perseverance and strong will, she managed to find suitable employment, and Rahmetüllah vanished from her life for good.

Another case of a strong-willed slave unfolded in Izmir during 1869 and was reported to London by the British consul in August of that

34. BOA/İrade/Meclis-i Vala/21316/the Grand Vezir to the Sultan, 31.7.1862, and Sultanic İrade, 1.8.1862, and related documents.

year.[35] Our protagonist here is Hacı Mehmet, a freed African man, who escaped to the consulate and sought refuge there. At the time, Mehmet was twenty-four years old. In 1854, when Mehmet was nine, he had been captured in his native land, transported into the Ottoman Empire, and sold into slavery in an unspecified location. He served the man who purchased him for seven years, and in 1861 this unnamed slaveholder properly manumitted him. Sixteen years old and freed, he chose to travel to the burgeoning Egyptian port city of Alexandria, where he settled down and got married. In the course of those years, he also made at least one pilgrimage to the Holy Cities in the Hijaz, as indicated by the title Hacı, which was attached to his name. However, his troubles were not over, and in 1863 a certain unspecified slave dealer began to "pursue" him, as the consul put it in his report.

We are not told if Mehmet and the slave dealer had known each other before, but the impression we get from the story is that this was not so. Had this man been either the slave dealer who had brought Mehmet into the Empire or the one who sold him to his first holder, it would have been unusual for Mehmet or the consul to omit that from the story; but we really do not know. If we exclude other motives, the only possible explanation for the man to be "pursuing" Mehmet would be that he wanted to reenslave him. An eighteen-year-old African man in Alexandria could have been safely assumed to be either a slave or a freed person. And, if perceived to be vulnerable, either physically or because unemployed and unable to fend for himself or care for his family, such a man could have been considered easy prey for the slave dealer. A dealer might try, then, to induce the ex-slave to return to slavery in a profitable deal, perhaps for a share of the purchase price, or as part of a scheme to be falsely sold and then run away, again for a share of the money. Whatever the purpose of the slave dealer in Mehmet's story, he was persistent and managed to harass the young man for a number of years to the point that Mehmet felt compelled to flee Alexandria, cross the eastern Mediterranean, and go to Izmir, where he found his way to the British consulate and asked for help.

Mehmet's last move lends support to the assumption that the Alexandrian slave dealer was trying to reenslave him against his will.

35. FO/84/1305/402–5, Cons. Cumberbatch (Izmir) to Foreign Sec. Clarendon, 28.8.1869.

Consul Cumberbatch's reputation as a zealous abolitionist who was always willing to help out runaway slaves spread beyond the port city of Izmir, and an African man, especially an ex-slave, would probably not have traveled all the way from Alexandria to that particular consulate unless an enslavement-related problem was involved. At the time, Alexandria and Izmir were two major Ottoman ports in the eastern Mediterranean, with a great deal of commerce moving between them, mostly—though not exclusively—aboard foreign and Ottoman steamers. Transporting slaves on board those steamers became a major issue for British consuls in these towns, and Consul Cumberbatch's actions to stop the traffic in Africans were well known among slave dealers and government officials. Potential absconders were also aware that the British consulate in Izmir was a safe place to escape to, and in Mehmet's case, as in many others, this indeed proved to be so.

The important point to notice in these two persistent harassment cases—Ferah's and Mehmet's—is how the enslaved individuals were saved by their own determination not to succumb to their abusers. In both these stories, the protagonists had to cope with unrelenting attempts by the abusers to deprive them of their freedom. Both Ferah and Mehmet had to reject importunate interference with their lives—Ferah refused to be put once again, through resale, in a vulnerable position that would expose her to Rahmetüllah's revenge, while Mehmet had to cope with nothing short of what we would today call stalking. In addition, both had to be fairly knowledgeable about the options available to them as enslaved persons in Ottoman society and were adept enough to take advantage of the intelligence they managed to gather, and use it to their advantage. But neither could do it without outside help, which for Ferah and Mehmet, as for many others, came from the Tanzimat-state and its officials: Ferah was helped by Ottoman law-enforcement agents and by top men in the Empire, including, ultimately, Sultan Abdülaziz himself; Mehmet received support from a British official, who provided both a temporary shelter and crucial intercession with the Ottoman government to obtain manumission.

Leaving to Escape Resale

One of the main motives for absconding was the desire of the enslaved to avoid being resold to another slaver. As already mentioned, manumitting slaves after a number of years, usually seven to ten, was regarded as a meritorious act in Ottoman society. Slaves came to expect to be freed within that general time frame, and they considered holders' attempts to evade manumission after that period as violations of the norm. This was especially so when slavers intended to put the enslaved on the market, thereby causing their years of service to be wiped out and the counting toward manumission to begin anew. There were several reasons for slavers to flout the norm, ranging from financial concerns, especially if they were not well off, to a lack of empathy or compassion for the enslaved person's pain and plight. The enslaved could try to negotiate with the slavers if the latter were at all amenable, especially when the enslaved could offer to pay the slavers some of the resale value, either after manumission or before. But if the slaveholder was adamant, the enslaved person had no legal recourse, since the law did not fix the term of servitude and since, in theory, slavers could keep their enslaved workers in perpetuity.

Many borderline cases occurred when slavers wished to sell a slave, for any reason, after a period of service shorter than seven years, say four to five years. If an enslaved person had any leverage to generate a self-manumission contract, these were the circumstances in which to use it. However, many slaves did not have much leverage, and the re-count to liberation would start all over again with a new, unfamiliar slaveholder. At such a point, as in attempts to resell after the full term of bondage had been completed, the only option available to an enslaved person who was determined not to remain in servitude for an additional term was absconding. Often, in fact, we find cases that display a combination of resale-related absconding and abuse. This was frequently the result of pre-sale altercations between an enslaved person desperate to convince a slaveholder to resolve the matter without resale and an adamant slaveholder seeking to force the enslaved person to submit to resale. When such conflicts escalated into severe violence, the enslaved person would opt for absconding, citing to the authorities *both* motives for the action— a desire to avoid abuse as well as resale. In addition, some long-serving slaves who failed to avert a resale escaped after they were transferred to the slave dealer.[36]

36. FO/84/1450/271–5, V. Cons. Jago (Damascus) to Amb. Elliot (Istanbul), 18.12.1876.

Long-serving slaves who opted for absconding before an impending resale often preferred to seek help from a foreign government representative, usually a British consul. This was so because until the 1880s the Ottoman authorities were reluctant to intervene in cases of this kind, given the want of a legal basis to enforce manumission upon reluctant slavers. The sultan's agents would intervene only if abuse was demonstrable, which might account for some of the abuse charges raised by enslaved persons in this category. Therefore, as in the following three examples, most of the evidence for this type of absconding comes from British consular sources.

At the end of 1860, the British consul in Canea, Crete, reported that an enslaved African woman escaped to the consulate and asked for help.[37] Conspicuously bruised, the woman claimed that she had been severely beaten by her holder, a certain Molla Mehmet. She added that the battering occurred because of her refusal to be sent to Istanbul for resale. The consul granted her asylum at the consulate and referred the matter to the local council. Following the council's deliberations, the slaveholder was induced to free the woman, and the case was closed. Despite the absence of further direct evidence, we may safely reconstruct the way the council handled the matter. The intended resale itself did not constitute grounds for interference, let alone for terminating the slaver-enslaved relationship, a fact of which the slaver must have been palpably aware. After all, he was a respectable figure in the community and—as his title of *molla* suggests—was possessed of ample knowledge of the Şeriat and Ottoman social praxis. However, the door for interference was opened by the enslaved person's charge and demonstration of abuse, and the council probably did not take much convincing to encourage Mehmet to free the woman, since he must have wished to avoid further public embarrassment and perhaps control the damage by performing a benevolent act of manumission.

Some two years later, in December of 1862, the British consul in the Balkan town of Manastir reported to London that an enslaved African woman had sought refuge in his consulate.[38] Her name was Gülfidem,

---

37. FO/84/1120/117–18, Cons. Guarracino (Canea) to Amb. Bulwer (Istanbul), 10.12.1860.
38. FO/84/1181/183–5, Cons. Calvert (Monastir) to Foreign Sec. Russell, 20.12.1862.

and she was thirty-four years old. The woman told the consul that she had already twice served seven-year terms of servitude and that although three of her holders had died, she still remained in slavery. With no liberation in sight she had simply had enough. There is no way of statistically knowing how typical Gülfidem's experience was in Ottoman society, but the clear impression is that it was not atypical. If we work backward through her life story, we have to assume that she actually served well over fourteen years, since she had at least three holders and was unlikely to have been enslaved only at the approximate age of twenty. A proper reconstruction of Gülfidem's life history as an enslaved woman leads us to the following sequence of events:

- born ca. 1828
- enslaved probably in mid-teens (early to mid 1840s)
- served seven years under first holder
- first holder dies but does not manumit her (around 1850)
- resold by first holder's heirs (or began to serve one of them)
- served seven years under second holder
- second holder dies but does not manumit her (around 1857)
- resold by second holder's heirs (or began to serve one of them)
- served about five years under third holder
- third holder dies but does not manumit her (1862)
- passed to one of third holder's heirs (no prospect of manumission)
- escaped to the British consulate

While referring her case to the Ottoman authorities, the consul let Gülfidem stay at the consulate. The governor reviewed the file and agreed to manumit her, which confirms our impression that her experience was seen as unusually harsh. Acting on humanitarian grounds, the government went one step further and arranged for Gülfidem to be employed in the nearby town of Scutari as a paid domestic servant at the house of Abdi Paşa, whose wife was described by the consul as a "benevolent lady."

In a case mentioned above, eight enslaved African men escaped in 1880 to HMS *Seagull* off the coast of Jidda.[39] The ship's commander

39. FO/84/1579/266–81, Hall (Admiralty) to Under Sec. of State (FO), including five letters from Commander Byles (HMS *Seagull*), 31.12.1880.

reported that two of those starved and abused men had an additional unhappy aspect to their life histories. One of them had been sold four
times over the past seven years within the Red Sea region, and the other
five times in as many years in same area. Apparently, frequent resale
was not that uncommon in the Hijaz, where enslaved African men were
being employed by Bedouins as pearl divers, masons, quarry diggers,
and other menial laborers at tasks requiring hard physical work. Under
those harsh conditions, the personal and extenuating slaver-enslaved relationships that were often found in urban households could not easily
be formed. This was especially so for the men, since women fared somewhat better if serving in a Hijazi urban domestic environment. Under-
standably, many enslaved people found disconcerting the instability that
frequent resales wreaked upon their lives. In urban areas, where the custom of fixed terms of servitude was more often respected by slavers, an
enslaved person could build up those years and look forward to being
manumitted. She or he could also invest in cultivating a long-term, mutually beneficial relationship with the holder. But a harsh environment
as in the Hijaz was noticeably disruptive to servile relations, causing
more frequently the kind of continuous neglect and abuse seen in this
and other stories, and ultimately took its toll mainly on the enslaved.

Some slaves also reacted against attempts to manipulate their lives
through sale and resale even when long service or disregard for fixed-
term practices were not the issue. In September 1861, for example, one
of the leaders of the Circassian tribe of Dikur, named Hacı İsmail Bey,
was on his way to Istanbul.[40] Recently, perhaps even after he had set out
on that trip, İsmail bought four young male Circassian slaves and took
them with him. One night, when he was staying at a place called
Hamamlı in the east Anatolian town of Kars, the four lads stole his belongings and escaped across the border to Russia, where they sought
refuge among their kin. Hacı İsmail Bey complained to the authorities,
and the matter was referred to the Refugees Commission, an Ottoman
agency set up to deal with the problems of the Circassian refugees who
were being driven out of the Caucasus by advancing Russian forces. Because the refugees were Muslim, the Ottoman Empire offered them safe

40. BOA/BEO/Mühacirin Komisyonu/vol. 758–38:1/# 126, 9–10.1861. (BEO,
used henceforth, stands for Bab-ı Alı Evrak Odası.)

haven and settled them with their agricultural serfs-slaves in unculti-
vated, often frontier regions of the Empire. One Ottoman report assessed the number of refugees who entered the Empire from the late
1850s to the late 1860s at 1.5 million, including some 150,000 agricultural slaves who came with their landlords (Adygé Circassian, *pshis;* Ottoman Turkish, *beys, emirs*).[41] In Russia, these people were considered
serfs, but once they entered the Ottoman Empire, the only applicable
legal category available for them was that of slaves.

The Refugees Commission referred İsmail Bey's complaint to the Ottoman Foreign Ministry, which was expected to take it up with the Russians later on. The Ottoman documents do not tell us whether the four absconders were indeed of "slave origin" (*köle cinsi*), which was a heritable
serf status, or whether they were free Circassians illegally sold to the bey
by slave dealers or by their own impoverished families. Their primary
motivation for absconding could have been to avoid slavery, but it is also
possible that all they wanted was to steal from the bey and then run
away. Despite the information gap in the records, we can still discover
the gist of this story. The four lads obviously knew that Hacı İsmail Bey
was heading for the imperial capital. He might have told them that he
intended to sell them there, but even if he did not, they could have
guessed as much, for why else would a Circassian bey who probably had
slaves on his own estate buy new ones and take them with him to Istanbul? We may also safely assume that the young men did not cherish the
idea of being resold there for a profit to some unknown buyers, who
could then move them anywhere in the vast Empire.

More likely, the main aim of the four escapees was to thwart İsmail's
plans and avert the plight he had in store for them; the stolen articles, in
all likelihood, were fringe benefits. But this episode can also teach us
something about what role the Tanzimat-state was seen to be playing—
by enslaved and slavers alike—with regard to the issue of enslavement.
In 1861, these enslaved Circassians and probably others as well preferred to seek refuge with their fellow tribespeople in Russia rather than
trust the Ottoman state to uphold their claims to freedom vis-à-vis the
proprietary rights of their slaving beys. Five years later courts were still

41. For a detailed discussion of the Circassian refugees question, see Toledano,
    Slavery and Abolition, Chapter 3.

leaning heavily in favor of slavers even when enslaved persons asserted that they were freeborn and had been illegally sold into slavery. But in less than two decades, attitudes changed significantly.

Leaving to Save the Family

Perhaps the most heart-wrenching cases of absconding were those in which the escapees struggled to avoid having their families split up by sale of one or more members to another slaver. These stories belie any notion of presumed weak family links among the enslaved or, indeed the nonexistence of strong enslaved families in Ottoman societies. In fact, the slavers themselves may have contributed to the emergence of such views so that they would have a ready justification for breaking up enslaved families.[42] Forcibly splitting up such families to realize a profit or reduce upkeep costs was a humanly unacceptable action, and slavers who did this looked for mitigating circumstances to defend their actions to themselves as well as to their families, friends, and neighbors. Here, slaves who fought against such acts could expect help not only from foreign consuls but also from the Ottoman authorities, despite the fact that Şeriat courts often sided with the slavers and endorsed such sales. Here, too, it seems that the obvious humanitarian argument enabled the government to find ways to help those enslaved families who chose to fight against the slavers' intentions to break them up.

In 1857, a family of three enslaved Africans, consisting of two parents and one child, appeared at the British consulate in the North African port city of Tripoli and told the staff that their holder had decided to sell the mother and the child and keep the father.[43] Rightly assuming that the family would refuse to cooperate, the slaveholder acted swiftly and deceptively: when the father was plowing the fields, the man sold the mother and the child to a slave dealer, who carried them off immediately. Upon returning from the fields, the father found out what had happened and vehemently

---

42. For slavery in literary sources during the Tanzimat period, see İsmail Parlatır, *Tanzimat edebiyatında kölelik*, Ankara: Türk Tarih Kurumu Basımevi, 1987; Börte Sagaster, *"Herren" und "Sklaven": Der Wandel im Sklavenbild türkischer Literaten in der Spätzeit des Osmanischen Reiches*, Wiesbaden: Harrasowitz, 1997.

43. FO/84/1029/85–92, Col. Herman (Cons. Tripoli) to Foreign Sec. Clarendon, 8.2.1857.

protested, but he was locked up by the slaveholder somewhere on the farm. After fifteen days, the father managed to escape, only to be told by another slaveholder that his wife and child had just been marched to the marina and were about to board the boat *Mesut,* which was heading for Izmir and Istanbul. The man ran to the docks and rescued his wife and child just before they boarded. After that he proceeded directly to the British consulate with his family and sought refuge. Vice-Consul Reade approached the governor-general of the province, who, upon reviewing the case, decided to liberate the entire family and put the slaveholders in jail.

In October 1866, the British consul in Damascus reported that an enslaved woman—probably an African, although this is not specifically stated—came to the consulate and asked for help.[44] She said that she had been serving the family of a *shaykh* in the village of Sbini for a very long time. Although she mentioned being in servitude for forty years, this seems perhaps somewhat overstated, as forty was a formulaic number often used to indicate "a very long time indeed." It turned out that during those long years, she married an enslaved man and had three children by him. Now her holder wanted to sell two of the children, so she desperately approached the consul to prevent that from happening. The consul duly represented the case to Edhem Paşa, the deputy governor-general (*kaymakam*), who reviewed the story and set the entire family free.

In late 1867, two Ottoman officials, Hafız Ahmet Efendi and İshak Bey, and their respective wives, Hamide and Zehra, brought six of their eleven Circassian slaves from their home in Tekfurdağ to Istanbul to be sold there.[45] All the enslaved persons were members of the Şumaf family. It appears that ownership rights over the Şumafs were shared between the two couples, since there is no reference to any other arrangement; it could even be that the four slaveholders were related to each other and that the households they maintained were located on the same plot of land, enabling them to keep the enslaved family together. In any

---

44. FO/84/1260/17–18, Cons. Rogers (Damascus) to Foreign Sec. Stanley, 31.10.1866.
45. BOA/İrade/Meclis-i Vala/25956/Enclosure #2, İdare-i Muhacirin to the Meclis-i Vala, 26.8.1867, and attached list of the slaves' names dated 30.9.1867; BOA/İrade/Meclis-i Vala Mazbatası, 21.10.1867; BOA/Ayniyat defterleri/1136, #675, Bab-ı Ali to Osman Paşa, member of the Meclis-i Vala, 7.10.1867.

event, the significant sociolegal point here is that the Şumaf family belonged to the class of enslaved Circassians, a heritable status that allowed trading in them across the Empire. Although originally enserfed
in the Caucasus, they had been classified as slaves upon entering Ottoman jurisdiction and were consequently also sold into harem and domestic slavery. The evidence shows that among members of this group,
selling family members outside the family did occur, usually in situations of dire economic need and in the hope of opening up for young
children, especially girls, the route to a better life in elite harems.

The breakup of the Şumaf family was supposed to affect both the extended family and a nuclear subunit thereof. That these persons were not
freeborn only endows their resistance with greater significance. When
they learned of their holders' intentions, the Şumafs mounted stiff opposition, as the official documents reveal. Already in Istanbul, they demanded
to be returned to their home and to their remaining five family members
in Tekfurdağ. The first round in the struggle took place at the Şeriat court,
where the slavers went to enforce their proprietary rights over the recalci-
trant family, including the right to sell some of them. Since the Şumafs
were not freeborn, no charge of illegal enslavement could be sustained in
their case. The alternative of allowing them to purchase their freedom was
also blocked, because they could not come up with the amount of money
estimated to have been their market value. Consequently the Şeriat court
decided to back the slaveholders and confirmed their right to sell the six,
thereby allowing them to split the extended Şumaf family.

The Şumaf family persisted: they petitioned the government to
prevent the break-up. Apparently, their supplications and determination
convinced the authorities to overrule the Şeriat court and offer a kind of
compromise: the Ottoman treasury undertook to compensate the slaveholders monetarily, thereby effectively purchasing the freedom of the
entire family, which facilitated the repatriation of its six members to Tekfurdağ. All the various Nizami courts and state councils that had reviewed the case cited both the humanitarian aspect and the perseverance
of the Şumafs—so much so that this was used to reaffirm the existing
regulations against splitting enslaved families by sale. This interdiction
was based on the customary and tacit understanding between the Circassian slavers and their enslaved tenants which prohibited family splitting. In the Şumaf case, however, the slavers tried to manipulate the

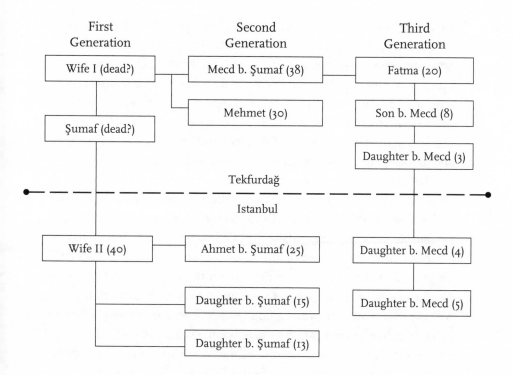

First Generation	Second Generation	Third Generation
Wife I (dead?)	Mecd b. Şumaf (38)	Fatma (20)
	Mehmet (30)	Son b. Mecd (8)
Şumaf (dead?)		Daughter b. Mecd (3)

Tekfurdağ
— — — — — — — — — — — — — — — —
Istanbul

Wife II (40)	Ahmet b. Şumaf (25)	Daughter b. Mecd (4)
	Daughter b. Şumaf (15)	Daughter b. Mecd (5)
	Daughter b. Şumaf (13)	

(number) = age
b. = bin/bint (son/daughter of)

FIGURE 2.1. The broken-up family of Şumaf

Şeriat court by exploiting a lacuna in Islamic law that did not block family splitting. They were also correct in relying on the general inclination of such courts to uphold the slavers' proprietary rights, except when flagrant abuse could be palpably demonstrated.

Our last example in this category comes from the Red Sea port of Jidda, where in July 1881 the British consul reported to London the case of an enslaved African family.[46] In this instance, the parents and their two daughters had come from an unspecified location outside the town to seek refuge at the consulate to avert separation by sale. Their saga, however, did not begin at that point. It became clear from their story that five years earlier, in 1876, their third child had been sold out of the family,

46. FO/84/1597/390–1, Cons. Zohrab (Jidda) to Foreign Sec. Granville, 1.7.1881.

which they were unable to prevent. This time, two days before absconding to Jidda, their holder sold one of their remaining two daughters, but the
father somehow managed to recover her—no details are provided by the
consul—and the whole family escaped to the consulate. No information is
given as to the outcome of this case, but the process probably took the same
course that other cases with similar exposure did: a consular representation was submitted to the local authorities and reviewed by the governor,
and ultimately a state-issued manumission would follow.

These cases illustrate our need to revise previous notions about the
enslaved family in Ottoman societies. Obviously, human relations and
the families they produce come in all shapes and forms. It would be unreasonable to expect that enslavement had no significant impact on the
structure and nature of the family. But we must be careful in assessing
the exact and likely character of that impact before assuming that families formed by enslaved persons were necessarily fragile, transient, and
with weak commitment among family members. The stories cited here
and others like them may lead us to doubt the validity of such hasty conclusions. Now let us examine some of the basic circumstances in which
Ottoman enslaved persons could form families.

Enslaved families were much more a phenomenon of rural than
urban society, which meant that they were not widespread. In urban elite
households and those of the somewhat lower strata, domestic slaves usually got married after manumission, often to other freed persons. Such
families of freed people should not be seen as different from other families in similar socioeconomic circumstances and will therefore not be
treated here. For the most part, household slaves were allowed to marry if
kept in servitude longer than usual and were allowed to stay together if
purchased as a couple or a family. Otherwise, concubinage and, in less affluent households, the physical limitations of space discouraged slave
marriages. But in the countryside, the organization of agricultural labor
on small or larger farms proved conducive to serfdom-type arrangements. Unfree families were both efficient and desirable.[47] Enserfment

47. In general, the Ottoman system did not favor agricultural enslavement, and the
    advent of Ottoman rule, as in the case of Cyprus, normally meant the extinction
    of cultivation by enslaved persons (Ronald C. Jennings, *Christians and Muslims
    in Ottoman Cyprus and the Mediterranean World, 1571–1640*, New York: New York

among the Circassians encouraged that type of family structure, as did the temporary rise of African agricultural enslavement in rural Egypt during the cotton boom of the 1860s. The case stories cited above from the hinterlands of Tripoli, Damascus, and Jidda indicate that in similar circumstances, enslaved Africans also formed families of their own. The family structure of the Şumafs in Tekfurdağ was common among the Circassian refugees and a familiar sight in the Ottoman countryside from the late 1850s onward, when these people were being settled with their landlords in the Ottoman Empire.

The very predicament of bondage exposed enslaved families to interference by outsiders, mostly slavers. However, this seems to have been a real factor in shaping family life only for household slaves in urban settings, where the space that could be allocated to such families was small, their living quarters were crowded, and the supervision and interference by other enslaved and free household members were great. We may reasonably assume that privacy, guidance of children, and other issues involving freedom of choice were a source of tension and friction within the household. Sexual access and harassment would also come up, especially when boundaries were not clearly drawn or when previous slaver-enslaved relationships had existed. In urban households, enslaved persons were normally allowed to form only nuclear families. These families were deprived of the protective and support system an extended family could provide, especially to offset and deter outside pressures. Literary sources may partially fill the evidence gap that we face regarding such questions, so at the present we are still treading very lightly on rather tentative ground.

University Press, 1993: 240–241). One of the few scholars to have studied Ottoman agricultural slavery is Halil Inalcik: "Servile Labor in the Ottoman Empire," in Abraham Ascher, Tibor Halasi-Kun, and Bela K. Kiraly (eds.), *The Mutual Effects of the Islamic and Judeo-Christian Worlds: The East European Pattern*, New York: Brooklyn College Press, 1979: 25–52, especially 30–35; and "Rice Cultivation and the Çeltukci-Re'âyâ System in the Ottoman Empire," *Turcica*, 14 (1982): 69–141, especially 88–94. See also Ehud R. Toledano, "Where Have All the Egyptian *Fallahin* Gone To? Labor in Mersin and Çukurova during the Second Half of the Nineteenth Century," in Mersin University, Center for Urban Studies, *Mersin, the Mediterranean, and Modernity: Heritage of the Long-Nineteenth Century*, Mersin: Mersin University Press, 2002: 21–28.

Compared to enslaved families in urban areas, families formed by enslaved persons in rural areas were less vulnerable to outside interference and could develop a reasonable autonomy vis-à-vis the slavers. An agricultural environment often afforded enslaved families the distance from the slaver's household required to protect their privacy and preferred life choices. The fact that multigenerational extended or joint families were common in such situations rendered the enslaved families more capable of resisting pressures and interference from outsiders, again mostly from their landlords.[48] The strong resistance displayed by the Şumaf family of Tekfurdağ demonstrates the strength of ties in extended enslaved families and the commitment of their members to each other. But it also stresses the exposure of enslaved families to slavers' interference even in rural areas, since forced splitting was one of the more brutal manifestations of their vulnerability. We should remember that splitting did occur and that not all heroic struggles ended in success. In fact, the Şumafs' resistance is even more striking when compared to other cases, in which Circassian paternal uncles sold their freeborn nephews into slavery (this resembles atalık).

Although more research is needed before we can draw broader conclusions on the strength of ties in the different types of families discussed thus far, we may for the moment respectfully recognize that in most cases, it was harder for enslaved persons than for free persons to form a family and protect its integrity. Because the enslaved family was socially and economically more dependent and more vulnerable than the free family, it required a stronger commitment from its members in order to survive and stay together. To appreciate this we need only imagine the father who was running as fast as he could, hoping to find and rescue his daughter from the men who had snatched her for sale; or the father who was locked in a dungeon for fifteen days but trying to escape to rescue his wife and child, and all that time being tormented by the

48. For family structure and definitions, see Alan Duben and Cem Behar, *Istanbul Households: Marriage, Family, and Fertility, 1880–1940*, Cambridge: Cambridge University Press, 1991: 48–86. Duben and Behar argue that the simple rather than the extended family was the common structure in Istanbul from the late nineteenth century and that family size was rather small. In rural areas simple families were larger. Here we talk about extended elite households and larger, multigenerational rural families.

fear that they were already far away; or the mother who ran to the consulate, desperate to prevent the sale and loss of her two daughters; or the six members of the Şumaf family, whom the kadi turned away and left exposed and defenseless but who remained defiant and unrelenting. It does not take much to appreciate the anger, frustration, pain, and fear that these enslaved Africans and Circassians experienced—but also their love, care, and commitment—in order to understand the heavy price demanded of them to keep their families together.

Severing the Bond of Enslavement to Be Free

Among the many absconders were also those who escaped to get out of enslavement, who left simply because they wished to be free, almost regardless of the specific circumstances of their own lives in bondage. They were admittedly few in number, but they deserve to be mentioned. Conspicuous members of this group of escapees are kul/harem slaves, those who normally preferred to work within the system rather than break away from it. But some harem women and eunuchs did choose to escape, which makes exploration of their person stories all the more intriguing. Before we do that, we should turn to an atypical but fascinating case of an unusual African absconder.

In 1870, the British consul in Corfu reported that a young enslaved African male came to the consulate and asked to be protected and liberated.[49] Sa'd ibn 'Abdallah was sixteen years old, and to the consul's surprise he could read and write Arabic and was also fluent in Turkish—which was rare among enslaved Africans. Determined to reach the British consulate, Sa'd escaped from an Ottoman schooner cruising in the vicinity, took a boat, and sailed by night to Corfu. At first the Ottoman consul in town demanded his return, but when he was convinced that Sa'd was not one of the schooner's sailors, he rescinded his request, making it possible for Sa'd to be liberated. None of the usual motives for escape seem to be present in this case, and none was mentioned by the consul or—for all we know—to him by the absconder. Nor are we made aware of any pressing problem, such as abuse or harassment, that might have impelled Sa'd to flee the schooner. We may assume, then, that this

49. FO/84/1324/327–40, Cons. Everton (Corfu) to Foreign Sec. Granville, 6.10.1870.

educated slave simply wanted to be liberated and live as a free man. To attain his objective, he planned a daring escape, overcame the risks involved, and was determined enough to carry his plan through with much success.

A similar motivation might have existed in the sensitive case that was reported to London by Hugo Marinitch, the dragoman (interpreter) in charge of slavery-related matters at the British consulate in Istanbul.[50] In his October 1879 memo, Marinitch wrote that three Circassian female slaves had escaped to the consulate in Salonika, northeast Greece, and taken refuge there. The women came from the harem of İskender Paşa, a senior Ottoman official in that province. What complicated matters was that the three were not recently imported slaves but longtime ones. This meant that the anti-slave-trade policy, which provided for the manumission of illegally enslaved and imported individuals, could not be applied. The Ottomans gave the case serious and high-level attention because it could set a precedent for the entire kul/harem system. In itself this indicates that the slaving elite was, after all, perhaps not so confident that long-serving harem women and eunuchs would voluntarily choose to remain under slavery if the door to manumission was thrown open. The governor-general of Salonika referred the matter to the Porte, whence it was sent to the Consultative Council (Şura-yı Devlet), later reaching the Council of Ministers for a policy decision. Unfortunately, the final word on this issue could not be located in the archives, but we know for certain that kul/harem slavery remained intact until the demise of the Empire.

In March 1881, the British consul in Jidda wrote to the ambassador in Istanbul about a fascinating case involving an Ethiopian eunuch who ran away from Mecca and sought refuge at the Jidda consulate.[51] The man, İhsan Ağa, who had already been freed, asked to be sent to Egypt, where he could, as a free man, earn a livelihood. His story begins in his native land, when in 1872, nine years prior to his appearance at the consulate, his father had to flee because he could not pay the heavy taxes imposed by King Yohannes. The tax collectors seized İhsan and sold him

50. FO/84/1543/279–80, memo by Dragoman Hugo Marinich (in charge of slave issues, Istanbul Consulate), 8.10.1879.
51. FO/84/1596/63–83, Cons. Zohrab (Jidda) to Amb. Goschen (Istanbul), and enclosures, 22.12.1880–14.3.1881.

into slavery. Those who purchased the boy made him a eunuch and brought him to Jidda, where he was purchased by Ömer Nasıf Efendi, agent to the late Sharif of Mecca, who sent him to Istanbul to Ali Paşa, probably the famous grand vezir. Ali Paşa gave him as a present to the *valide* sultan, the sultan's mother (and hence the head of the harem), who passed him on to (her son?) Prince Murat, later Sultan Murat V, in whose service he remained until the sultan was deposed during the tumultuous events of 1876. At that point, İhsan and five other eunuchs were manumitted and sent to Mecca, where many imperial eunuchs were sent to serve in retirement as a special corps at the grand mosque.[52]

For about three years, İhsan continued to receive a comfortable monthly stipend of 450 piasters, but six months before seeking refuge at the Jidda consulate, he and two other eunuchs were sent to Medina, and their pay was severed. Apparently, this was quite common, as old eunuchs would be allocated the wages of young ones in return for feeding and clothing them until the junior eunuchs became senior enough to merit a stipend of their own, which was then taken from other incoming junior ones.[53] Having spent all his savings, İhsan made up his mind to escape. His plan was to ask for permission to make the pilgrimage to Mecca and from there to head for Jidda, which was what he managed to do. Although he was technically a free man, the Ottoman authorities ordered İhsan to return to Mecca so that matters could be sorted out there, since the sultan manumitted his eunuchs on the condition that they serve at the Mecca holy site, and for all intents and purposes they were still treated as unfree. İhsan refused to do that and threatened to take his life if the consul turned him over to Ottoman hands. He argued that once in Ottoman custody, he would be considered a traitor and therefore would be tortured and killed.

52. Some information about the imperial eunuchs in the Holy Cities can be found in Richard Francis Burton, *Personal Narrative of a Pilgrimage to al-Madina and Meccah* (ed. Isabel Burton), New York: Dover, 1964. Jane Hathaway studied the history of the Chief Black Eunuch and his strong ties to Egypt in the eighteenth century (Hathaway, *The Politics of Households in Ottoman Egypt: The Rise of the Qazdaglis*, Cambridge: Cambridge University Press, 1997:139–164), and she is currently preparing a major study of the Chief Black Eunuchs in the Ottoman Empire.
53. This practice is described in Zohrab's report, FO/84/1596/63–83, Cons. Zohrab (Jidda) to Amb. Goschen (Istanbul), cited above.

Despite high-level contacts and pressures going all the way to the grand vezir and Council of Ministers in Istanbul, the British refused to turn him in and finally facilitated İhsan's passage to Egypt, as he had wished. Here is a summary of his life history up to his escape:

- about 1862: İhsan (under a different name) is born in Ethiopia
- 1870s: King Yohannes imposes new taxes
- about 1872: İhsan's father runs away and İhsan is seized, enslaved, and castrated
- 1872: İhsan is bought in Jidda by an agent of the Sharif of Mecca, sent to Istanbul and given to the grand vezir(?) Ali Paşa, then given by Ali Paşa to the sultan's mother (probably Murat's), and then given by the sultan's mother to Prince Murat
- 1872–1876: İhsan serves Murat
- 1876: Murat V becomes sultan but is deposed; İhsan is freed and sent to Mecca
- Late 1876 to early 1880: İhsan lives comfortably in Mecca
- Early 1880: İhsan is transferred to Medina, and his pay is stopped
- Mid to late 1880: İhsan is permitted to make the pilgrimage to Mecca
- Late 1880: İhsan escapes to the British consulate in Jidda
- Early 1881: İhsan is safely transported to Egypt

[Rationale: castration had to occur before puberty, here set at about ten]

İhsan's story is about the refusal to settle for less and the determination to maximize options in unfriendly circumstances. Notice that had he been willing to accept the dependent status of a junior eunuch in Medina until he reached seniority, he would not have been exposed to a threat that caused him to abscond. There was no imminent danger of abuse, and life was probably fairly easy, quiet, and slow-moving for a eunuch in that situation. Nonetheless, he was confident of his ability to earn a better living and enjoy the benefits of a free person in Egypt and was prepared to risk a great deal, including perhaps his life, in order to realize that option.

The story brings out the remarkable strength of this young man, who must have been only in his late teens when he made these crucial decisions in life. But it also highlights İhsan's considerable capacity to gather information and plan the deceptive pilgrimage to Mecca that enabled him to get out of Medina and flee to Jidda via Mecca. His suicide threat was also a clever move to harden the consul's resistance to the high-level Ottoman pressures under which he was operating in this case. An intelligent and ambitious young man, İhsan had been exposed to life in the imperial harem, where he probably heard of the good life in Egypt. That life experience gave him a wider view of the world and broadened the options he was willing to entertain for his future, an invaluable advantage that many non-kul/harem slaves did not have.

With İhsan's story we have completed our review of absconding, a diverse phenomenon ensuing from a number of situations that, each in its own special circumstances, impelled our protagonists to leave their relationship with slavers and seek major changes in their lives. Before we consider the other options available to the enslaved, however, we need to evaluate the role of the Tanzimat-state in the slaver-enslaved relationship. This task will be undertaken in Chapter 3, again deliberately from the perspective of the enslaved, not that of the state and its agents. How the Tanzimat-state came to be seen by the enslaved as their patron and why some of them later came to feel betrayed by that new and promising patron are two of the questions that will be addressed.

CHAPTER THREE

Turning to the "Patron State" for Redress

THE TERM "PATRON STATE," which will be used hereafter, calls for some clarification. If "state" is taken to reflect a well-integrated modern entity, much in the way we think of present-day or even late-nineteenth-century European states, then this is not what the Ottoman Empire was during the period reviewed in this book.[1] Rather, it was a "compound" polity, made up of a coalition of the interest groups that formed its imperial elite. That elite was mostly male and Muslim, multiethnic, kul/harem and freeborn, military-administrative-legal-learned, urban and rural, officeholding and propertied, Ottoman-imperial and Ottoman-Local. While ruling a sprawling world empire, members of that elite were embedded in households, which were tied into sociopolitical networks, which linked estates to provincial capitals, and urban centers to Istanbul.

All this complex web flourished under the sultans, who in the long nineteenth century were, for the most part, reform-oriented, and

1. For the debate about the nature of the Ottoman state in the seventeenth and eighteenth centuries, see Rifaat Ali Abou-El-Haj, *Formation of the Modern State: The Ottoman Empire, Sixteenth to Eighteenth Centuries*, Albany: State University of New York Press, 1991. For the state in the long nineteenth century, see Carter V. Findley, *Bureaucratic Reform in the Ottoman Empire*, Princeton, N.J.: Princeton University Press, 1980; and Findley, *Ottoman Civil Officialdom: A Social History*, Princeton, N.J.: Princeton University Press, 1989.

hands-on leaders. The center of that composite polity moved with changing political circumstances from the palace to the seat of the grand vezir and back, with shifting coalitions forming, collapsing, and re-forming among interest groups and leading elite members. It is in that sense of a composite polity that we use here the term Ottoman "state," which also jibes with the notion of a "classical tributary empire." In a recently conceived research project, it has been suggested that the Ottoman Empire, like contemporary and earlier entities such as the Mughal and the Roman, consisted of "segmented, loosely integrated, and partly overlapping forms of power and authority."[2] Regardless of how precise the definition used here can or should be, all these attempts veer away from the well-integrated, uniform, tightly structured view of the modern state developed for Europe during the nineteenth and twentieth centuries.

"Patron" is added to "state" to convey the notion, developed throughout this book, that the slaver-enslaved relationship was an instance of patronage, that is, essentially a bond of reciprocity between unequal participants. Here I extend this concept to include the Ottoman state during the Tanzimat period (1830s–1880s). I shall argue that the Tanzimat-state gradually assumed the role of a patron vis-à-vis the enslaved. In other words, it intervened in the slaver-enslaved relationship when the enslaved removed themselves from, or sought to sever, the bond with the slavers. The Tanzimat-state, a composite polity, withdrew its traditional support from the slavers and took on a certain wardship over those enslaved persons who approached its agents and sought reattachment or manumission.

Despite differences regarding the nature of the Ottoman state in earlier periods, most scholars seem to agree that during the Tanzimat, the central authority as embodied in the sultan's government gained strength and became more centralized. The new technologies imported from Europe—the telegraph, steam shipping, the railway—were increasing the power of the state and its ability to exercise a growing degree of control. State and society were neither separate nor opposing entities; rather, they were intertwined in a web of dependencies, with the

2. "Royal Courts and Capitals" conference, Sabanci University, Istanbul, 14–16 October 2005 (part of the COST Action "Tributary Empires Compared: Romans, Mughals and Ottomans in the Pre-industrial World from Antiquity till the Transition to Modernity").

state being the vehicle for securing and perpetuating the power structure and the dominant social groups that constituted it. As the state grew in coherence and articulation, it was being faced with new challenges both from the outside and from within. The survival of the Ottoman Empire as an independent member of the Concert of Europe was constantly on the agenda of European powers in what came to be known as the Eastern Question.[3]

Britain, France, Russia, the Habsburgs, were all trying to affect matters in Ottoman-controlled territories in which they held—or wished to build—vested interests. Extending protection to non-Muslim minorities within the Empire, whether invited to or not, they vied for a foothold in Ottoman domestic affairs, promoting certain causes and opposing others. The Tanzimat reformers maneuvered effectively among all these constraints, managing most of the time to ward off unwanted pressures or, better still, to manipulate outside intervention to advance their own policies and achieve their own goals. With Ottoman-imperial households in the capital and Ottoman-Local households in the provinces gaining in power and wealth, pressures on the state also mounted internally. The capacity to juggle several balls simultaneously—the economic, the political, the social, the international—thus became a sine qua non for Tanzimat officeholders from the sultan through the vezirs and to the paşas and beys. The issue of enslavement lay at the crossroads of interests and passions.

In the second half of the nineteenth century the British used the slave trade as a tool for intervening in Ottoman domestic affairs, pushing first for suppression and later for manumission.[4] Skillfully maneuvering to ward off British pressures by prohibiting the traffic in Africans, Tanzimat leaders rejected foreign attempts to block the inflow

3. Still the best surveys of the Tanzimat period, both internally and externally, are Bernard Lewis, *The Emergence of Modern Turkey*, 2nd ed., London: Oxford University Press, 1968; Roderic H. Davison, *Reform in the Ottoman Empire, 1856–1876*, Princeton, N.J.: Princeton University Press, 1963. For the Eastern Question, an old classic is M. S. Anderson, *The Eastern Question, 1774–1923: A Study in International Relations*, London: Macmillan, 1966; for a more recent work, see Stefanos Yerasimos, *Questions d'Orient: Frontieres et minorites des Balkans au Caucase*, Paris: Livres Herodote, Editions La Decouverte, 1993.
4. For an account, see Ehud R. Toledano, *The Ottoman Slave Trade and Its Suppression, 1840–1890*, Princeton: Princeton University Press, 1982.

of enslaved persons from the Caucasus and to tamper with kul/harem slavery. At the same time, however, the same reformers used legislation, the courts, and law enforcement agents to mitigate the circumstances of enslavement and check the power of slavers over the enslaved. By interjecting the state into the slaver-enslaved relationship, they were sending a signal to the households and their all-encompassing networks that the Tanzimat-state was asserting itself as a power broker in the Ottoman polity. The ambivalence that is constantly apparent in their actions, though, stemmed from the fact that they themselves were household heads, movers and shakers in network politics, and slavers to boot.

Not embedded in the main building blocks of Ottoman society—guilds, Sufi brotherhoods, village communities, urban quarters, tribal formations, local mosques, and local associations—the enslaved were more easily accessible and manipulable. When approached by absconding enslaved persons, the Tanzimat-state offered protection and benevolence—that is, manumission and responsible placement. It seized the opportunity to extend patronage, replace the slavers in failed and betrayed bonds of enslavement, and remind the imperial elite of its growing role and power. But the enslaved should not be seen here as mere victims of manipulation, since they, too, soon learned how to use the system and manipulate the composite state to their advantage. That they did through the use of the very tools developed and deployed by the Ottoman government as part of its centralizing reforms.

With the growing bureaucratization that accompanied the centralization of the Tanzimat-state, the demand for detailed and more reliable recording methods, registration, certification, and licensing markedly increased.[5] Like contemporary empires and later colonial states, the Tanzimat-state proceeded to impose more and more control over their subjects' bodies and minds, creating a new realm of order. Its agents sought to regulate and regiment life in the Empire, to make sovereign power diffuse and all-encompassing but less directly linked to the person of the

5. On the Ottoman central bureaucracy, see Findley, *Bureaucratic Reform;* and Findley, *Ottoman Civil Officialdom;* on the parallel development in Ottoman Egypt, see F. Robert Hunter, *Egypt under the Khedives, 1805–1879,* Pittsburgh: University of Pittsburgh Press, 1984.

sultan.[6] As the century wore on, the sultan's subjects needed more certificates, more licenses, more state-issued documents, to conduct their daily lives. They needed official papers to travel, to trade, to practice a profession, to get assistance from the state and its bureaucrats. The overwhelming majority, who could not read those papers, nor present a written petition to the authorities, needed the help of those who could. Literacy, more than ever before in Ottoman history, became an important asset. As with other resources in society, such skills were not possessed by most of the enslaved either, but state-issued papers acquired vital importance for them too.

Much like other societies with slaves, the Ottoman state upheld the rights of slavers and refrained as much as possible from intervening in slaver-enslaved relationships. When it intervened, this was in most cases to help slaveholders to recover their absconding slaves or, conversely, to liberate severely abused enslaved persons from abusive slaveholders. Until 1845, the Tanzimat-state was also reluctant to impose its criminal system upon enslaved persons, leaving the responsibility for punishment in the hands of slaveholders. However, that changed as part of the growing role the state assumed in criminal matters in general. In August of the same year, while reviewing a theft case in which an enslaved African male was accused of stealing from his master, a certain Mustafa Bey, the Council of Ministers decided that unfree offenders should be treated like free ones.[7] Those cases, too, were henceforth to be handled by the state—not by the slaveholders, as stipulated in the Şeriat—and receive the same penalties as free offenders. Having served their term in prison, enslaved convicts would be returned to their holders, the council ruled.

With this ruling, the Ottoman state opened the door to greater involvement in slaver-enslaved relationships, setting aside in the process

6. In this sense, I adopt here some of the views developed by Timothy Mitchell for Egypt under the British in his *Colonizing Egypt*, Cambridge: Cambridge University Press, 1988. A similar analysis for Ottoman Egypt is in Ehud R. Toledano, *State and Society in Mid-Nineteenth-Century Egypt*, Cambridge: Cambridge University Press, 1990: 98–101. Khaled Fahmy applies Mitchell's ideas, with some additions, to Egypt under Mehmet Ali Paşa in Fahmy, *All the Pasha's Men: Mehmed Ali, His Army and the Making of Modern Egypt*, Cambridge: Cambridge University Press, 1997: 29–32.

7. BOA/İrade/Meclis-i Vala/1280/*Mazbata*, 23.7.1845, the Grand Vezir to the Sultan, 5.8.1845.

some of the basic notions enshrined in the Şeriat. The government allowed kadi courts to be bypassed on enslavement-related matters by two main paths:

1. The various councils it established as part of the Tanzimat reforms, which served as high administrative courts, adjudicated cases in which ill-treatment of enslaved persons by slavers was alleged.
2. The police and other law-enforcement agencies—both in Istanbul and in the provinces—agreed to entertain complaints from British consuls regarding runaway slaves who claimed to have been abused.

With either path, the result often was that the enslaved were set free against the will of the slaveholder, an act that nibbled into the Şeriat-sanctioned bond between slaver and enslaved. While in the first decade and a half after that development these cases just trickled in, from the 1860s onward setting the enslaved free became a well-established practice and perceptibly affected the experience of slavery.[8]

The state developed its own emancipation procedures, with official certificates of manumission being issued by the government on pre-printed forms (see the figure 3.1 on page 121). At the same time, Şeriat courts continued to handle matters involving enslaved persons, more often in procedural cases than in criminal ones. Thus, the state regulated, through the Tanzimat Council, the types of certificates that these courts were authorized to issue and determined the fees they were allowed to collect for their services. The following articles in the procedure code[9] set the appropriate legal fees for issuing the following slavery-related documents:

Article 34

Certificate confirming status of a free person	225	Kuruş
Certificate of manumission	75	Kuruş

8. On how the state acted in term-related manumission issues, see Y. Hakan Erdem, *Slavery in the Ottoman Empire and Its Demise, 1800–1909*, Basingstoke, England: Macmillan in association with St. Antony's College, Oxford, 1996: 154–160.
9. BOA/Meclis-i Tanzimat defterleri/#1/p. 150, Regulations governing the operation of Şeriat courts in the Empire, n.d. but probably the last quarter of the nineteenth century.

Article 36

No fixed fees are to be imposed for confirmation of a [regular] certificate of manumission, a certificate of manumission after the death of the slaveholder [*tedbir*], or a certificate of contracted manumission [*mükatebe*].

Fees are to be assessed at 5 to 30 Kuruş, according to the applicant's ability to pay.

Article 39

Certificates confirming legal ownership over an enslaved person are to be charged at 2 percent of his or her value.

A slaver-enslaved interest analysis of these fees is not very conclusive. Article 36 is pro-enslaved in that it imposes no or very low fees for a service required only by enslaved persons, who made up an overwhelmingly poor population. Certificates to be issued by courts under this article were based on manumission contracts already on file at court archives, and enslaved persons were likely to request such copies in order to protect themselves from retraction by slavers. On the other hand, Article 39 is heavily pro-slaver in that it imposes a very low fee for a service only slavers would apply for. Article 34 is not easily classified as favoring either the enslaved or the slaver. Only *freed* persons needed a certificate of manumission, but the article also applied to *free* persons who wished to have proof of their freedom in case they might be taken for slaves. The risky latter state was relevant mainly to two categories of people: *freed Africans*, because of the color of their skin, and *freeborn Circassians*, because of the existence of a heritable slave or serf status. The fees imposed under Article 34, especially for confirmation of free status, were rather steep.

The overall impression is thus rather mixed. Article 36 enabled enslaved persons—whether freed or expecting to be freed through some form of a contract—to assert their legitimately obtained legal position. On the other hand, Article 39 allowed the slavers to assert their proprietary rights over enslaved persons without financial penalty. We are then left with the apparent contradiction within Article 34, which can perhaps be explained by a desire to discourage false assertions of freedom by legally enslaved people while according preference to all Şeriat-sanctioned procedures for obtaining manumission.

But state-imposed manumission took hold only gradually and in many ways was still in a state of flux even during the last quarter of the nineteenth century. It is possible that the authorities were ambivalent about the entire process, partly because they did identify with the slavers more than with the enslaved, but partly also because state-imposed manusmission was seen by many officials on all levels as yielding to foreign, mainly British pressure, which they regarded as intrusive and patronizing. In any event, lack of determination on the part of the Ottoman state left the door open for exploitation by slaveholders and slave dealers at the expense of the enslaved and the freed. Freed slaves, however, proved to be great believers in the Tanzimat-state and its official documents; to them the documents came to embody freedom itself. The enslaved and freed expected law-enforcement officers to respect the papers that the government had issued to them, even if those papers were mocked by slaveholders and dealers and taken lightly by many state officials.

ATTITUDES TOWARD MANUMISSION PAPERS

In early December 1869, the British consul at the port town of Bengazi (in present-day Libya) reported to London about his frustrating correspondence with the governor-general of that Ottoman province.[10] The document reveals insidious activities by some slaveholders, probably resulting from the application of measures to suppress the traffic in Africans, which included the seizing and manumitting of enslaved persons. Along with Tripoli and Tunis, Bengazi was one of the main entrepôts for the slave trade going into the Ottoman ports of the eastern Mediterranean, and it is not impossible that many of the slaveholders mentioned were slave dealers. Reports circulated that these men were kidnapping and reselling manumitted Africans. The consul complained to Ali Rıza Paşa, governor-general of Bengazi, that the authorities were doing nothing to stop this activity or to punish the perpetrators. Such a seemingly organized and large-scale disregard of state-sponsored manumission was perhaps rare, but it did reportedly happen on a smaller, more private level. Perpetrators hoped that they would not be apprehended or, if they were caught, that conniving Ottoman officials would wink at their deeds. This occurred more frequently in the remote provinces, where local

10. FO/84/1305/512 ff., Cons. Hay (Tripoli) to Governor-General Ali Rıza (Tripoli), correspondence and telegrams, 4–7.12.1869.

officeholders had more discretionary powers than at the center and in core metropolitan areas.

In peripheral regions and perhaps somewhat more generally, Ottoman slaveholders seem to have considered manumission papers a mere formality and did not hesitate to repossess freed persons who had been forcibly liberated. "Allah, Allah," said the chief financial officer (*defterdar*) of Bengazi when such a case was brought to his attention as late as 1883, "what does it matter, when once we have signed and delivered their emancipation papers, what becomes of the slaves, or whether they are re-captured or not by their late owners?"[11] This statement stands in stark contrast to the view taken by the enslaved themselves, who remained keen on obtaining official papers of manumission, trying as best they could to hang on to them or—if the papers were taken and torn—to reclaim their freedom on the basis of the destroyed papers. In the specific case referred to by the Bengazi official, the person concerned was an aged African male slave named Jumʻa who had been officially manumitted, then recaptured and severely beaten. His papers were shredded, and he himself was locked up outside Bengazi city limits. Jumʻa managed to escape but was imprisoned by the police because he was unable to produce his stolen manumission papers and was hence assumed to be a slave. The following day, he was released but not given new papers, which meant that, lacking an acceptable social identity, he was left exposed to further abuse.

This brings up the issue of the slaves' awareness of their entitlements under Ottoman law, given that most of them were illiterate and could not possibly read these documents. Yet it is truly remarkable how seriously they regarded the papers, refusing to part with them as though they were freedom itself. Abuse of freed slaves through their entitlement papers was more widespread in the provinces, much less so in the capital. This conformed to the willingness to grant manumission on the basis of ill-treatment, which was more acceptable in Istanbul, less so in some provinces. In both matters, a great deal was left to the discretion of individual governors of provinces and subdistricts, some of whom were more lenient than others. This was also related to the reaction of the

11. FO/541/25 (Confidential 4914)/68, Cons. C. Wood (Bengazi) to Foreign Sec. Granville, 10.6.1883.

slavers, who, in some provinces, notably in the Hijaz, were less willing to accommodate the desire of the enslaved to free themselves. Indeed, some Bedouins in that province resorted to violence in order to put an end to British consular intervention in what they considered their domestic affairs. For example, it was reported in March 1879 that tensions were rising in Jidda following the arrival in town of three hundred armed Bedouins demanding the return of their runaway slaves, who had been allowed to board the HMS *Ready*.[12]

In the late 1870s and early 1880s, Jidda particularly, though certainly not exclusively, supplied a larger-than-usual number of cases in which manumission was not taken seriously. Now a burgeoning Saudi city with flourishing international business activities, Jidda was then a Red Sea slaving port and one of the main gateways to the Hijaz and the holy cities of Mecca and Medina. The following three stories illustrate the situation in Jidda at the time.

In 1881, the British consul there reported two cases of enslaved persons who fell victim to deceptions that affected their status as free persons.[13] The first case concerned Bilal, a twenty-year-old enslaved Ethiopian man who had been freed by his master, Bakır Efendi, in Cairo and who later moved to the port of Sawakin, on the opposite coast of the Red Sea. There he worked as a servant for a slave dealer named Ali, then for another slave dealer by the name of Muhammad Kayl. At one point, Muhammad Kayl sent Bilal to Jidda to accompany a group of three hundred slaves, but upon reaching Jidda, Bilal was seized, probably by some local slave dealer. He was sold as a slave together with the group he had accompanied on the crossing from Sawakin. The report does not specify whether he had with him his manumission papers or whether he resisted being enslaved but received no assistance from any Ottoman officer on the spot. Whoever ignored his pleas did so either knowingly or out of the conviction that all Africans were slaves, regardless of what they claimed. Later Bilal managed to escape to the consulate, and the consul succeeded in getting him freed, yet again, and then sent him safely to Egypt.

In the second case, the man who sought refuge at the Jidda consulate was Yusuf, also a twenty-year-old enslaved Ethiopian. Yusuf had worked

12. FO/84/1544/111–19, Wylde (FO, London) to Cons. Beyts (Jidda), 15.3.1879.
13. FO/84/1597/390–1, Cons. Zohrab (Jidda) to Foreign Sec. Granville, 1.7.1881.

for an unnamed man in the Red Sea port of Yanbuʿ, and the consul wrote that he was "a very intelligent lad" but apparently also too naive and trusting. During a long period of service, which lasted some twelve years, Yusuf managed to save 100 dollars (probably Austrian, Dutch, or Spanish), a very large sum indeed. To buy his way out of slavery, he offered the money to his holder in exchange for freedom. The man took the money, and then—shamelessly—sold Yusuf to another man, who brought him to Jidda. In this case, too, the consul succeeded in having Yusuf manumitted and sent safely to Egypt, but there is no mention of the culprit in this case. We must assume that the man was never punished, nor asked to return the money he had falsely taken from Yusuf; in the Jidda of those days, the consul must have considered Yusuf very fortunate to have been able to secure freedom and a way out to Egypt. There, it seems, matters were getting better for freed persons, and manumission papers were respected more than in other places, especially in Jidda, as the following story shows once again.

In January 1883, the British consul reported that a young enslaved African woman escaped to the consulate.[14] This unnamed seventeen-year-old told the consul that she had been held in slavery by a senior Ottoman official named Saidi Efendi, head of the Customs House in town. On his deathbed, Saidi freed the young woman and granted her 20 British pounds, a very large amount of money for anyone in her position. However, either his heirs or the executor of the estate took away her certificate of manumission and refused to pay the money. Presumably, whoever did this was confident that he could act with impunity, that a young African slave would take the perfidy without protest, a belief that reflects the kind of attitude that prevailed in the region toward the Anglo-Ottoman anti-slave trade measures. Still, in this case at least, as in the previous two, the consul was able to restore the young woman to freedom. In addition, she was paid 25 pounds, more than had originally been granted by Saidi Efendi, and was placed in paid service at the house of the acting deputy-governor of Jidda.

WORKING WITH THE TANZIMAT-STATE

Reconstructing the mindset of enslaved Africans and Circassians—and Georgians, Greeks, and Slavs—in Ottoman societies is an admittedly

14. FO/84/1642/73–81, Cons. Moncrieff's report (Jidda) on runaway slaves for 1882, dated 12.1.1883.

risky venture, but we can be certain that the *enslaved* saw themselves as inhabiting the lowest rung in society, with a towering social edifice rising above them, Straight above and with direct power over their daily lives were the men and women who had bought them and whom they served at home or worked for in the fields—*slavers*. As the evidence adduced in this book attempts to show, the enslaved realized that on the next rung up after that, there were higher powers to which the slaveholders were answerable. Foremost among these was the *state*, or, as the enslaved saw it, the officeholders who represented the state and acted as its agents: from the police officer at the nearby urban precinct to the village headman all the way up to the sultan himself. Separate from the state were the representatives of *foreign powers, including* consuls and others to whom the enslaved knew they could escape for help in dire circumstances.

Up and along this hierarchy there was always room for negotiation, and when grievances developed, redress could first be demanded from its immediate source, the slaveholders. Failing that, enslaved persons could try to get justice and succor from the state or foreign consuls, who had the power to overrule the slaveholders but used it sparingly and only when matters got really bad. Beyond that, an enslaved person could appeal to a deity, but this was often done through intermediaries, such as figures in the community believed to possess special powers to intercede with God or gods—figures such as a *kolbaşı* (headwoman of an African lodge), an *imam*, or a Sufi shaykh, the latter two Muslim personages being present in most neighborhoods.

As the reforming Tanzimat-state gradually assumed greater responsibility for the enslaved, reluctantly but persistently stepping into the slaveholder-enslaved relationship, it developed a new and direct dialogue with the enslaved, which was less and less mediated by the slaveholders. The official document that most embodied this relationship was the *certificate of manumission* issued by the state to freed persons. Notwithstanding the often dismissive attitude of slavers—and some officials—to this document, the enslaved took it seriously. When the certificate was unlawfully taken from them, they repeatedly demanded its restitution, fully aware that these state-issued papers stood between them and illegal enslavement.

Freed persons realized that reenslavement could occur either because they were African-looking or, if Circassian, because they might be presumed unfree by birth as opposed to freeborn (*pshitl* versus *thfokotl*, in Adygé Circassian; *köle* versus *hür*, in Ottoman Turkish). Various archives contain several types of manumission papers issued to freed persons by the Ottoman state. Three examples are discussed below: a blank certificate of manumission (*azatname*), meant to be filled out when illegally transported Africans were seized by Ottoman naval ships; a certificate of manumission issued by a court in Istanbul to a specific person; and a manumission document issued by the local council in Salonika to a freed woman.[15]

At the top of the blank form provided through the Ottoman navy, it is clearly stated that the document is issued according to the law (*kanun*) by Ottoman officials and the Ottoman courts. Significantly, the Tanzimat-state hereby assumed an authority that was, until the third quarter of the nineteenth century, invested in the Şeriat courts and executed according to the Şeriat. The following section includes eight categories designed to mark the recipient of the document and identify him or her to any person who might need to examine the paper. The top four categories are, in order of appearance: name, country (of origin), age, and trade. The remaining four provide physical descriptions of the certificate holder: height, moustache (whether he has one or not), beard (whether he has one or not), and eyes (color of). Two of the last four refer only to men, and color of hair is curiously missing, although that category was often used by the Ottomans in physical descriptions of people.

The text of the certificate makes it clear from the outset that it applied only to Africans, since the description "black" is part of the printed text of the form, not left to be filled in. It also becomes clear that the form was intended to be used by captains of Ottoman naval vessels who seized illegally transported enslaved Africans, and a blank space was even reserved for the name of the captain to be filled in. The enslaved person whose name and description were provided in the document, the text reads, was to be "rescued from the bond of slavery" by the "sublime Ottoman state," and thereafter no one was to be allowed by any means to claim that he or she was still a slave. It was further stated that this certificate of manumission was herewith given to the named person. The

15. All three documents are grouped under FO 198/82, X/M 00518, dating from the late 1880s–early 1890s.

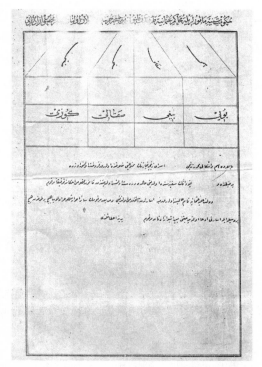

FIGURE 3.1. A blank certificate of manumission

act of handing the document to the freed confirmed the state-sponsored manumission and came to symbolize freedom itself. In the absence of identity papers in Ottoman society, these certificates served to identify, place, and classify the freed individuals who carried them. The certificates told officials and employers much of what they needed to know about the bearers, and they were the only barrier standing between the category of "African" and that of "slave."

The second example is a certificate of manumission issued by the first criminal section of the lower court in Istanbul. This was a Nizami court, not a Şeriat one; Nizami courts were established by the Tanzimat-state as part of its legal reforms. The document states that in Safer 1308 (ca. mid-1890), Bahtyar bint Abdüllah, a twenty-five-year-old enslaved Sudanese woman, tall with black eyes, applied to the court to be manumitted. She was the slave of Ali Efendi, a clerk at the Şeriat court in the Mahmut Paşa area of Istanbul. The woman addressed the court in

FIGURE 3.2. A certificate of manumission (Istanbul Court)

order "to benefit from" the 1857 prohibition of the slave trade in Africans and the "recent" imperial law which reaffirmed it. The court stated that the policy was to liberate enslaved persons who applied to the authorities even if they did not have in their possession a manumission certificate or other documents testifying to their being free. Therefore, the court decided to manumit Bahtyar and to give her the necessary document so that she could henceforward enjoy the benefits of freedom like all other Muslims in the Empire and be free to choose where to move and live. The language deployed here leaves no doubt that the state, here through the court, was fully aware of the disadvantages of slavery and the benefits of freedom, regardless of how hard defenders of the Islamic version of servility tried to portray its nature as mild and integrative.

Our third example of a state-issued manumission paper comes from the important province of Salonika, in present-day Greece. There, in January 1888, the Administrative Council of the province, acting as a Nizami court, issued a manumission document to Zubur bin Abdüllah, an enslaved African man. For the previous nine years, Zubur had been in the service of Osman Bey, son of Hacı Hüseyin Ağa of Salonika, whose family

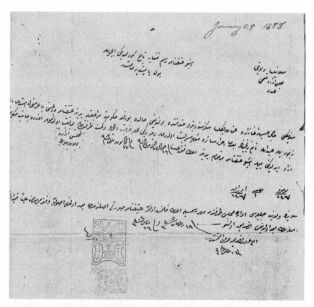

FIGURE 3.3. A certificate of manumission (Salonika Court)

belonged to the military-administrative elite in the province. He was not
manumitted by the slaveholder despite his long period of service, and
Zubur had to petition the council to obtain his freedom. The phrase used
in the document is that he wanted "to go freely where[ever] he wished, like
all free persons, without being prevented by anyone."[16] Movement without restriction seems to have embodied liberation itself, as the other papers also indicate. Not surprisingly, the council decided to give Zubur his
manumission certificate and set him free.

The issuing of these Ottoman documents reflects the end of a long
and painful process that began in midcentury and shifted the position of
the Tanzimat-state from unequivocal support for the slaveholders first to
an intermediary stance between the enslaved and the slaveholders and
then to a position that favored the emancipation of enslaved Africans.

The enslaved of course noticed the shifting position of the Tanzimat-
state from the middle decades of the nineteenth century onward. Even
young teenagers among the enslaved quickly discovered how to use the

16. *Ahrar-ı saire misillu serbest olarak dilediği mahale azimet eylemek ve kimesne
tarafından mümaneet olunmamak üzere.*

system and manipulate it to their advantage. In 1857, seven free Turkish boys were sent by their families to Istanbul to learn a trade.[17] Soon after their arrival, they began to work as servants or apprentices in several shops. Some time later, each one of them was separately approached and offered an opportunity to participate in the following scam. The boys were asked to pose as Circassian slaves, be transported to Egypt and sold there. In return, they would receive part of their sale value in two installments, a smaller amount—though still considerable in their terms—before leaving Istanbul, the rest upon arrival in Egypt and sale. The argument presented to them was that being sold as Circassian slaves in Egypt would give them each a chance to advance in life and become "a personage" (adam olursun). One of the boys was told that if he stayed in Istanbul, the authorities would draft him into the army. All of the boys agreed to take part in this adventure and were transported to Alexandria. They were later sold into the household of Sait Paşa, governor-general of Egypt (1854–1863), fetching high prices.[18]

However, one of them, named Hasan, was given a relatively small amount in Istanbul, and even that was taken away from him upon arrival in Egypt. He was not going to accept that deception, and when the bunch arrived in Cairo, he took with him one of the other boys, and together they walked to the borough of Hilmiyya, where he knew his brother was working as a cook. When Hasan told the story to his brother, the latter went to the head of the slave dealers' guild and exposed the entire scam. All seven boys were liberated from Sait Paşa's household, and the slave dealers involved in the affair were tried, convicted of fraud, deported from Egypt, and required to pay damages to Sait Paşa for the vacated deal.

The first thing we learn from this story is that in the 1850s it was still possible to convince young, inexperienced boys, coming from the provinces to the imperial capital, that enslavement could offer upward social mobility and improvement in life. This was certainly true of kul/harem slavery, and young men recruited to serve in elite households as retainers could indeed rise to officeholding positions within the administration.

17. BOA/İrade/Meclis-i Vala/16542/Mazbata, 17.8.1857, the Grand Vezir to the Sultan, 28.8.1857, and the Sultan's response, same date.
18. For a discussion of his reign and the Ottoman Egypt in the middle years of the nineteenth century, see Toledano, State and Society, 39–148.

But the officeholding career track was open only to white, mostly Circassian men, not to enslaved Africans, nor to freeborn persons of other ethnic
groups. In any case, the incentive was not strong enough to convince
Hasan, once cheated out of his money, to stick to the deal. Instead, he decided to act to reverse the situation and extricate himself from the new
predicament he found himself in. The young boy's brother trusted the authorities enough to submit a complaint to the guild's head, who in fact
acted according to the law. The decisive action taken here by the Tanzimat-
state sent a clear message to slave dealers and slaveholders alike, but also
to potentially enslavable individuals, that unlawful enslavement of free persons, even when it involved the most powerful elite household in Egypt,
that of the governor-general, would not be tolerated.

The following story also pits powerless enslaved people against powerful slaveholders, with the state negotiating a position in between. In
October 1861, an interesting case was brought before the Refugees Commission, which often in the 1860s had to deal with problems arising
from enslavement among Circassian refugees.[19] Here, five enslaved Circassian men and women from the district of Kostança (Constanța) in Ro-
mania petitioned the commission, asserting that they were freeborn and
should not be considered slaves. In those years, the commission was establishing itself as the main government agency handling such applications, but potential applicants needed to develop skills—such as how to
get literate people to compile and submit their petitions through the
right channels—in order to take advantage of this emerging option. An
enslaved person also needed to wait a few months, sometimes more,
until a decision was made, all the while being exposed to recriminations
from his or her landlord—here, Canpulad Bey.

Canpulad was one of the more influential officials in the province,
and to attempt to enlist the power of the state to enforce manumission
upon a person of that caliber was surely a brave move on the part of the
five enslaved men and women. We do not know whether all five belonged
to one family of Circassian cultivators working on the Canpulad estate,
but this was a possibility. If so, the ability to act together rather than separately certainly helped them to make such a bold move. While trying to
change their status, the five undoubtedly risked damaging their patronage

19. BOA/BEO/Mühacirin Komisyonu/vol. 758–38:1/# 179, 10–11.1861.

relationship with one of the strongest households in the province. This case also provides a good indication of the importance of status differences among Circassians—namely, between the freeborn and the heritably unfree. We have no information as to how the case was adjudicated, but in any event the five would have had to produce witnesses from their home villages to testify that they were freeborn. Given the chaos in the wake of the forced relocation of the Circassians from the Caucasus, this would not have been an easy task. Since they chose that path, the five may have had such proof of status already lined up. The clear choice the Canpulad dependents made was to prefer freedom to enslavement, despite the high risks and obvious costs entailed in the process.

A similar question was put before the Refugees Commission some six months after the Canpulad case.[20] An unnamed Circassian man was brought to Istanbul by Hanife, a woman residing in the district of Amasya in Anatolia and was offered for sale as a slave. The man petitioned to have his freeborn status recognized officially in order to prevent his enslavement, and in 1862, after an inquiry into the matter, the commission issued an order to free him. Moreover, orders were then given to prevent such attempted sales of freeborn persons in the future. Thus, the Tanzimat-state stepped in to prevent people from taking advantage of the Circassian mass migration into the Ottoman Empire by enslaving freeborn immigrants, who were often young children. In the bedlam that accompanied the Russian ethnic cleansing in the Caucasus, freeborn persons sometimes sold their own children or children of their immediate relatives into slavery. In many cases, this was motivated by sheer want and the hope of securing a better future for those children as kul/harem elite slaves in the Ottoman Empire than they would have in a zone of danger and poverty.

In the late 1850–early 1860s, Circassian tribal leaders and landlords continued to hold, sell, and otherwise dispose of their formerly enserfed families who had turned into Ottoman agricultural slaves. It was, then, not at all unusual that one of these leaders, named Hüseyin Bey, would make to his sister Arslan Koz Hanım, a resident of the Bulgarian port town of Varna, a gift consisting of five such individuals.[21] At a later

20. BOA/BEO/Mühacirin Komisyonu/vol. 758–38:1/# 371, 4–5.1862.
21. BOA/BEO/Mühacirin Komisyonu/vol. 758 (gelen)/# 1 (fevkalade), Petition, 6–7.1865.

point, these enslaved persons claimed to be freeborn, and in 1865 the matter was brought before the Refugees Commission to be sorted out. The High Court in Istanbul, to which the commission referred the case, requested that the five be delivered to the capital in order for their claim to be verified. Verification usually involved soliciting testimonies at their home villages in the Caucasus. Again, unfortunately, we do not know how the case was resolved, but we can safely assume that if credible witnesses were found who confirmed their assertion of status, or if doubt could be cast upon the slaver's statement, the court would lean toward a presumption of freedom and grant them manumission papers.

THE TWILIGHT ZONE OF FREEBORN STATUS

By the mid-1860s, this tendency of the Tanzimat-state to favor freedom claims put forth by the enslaved became well known among Circassian agricultural slaves; rumors about such cases must have circulated among Circassian communities throughout the Empire. It is quite possible that enslaved agricultural workers, individually or as families, were also trying their luck with the courts, even if they had not been born free. If successful, a petitioner received court-approved manumission papers—and also a tract of land and basic means to cultivate it, making it possible to become a productive subject of the sultan. By then, such briefly recorded cases became fairly common in the registers of the Refugees Commission. One typical entry simply states that two freeborn Circassian refugees who had been unlawfully enslaved asserted that they were not of slave origin.[22] Having succeeded in substantiating their claims, they were declared free, and an order was issued on 13 September 1864 to the deputy governor-general of the province of İzmit, not far from Istanbul, to facilitate their settlement in the district with their families. Not all cases were so uncomplicated, as the next and unusually severe story of Fatime and Ahmet Ağa will illustrate.

In December 1864, the Refugees Commission sent to the administrative High Court in Istanbul the following manslaughter case.[23] Ahmet Ağa,

22. BOA/BEO/Mühacirin Komisyonu/vol. 758 (gelen)/# 91, order to the Kaymakam of İzmit, 13.9.1864.
23. BOA/BEO/Mühacirin Komisyonu/vol. 758 (gelen)/# 167, case report to the Meclis-i Vala, 11–12.1864.

an Abkhazian residing in Aydıncık, tried to force into his house a woman named Fatime and her children, claiming that she was his slave. Fatime and the children resisted, and in the ensuing confrontation—which evidently also involved members of Ahmet Ağa's family—his brother, Ömer Ağa, was killed. The matter was reported by the local authorities to the High Court, and although we do not know how the court ruled, we may surmise that the case was treated as manslaughter with extenuating circumstances, possibly as involuntary manslaughter. From the evidence we do possess, however, it is not difficult to classify this incident under resistance to slavery without recourse to the state. The Abkhazians, like their neighbors the Circassians, were also driven out of the Caucasus by the Russians during the same period, and they, too, were allowed to bring their serfs with them into the Empire. The two brothers, Ahmet and Ömer, had some standing in their village community, enjoying the state endorsement signified by the military title of Ağa that was attached to both their names.

In the disarray of the times, false claims to freeborn status were made by unfree refugees, and false claims were made by slaveholders against freeborn refugees. But the two sides were very unevenly matched, and it was up to the state to bring in a more balanced approach. The commission and the courts were expected by the poor and weaker members among the refugees to protect them against unlawful—and later even lawful—enslavement. To avoid losing their freedom, vulnerable individuals and families tried to escape to another town or village and, when possible, approached the authorities for help. Fatime and her children could have been either wrongly enslaved freeborn persons or unfree persons falsely seeking freedom. In any event, her family was already weakened by the absence of a father due to circumstances unknown to us and had to face a powerful family of ağas in a tough struggle between unequal forces.

With odds not in their favor, Fatime's family nevertheless chose to act against the ağas; even when met with violence, they responded with defiant self-defense, causing the death of Ömer Ağa. Only at that point—too late—did the Tanzimat-state step in. Perhaps because Fatime and her children did not fully trust the authorities to do justice by them, they had not approached the Refugees Commission or the police earlier—that is, when Ahmet Ağa's intentions became clear to them. Consequently, they set in motion a series of events that spiraled out of control with dire consequences.

If Fatime perceived the state as untrustworthy, the persons involved in the next case, in contrast, trusted the Ottoman system of justice and expected it to protect them from wrongful enslavement and from the slave dealer who claimed to have proprietary rights over them. The authorities' performance here was mixed. So the issue of *trust* was clearly a major factor in the Tanzimat-state's mediation between slaveholders and the enslaved. The image of the state as an honest broker between these unequal partners depended on the outcome of its intervention in past cases, both locally and regionally.

In early July 1866, a slave dealer named Süleyman Ağa—variously described as an Arab and an Egyptian—was caught in Istanbul trying to take five Circassian boys to Egypt for sale.[24] The boys were taken to a police station, where they claimed that they were freeborn, hence illegally sold into slavery. On 5 July, the dealer petitioned the office of the Şeyhülislam, the highest official authority on Islamic law in the Empire, for a ruling on the boys' status and his proprietary rights. Although four of the boys asserted that they were not from enslaved families, the Şeriat court did not act to verify their claims; it merely stated that the boys had failed to prove their claim and consequently affirmed the dealer's ownership rights over them. However, the authorities concluded later that matters in this case were not handled according to the proper procedures. The Şeriat court should have conducted interviews in the boys' home villages with people who knew them and could have attested to their legal status. In any event, the authorities asserted, it was a mistake to turn the boys over to Süleyman Ağa even if they were deemed to have been unfree, since Ottoman regulations prohibited the splitting of families by sale. Following are the stories of the five boys—all from towns in Anatolia—paraphrased using the language and terminology of the Ottoman documents.

> *Ahmet,* nine years old, belongs to the Şabigh tribe. Lived with his parents and two paternal uncles in the town of Çarşamba. The two uncles took him to the city of Samsun, where he was sold to a Turk who sold him to another Turk in Istanbul.

24. BOA/Yıldız/33/33:28/71/94, Petition, Şeriat Court documents, and İrades, 5.7.1866–31.6.1867, re the case of the five Circassian boys (their statements are in Enclosure #8).

Claims he is free and that there are two persons who can attest
to that, as required.

İzzet, seven years old, from the same tribe. His father lives
in the city of Trabzon, and he has an older brother, who sold
him in Trabzon to a Circassian. The latter sold İzzet to another
Circassian in Trabzon, and the boy later ended up in Istanbul
in the hands of Süleyman the slave dealer. İzzet, too, asserts
that he is freeborn and that he can name two witnesses who
are able to confirm that.

Hatuk Osman, eleven years old, from the same tribe, has a
mother and paternal cousins in Samsun. His cousins sold him
in Samsun to a Circassian slave dealer, who then sold him
there to another dealer named Hafız. Hafız sent him to his
brother in Istanbul, where the boy—who claims to be freeborn—was sold to Süleyman Ağa.

İshak, seven years old, belongs to the Abazkha tribe and has
a paternal uncle and a sister in Samsun and another free sister
in Kılıçhane. His cousin (the paternal uncle's son) sold him in
Samsun to a Circassian slave dealer from the same tribe. The
slave dealer took İshak to Batum, then to Istanbul, where he
sold him to another dealer, who then sold him to Süleyman
Ağa. The boy claims to be freeborn.

Feyzi, seven years old, from the same tribe, has a mother
and a brother in Çarşamba. His brother brought him to Istanbul and handed him over to a slave dealer. The dealer sold him
to another dealer. He is the only one who actually stated that he
was born a slave.

In this case, the state acted through two separate but closely linked
arms of the law: the Şeriat courts under the Şeyhülislam's bureau and
the new Nizami court system set up by the Tanzimat reformers. Other
agents were also involved, especially police, who seized the five boys and
began investigating the matter. In the first instance, the Şeriat system
backed the dealer, as it consistently gave preference to slaveholders'
interests. The boys were then given to the dealer, but they apparently
continued to defy the ruling, since they soon found themselves giving
statements before the Nizami court clerk and in the presence of the slave

dealer himself. This indicates that they were willing to stand up to a man who had absolute power over them and who could punish them severely if they failed to convince the Nizami court to overrule the Şeriat one. The five boys' action took not only courage but also a measure of trust in the Ottoman state and its ability to deliver justice by restoring them to freedom. In this instance, the Tanzimat-state did not let them down. In order to vacate the earlier Şeriat court decision, the Nizami court criticized the kadi on procedure, but it also reiterated government policy against splitting families. In effect, the state thus interfered with the sale of Circassian children by members of their own families, thereby setting a clear limit on parental rights.

Even high-ranking Ottoman officials were not spared state interference in their dealings with slaves. In August 1867, Muhsin Efendi, one of the top aides (the *mühürdar,* or seal bearer) to Muhlis Paşa, the governor-general of Trabzon, inherited from his father twenty-four male and female Circassian slaves.[25] Having taken possession of them, he decided to send two of the enslaved women and one of the enslaved men to Istanbul for resale. The report contained in the Ottoman state archives maintains that owing to Muhsin Efendi's lack of attention or care, the enslaved persons managed to sneak away and approach the authorities. Presumably at court, the three claimed that they were freeborn, an implausible assertion given that Muhsin Efendi had inherited them from his father. The enslaved persons in question undoubtedly knew that their owner was well connected and that their claims were false. Nevertheless, they pressed ahead with their attempt to gain freedom, and, no less significantly, their case was not dismissed out of hand but was processed through the system and further investigated.

Muhsin Efendi had to work hard to refute the three's assertion of freedom, apparently recruiting for that purpose another Circassian refugee, who was serving in the military artisan corps. The man petitioned the office of the grand vezir to have the matter of the three absconders investigated and resolved. Wondering what his stake in the case was, we may surmise that he had been freed earlier—perhaps even by Muhsin Efendi himself—and placed in the army, which was not infrequently

25. BOA/Ayniyat defterleri/1136/# 398, Bab-ı Ali to the Mühacirin İdaresi, 29.8.1869.

done with freed men after manumission. The man must have known the three and their families and therefore was able to testify to their status, namely, that they were not freeborn but the property first of Muhsin's father and then of Muhsin himself. By producing this witness, Muhsin Efendi was trying to persuade the court to restore the three runaways to his possession. The fact that the grand vezir's office and the court enabled the whole process to take place in earnest suggests that, by the mid or late 1860s, due process was well in place regarding cases of absconding and freedom assertion.

As already noted, in the following decades, the Ottoman state found itself increasingly called upon by the enslaved to limit the slaveholders' proprietary rights and restore to freedom more and more enslaved persons, here mainly enserfed Circassian refugees. The number of enslaved Circassians who approached the government and demanded to be liberated increased markedly. For example, in January 1872, the governorate of Trabzon sent a telegram to the office of the grand vezir, asking for policy guidance regarding Circassian refugees from the district of Çarşamba, who had come to the town of Samsun and requested to be "rescued from slavery."[26] In the regions on the Black Sea shores of northeastern Anatolia, and in other areas as well, the number of people petitioning the government regarding manumission required specific instructions from Istanbul to provincial authorities.

In August 1878, a group of forty-three Abkhazian individuals from the district of Atapazarı petitioned the Ottoman Refugees Commission to assist them in asserting their freedom.[27] The group, consisting of six families, reported that they had been enserfed in their country of origin but set free there, remaining, it appears, on the property of their former landlords as free persons. However, following their emigration into the Empire, most probably with their landlords, the latter continued "to interfere with their lives," meaning, in effect, that they continued to treat them as if they were still their serfs-turned-slaves. On 2 September 1878, the matter was referred to the Consultative Council, but we do not know how the case was decided. However, especially if we consider the trend,

26. BOA/Ayniyat defterleri/1136/# 265, Bab-ı Ali to the Mühacirin İdaresi, 24.1.1872.
27. BOA/BEO/Mühacirin Komisyonu/vol. 762 (gelen)/# 89, Petition, 28.8.1878.

we may safely assume—barring special circumstances, not stated in this case—that even if these six families could not produce proof that they had been liberated in the Caucasus, the Tanzimat-state would lean heavily toward affirming their freedom and would release them from the control of their beys.

This petition is a form of group action, organized by the former serfs in order to change their status. Six families from the same subdistrict, working for several landlords, cooperated on this initiative. It is not clear how they expected their lives to change as a result, but since they specifically protested against their landlords' interference, they may have expected to be allowed to continue cultivating the land as freeholders. In that case, much more would be involved, since the issue of usufruct rights would have to be resolved first. Circassian refugees coming into the Empire in the 1860s received cultivation rights over government-owned land, often in frontier or undercultivated areas, and also initial means of production to enable them to make a living. Such rights were given to free refugees and to former landlords in the Caucasus, who were allowed to continue using their enslaved families to till the land.

Presumably, the petitioners in this case had hoped that if interference from their former masters were stopped by the authorities, they would be able to get cultivation rights over the plots they were already cultivating. The significance of such a change could have played a role in the decision by these six families to undertake an organized initiative, rather than act separately, which would have made it more difficult to face the landlords. They obviously knew of cases in which the government had not only freed people in their situation but also used its considerable economic power to set them up as free cultivators.

During the same year, 1878, another interesting case was brought before the Refugees Commission, further illustrating the pivotal role now being assumed by the Tanzimat-state at the expense of the Circassian landlords. A number of the enslaved Circassians who had migrated into the Empire with their beys requested permission to return to their country of origin.[28] No further details are provided, but the very action on the part of these enslaved persons is significant. Again, it expresses

28. BOA/BEO/Mühacirin Komisyonu/vol. 762 (gelen)/# 196, memo to the
    Refugees Commission, 17.11.1878.

a desire to change their predicament by making a fairly drastic move and choosing repatriation. They must have asked to travel without their beys, or the entire petition would have been superfluous. Hence, the petitioners were hoping, we may safely assume, to be liberated from their landlords and live as free persons in the Caucasus, whence they had come. There does not seem to be an issue of status change from enslaved to freed, nor any mention of beys who might have opposed the request. So we can only speculate as to the motives that may have propelled the enslaved persons in question to seek repatriation. Getting out of slavery may have been one, but a desire to improve their economic lot must have been another, if not the more pressing. Otherwise, we could expect them have tried a change of status where they were, rather than seek to go back to the Caucasus. The landlords, it appears, could no longer rely on the state to automatically protect their proprietary rights; otherwise, such a petition would not have been served at the Refugees Commission.

Indeed, a serious struggle was taking place within the government, with some officials advocating a blanket emancipation of former Circassian serfs, which was tantamount to a de facto abolition of agricultural slavery in the Empire. Ottoman cabinet minutes mention that on 30 October 1878, the Consultative Council had issued a memo to the effect that from then on, all Circassian refugees in the Ottoman Empire were to be considered free and that claims of slaveholders seeking to affirm their proprietary rights regarding various individuals would not be heard, including pending ones.[29] In fact, the ruling meant that claims from *unfree* persons asserting their right to freedom could not be challenged in Ottoman courts. This significant decision attests to the ongoing desire of enslaved individuals to shed their social disability not only was evident in sporadic and isolated cases but had reached such proportions that the tide could no longer be contained by the slaveholders, especially with a state growing increasingly ambivalent about supporting Circassian agricultural enslavement.

For two decades, from the mid-1860s to the mid-1880s, support for slaveholders' rights came from Şeriat courts while, at the same time, the Tanzimat government was nibbling away at those rights. This ambivalence

29. BOA/Meclis-i Vükela Mazbata ve İrade Dosyaları/Cabinet minutes of
    Wednesday, 8.2.1882.

within the Ottoman administration resulted in shifts from a more conservative stance to a more liberal position and vice versa. The struggle was not over with the Consultative Council's 1878 decision, which was overturned by the Council of Ministers a while later. Fearing the negative reaction of slaveholders and conservative forces in Ottoman society to a blanket emancipation—rather than liberation on an individual basis—the government devised another way out of the quagmire. The preferred solution was a government-supported and state-financed individual contract of purchased manumission (mükatebe) between the landlords and their enslaved cultivators.[30] Accordingly, enslaved persons and families were granted land and tools by the authorities where they resided, and could buy their freedom from the beys, paying a share of the produce they grew.

During the 1880s, the state became actively involved in this manumission mechanism, which in effect broke the chains of bondage within Ottoman-Circassian agrarian society. The Tanzimat-state also began recruiting these freedmen into the Ottoman army, which it could not do when they had been legally slaves, so there was a clear interest on the government side in encouraging the manumission of enslaved Circassians, which in turn drew protests from the beys. In 1883, for example, eleven of these beys, nine retainer-warriors (Adygé Circassian, werks) and four ulema, all slavers, petitioned the sultan by telegram. They strongly objected to the fact that their enslaved clients were enlisted in the military and demanded compensation.[31] The government was here still treading a fine line between the slavers and the enslaved: it did not initiate such manumissions, nor did it move to unilaterally impose mükatebe procedures if the enslaved did not actively seek government involvement. Where enslaved Circassians refrained from challenging the slavers' "proprietary rights"—in effect, accepting the terms of bondage—the state let sleeping dogs lie.

It was not unusual, then, for a large slaver named Ahmet Kamupulan Bey to arrange through the Refugees Commission the transfer and settlement in the district of Atapazarı of his forty-five enslaved agricultural

---

30. The solution is outlined in Toledano, *Slave Trade*, 95–111.
31. BOA/Irade/Dahiliye/88412 (cited in Seteney Khalid Shami, *Ethnicity and Leadership: The Circassians in Jordan*, Ann Arbor, Mich.: University Microfilms International, 1985: 44).

laborers.[32] In September 1879, such an application was recorded in the registers, and although this concerned a large number of individuals, very likely a number of families, the government did not interfere in the bey's business. We can also assume that no families were split up in this move, because the enslaved would have been likely to protest such a step, and the government would probably have intervened on their behalf. However, claiming to be freeborn, hence unlawfully sold into slavery, was a ploy so commonly resorted to by enslaved persons to achieve liberation that the government had no shortage of opportunity if it wanted to support manumission.

Indeed, sellers tried to protect themselves by stating and proving that the enslaved person being traded indeed belonged to the Circassian enserfed, unfree class. On 16 March 1893, a man named Osman sold his nineteen-year-old female slave Cemile to the deputy minister of the interior, Ahmet Refik Bey.[33] In addition to the certificate of sale, Osman provided two statements signed by six respectable witnesses—some of them local officials in the woman's village of origin—attesting to the fact that Cemile, daughter of İsmail, was of slave origin (köle cinsi). Osman stated that he had owned her for a long time and that she was a Muslim and a slave. He undertook to refund the amount paid to him if anybody tried to take possession of her or if the buyer lost possession over Cemile because she—falsely—claimed to be freeborn. Perhaps to reduce the likelihood of her doing so, and in partial recognition of her legitimate family needs, he added that it was agreed that she would be allowed to see her parents twice a year. It is significant, however, that as late as the 1890s, and despite wide-scale emancipation of enslaved individuals in various categories who asserted their freedom, the state had not enacted a full-fledged abolition of ownership rights over formerly enserfed Circassians.

Despite the state's failure to make the final leap, both the enslaved and the slaveholders recognized the central place the Ottoman government, along with foreign consuls, assumed in bondage relationships. In 1888, an enslaved Circassian woman sought refuge at the British consulate in

32. BOA/BEO/Mühacirin Komisyonu/vol. 762 (gelen)/# 168, memo, 29.9.1879.
33. BOA/Yıldız/18/480:141/123/53, three documents relating to the sale of a Circassian female slave to the Dahiliye Müsteşarı, 16.3.1893.

Istanbul.[34] She claimed to be freeborn and asked Dragoman Marinitch, who for years was in charge of slavery-related matters, to assist her in obtaining official endorsement of her status and extricating her from the slaver. At the same time, however, the slaver applied to the Ottoman Nizami court to have the woman recognized as his lawful slave. Since white slaves were not covered by the 1880 Anglo-Ottoman Anti-Slavery Convention, Marinitch reported in December 1888, he had to act unofficially vis-à-vis the Ottoman authorities. Nonetheless, he was ultimately successful in persuading the court to accept the woman's assertion and declare her free. Thus, the Tanzimat-state came to occupy an indispensable position in relationships of servitude, an area that had been fiercely guarded as private and strictly within the Şeriat sphere only half a century earlier.

THE VULNERABILITY OF THE FREED

The Tanzimat-state was fully aware of the risks accompanying manumission, as were the foreign agents and consuls who often helped freed persons in the Empire. Hakan Erdem has written about government care of emancipated slaves, pointing out that Sultan Abdülhamit II (1876–1908) took a personal interest in finding proper arrangements and funding to support liberated persons.[35] However, Erdem believes that despite the good intentions of the authorities, freed persons were not always protected and cared for in the most efficient way. The main reason seems to have been the chronic want of money in the state coffers and the failure, in some of the peripheral provinces, of officials to vigorously carry out the instructions issued by Istanbul. For our microhistorical purposes, however, it is the attitudes of the enslaved and the freed toward the stance taken by the authorities that we need to examine. As the role of the Tanzimat-state in slavery-related matters was growing, the issue of the state's credibility in the eyes of the target population became more important.

Much though the Ottoman state tended to favor the interests of slavers, it is hard to ignore the fact that its agents displayed compassion in treating hardship cases among the enslaved. Kindness and generosity

34. FO/84/1903/147, Cons. White (Istanbul) to Foreign Sec. Salisbury, 7.12.1888.
35. Erdem, *Slavery*, 173–184.

were not infrequently bestowed upon enslaved persons pleading for the sultan's mercy. At the same time, until the 1860s at least, the sovereign's officials seemed reluctant to entertain demands from enslaved people on the basis of a claimed entitlement. Thus, for example, appeals for sultan-imposed manumission (azad-ı padişahi) based on length of service were not frequently granted. As Erdem has argued, manumission was not automatic after a fixed period of time, although it was considered meritorious following seven to ten years of service.[36] But the state intervened on behalf of enslaved people only in cases of blatant denial of liberation after many years of service, much in the same way it showed consideration toward suffering individuals in other kinds of cases. The following four stories illustrate the attitude of the government toward freed persons who had special needs after the death of their former masters.

İsmail Efendi was a middle-level official in the province of Diyarbekir, with an annual salary of 2,250 Kuruş.[37] When he died in 1851, he was survived by his wife, Ayşe Hanım, who was living in Istanbul, and by his enslaved concubine, who resided with their daughter in the province. Upon İsmail's death, the enslaved woman became free, but both she and her daughter remained without income. The government decided that the official who replaced İsmail in his capacity, Ahmet Raif Efendi, would receive an annual salary of just 2,000 Kuruş, the remaining 250 Kuruş to be divided between the widow in Istanbul (100 Kuruş) and the freed concubine and her daughter (150 Kuruş). The government not only assumed responsibility for freed slaves but also apportioned the pension between the wife and the concubine without discriminating. In another example, in mid-1853, the daughter of a deceased Ottoman official who had enjoyed a state pension died. The government decided to allocate more than half of the pension to her freed African female slave, who was suffering from a chronic eye disease.[38]

The third story is that of Zarafet, a freed African woman who had belonged to Pembe Hanım, the wife of an Ottoman scribe living near the

36. Ibid., 154–160.
37. BOA/İrade/Meclis-i Vala/7020/*Mazbata*, 4.6.1851, the Grand Vezir to the Sultan, 19.6.1851, and the Sultan's response, 21.6.1851.
38. BOA/İrade/Meclis-i Vala/9663/*Mazbata*, 17.6.1853, the Grand Vezir to the Sultan, 29.6.1853, and the Sultan's response, 1.7.1853.

main mosque in the Istanbul quarter of Cihangir.[39] Since Pembe designated the house as an endowed charity (vakıf), when she died it passed into the hands of the authorities in charge of such charities. The house remained vacant, and the freed woman was entitled to reside in it, probably according to the wishes of her deceased lady. Because it was in need of repairs, Zarafet petitioned the government to grant her money to renovate the house. Considering the request, the authorities noted that the woman was poor and decided to grant her 55 percent of the amount she had applied for. Again, this was a case of pure charity; even though the petitioner did not claim entitlement by Şeriat law or Ottoman custom, the appeal was still duly met with sovereign compassion. Finally, we have the case of an enslaved African man who belonged to a high-ranking military officer (mirliva) in the Ottoman army's Anatolian Division.[40] Upon the death of the officer, the state granted the slave a modest monthly subvention, although there is no mention of manumission. When the slave died, the pension was transferred to another person in need. The government must have realized that it had to take care of the man on humanitarian grounds; he might have been old at the time the officer died, or might have served with him long enough not to be put on the market again.

PLACING AND REATTACHING THE FREED

Humanitarian considerations motivated the Tanzimat-state also with regard to the slave trade. From the outset, the government realized that suppression of the traffic in enslaved Africans incurred care of illegally imported persons. In early 1857, the first edicts (fermans) were dispatched to provincial governors-general, instructing them to prohibit the trade in Africans.[41] In these edicts, the government clearly assumed responsibility for the fate of illegally imported persons. Each governor-general was ordered to manumit such Africans immediately and give them the necessary

39. BOA/İrade/Meclis-i Vala/14366/Mazbata, 5.6.1855, the Grand Vezir to the Sultan, 26.6.1855, and the Sultan's response, same date.
40. BOA/İrade/Meclis-i Vala/19417/the Grand Vezir to the Sultan, 28.10.1860, and the Sultan's response, 29.10.1860.
41. BOA/Yıldız/33/73/1403/91, Draft of Imperial Ferman sent to the Vali of Tripoli, 27.1.1857; BOA/İrade/Meclis-i Vala/16623/Enclosure 70, similar fermans to the Valis of Egypt, Iraq, and the Hijaz, late January, early February 1857.

lodgings and facilities so that they could settle down in the province. These freed individuals were to receive maintenance until they were given proper employment and achieved self-sufficiency. These measures were needed, the edict asserted, because it was too dangerous to repatriate the liberated men and women to their countries of origin; therefore they had to be cared for on Ottoman soil. Although from time to time, repatriation would be considered by the government, it seems to have rarely been a realistic option; it was expensive for the government and further exposed returning Africans to the possibility of reenslavement at the ports of origin, which in most cases were quite a distance from their homelands in the interior.

In the decades that followed the 1857 prohibition of the traffic in enslaved Africans, the Tanzimat-state continued to recognize its responsibility for the well-being of the women and men whom it freed as a result of the prohibition. Although practice did not always match intentions, the authorities realized that unless they actively protected such persons and placed them in gainful jobs, the freed would soon be exploited, abused, and, often, reenslaved. Here again, the notion of *attachment* becomes useful, as it helps explain the social vulnerability of individuals lacking association with any legitimate patronage-providing unit, such as a household or a kin group. Africans were especially exposed after emancipation, because they lacked the basic language skills to fend for themselves, yet the color of their skin invited ill-intentioned persons to capture them, often by force, and resell them as slaves. Women were more vulnerable to sexual abuse, men to physical violence. Reattaching freed Africans to private households or government agencies as free protégés was the solution that the authorities adopted from the very beginning. The most common employment offered to the women was domestic service in elite households, although some of them were also enrolled in state vocational schools.[42] The men were offered unskilled service jobs, or drafted into the army and taught a trade.

42. For a thorough analysis of domestic service in Ottoman elite households and its relation to slavery, see Madeline C. Zilfi's recent contribution, "Servants, Slaves, and the Domestic Order in the Ottoman Middle East," *Hawwa*, 2/1 (2004). The author stresses the impact of nineteenth-century developments in the domestic labor market on women, and notes (5) that female labor in the household was, as elsewhere, highly devalued.

The desire to integrate freed persons into Ottoman society as soon as possible was fully shared by the British consuls who dealt with the enforcement of the prohibition on the trade in Africans. In Cairo, for example, the consul reported in 1877 that his staff were directly involved in ensuring that enslaved Africans seized by the Ottoman authorities were manumitted in their presence. They then saw to it that these people were placed as domestic servants in homes, although if freed individuals chose rather to go where they pleased, they would not normally interfere.[43] But stated British policy was "to find protection and employment for fugitive slaves after they secure manumission," and they did that either through the Ottoman authorities on the spot or through their own contacts in the local community.[44] The key to the struggle against slavery and the slave trade, wrote Consul Moncrieff from Jidda in 1883—using almost the same language—was to find employment and protection for slaves after liberation. "It cannot be overlooked by a responsible person on the spot," he added, "that reckless enfranchisement would create want, suffering, and consequent crime."[45]

Thus, too, in mid-1877, a small distance farther to the south, twenty-two enslaved African women and eighteen such men were transported from the east African coast to the port of Hudayda in Yemen.[46] There, according to Anglo-Ottoman policy, they were detained by the Ottoman governor-general of the province, and their case was presented to the local court. The judge liberated the forty enslaved Africans and gave them manumission papers, after which they were distributed to households in town as wage earners. However, the governor-general went even further, petitioning the Porte to instate a government-funded program that would provide a daily allowance to each liberated person until he or she could be placed in suitable service. The grand vezir and the sultan approved the initiative, and the finance minister was instructed to provide the necessary funds to the province (*vilayet*) of Yemen. In this, the state took measures

43. FO/84/881/3184/4, Vivian (Cairo) to Foreign Sec. Derby, 17.3.1877.
44. FO/84/1482/169–70, Foreign Sec. Derby to Cons. Fawcett (Istanbul), 15.6.1877.
45. FO/541/25/81, Cons. Moncrieff (Jidda) to Foreign Sec. Granville, 19.2.1883.
46. BOA/İrade/Dahiliye/61192/the Grand Vezir to the Sultan, 12.6.1877, and the Sultan's response, 25.6.1877. Cf. Erdem, *Slavery*, 177.

to cover the transition period between manumission and placement in case the job market did not offer enough jobs for these freed persons. The same thought also guided the authorities in the imperial capital.

In Istanbul, the Ministry of Police, which was put in charge of slavery-related matters, established a hostel (misafirhane) for liberated persons. This was a sort of halfway house intended to temporarily host such people until proper employment could be found for them. The facility was also used for accommodating enslaved persons who ran away from slaveholders. However, this sensible idea soon turned sour, and absconders found themselves spending long periods, sometimes six to nine months, at the hostel. Conditions at the facility were described by the British consul in Istanbul as "dreadful," and the police experienced difficulties in placing its "guests." The view taken by the authorities was that the environment outside, in free society, was not safe for freed women and men without employment and respectable patronage. The assistant minister of police said on one occasion in 1880 that the issue was how to dispose of the freed, since "if simply liberated, they will starve in the streets." The minister of police told a British official that, in addition, runaway African women had to be detained for several months to prevent them from abusing the emancipation system.[47] As we saw, when liberated and let go without proper reattachment, many of them turned themselves in to slave dealers to be resold, pocketing half the money. Others turned to prostitution.

To partially redress grievances stemming from poor conditions and lengthy stays at the hostel, the British Embassy established its own safe house, which was referred to as an "asylum" for freed and runaway slaves. The man put in charge of it was the dragoman of the Istanbul consulate, Hugo Marinitch, who for years had been taking care of problems concerning the enslaved in the capital. His work consisted of intercession with the Ottoman authorities, usually the police, on behalf of those persons who sought refuge at the consulate. Such an individual was cared for at the asylum for two or three days, as Marinitch reported, until he could find "a suitable situation," that is, placement with a Muslim family.

47. FO/84/1570/251–2, Cons. Fawcett (Istanbul) to Amb. Goschen (Istanbul), 8.9.1880; FO/84/1570/255–6, Eyres to Fawcett, 9.9.1880; FO/84/1570/240–50, Amb. Goschen (Istanbul) to Foreign Sec. Granville, 25.10.1880.

The refugee would then wait at the asylum for Marinitch to present his or her case and for the police, court, or former slaveholder to issue a certificate of manumission. Hakan Erdem has shown that, contrary to English government's impression, it was the Ottoman government that defrayed the cost of Marinitch's asylum, in what appears to be a demonstration of pragmatism and a further recognition of responsibility on the part of the Istanbul police.[48]

At the end of 1890, the establishment of halfway houses to care for freed Africans became an official Empire-wide policy of the sultan.[49] There had been a few earlier attempts from the late 1870s to the early 1880s—most notably in the Yemen, the Hijaz, and Bengazi—to devise a system of funding for feeding, clothing, and sheltering freed Africans, partly to be paid for by the central government, partly by the local authorities, and partly through financing by local employers who would undertake payment for the free laborers they were gaining through the government emancipation program. In 1884, Sultan Abdülhamit II moved one step forward, ordering that freed Africans be brought from Bengazi to Istanbul and Izmir to avoid a lengthy wait in the province; the women were to be placed in domestic service, the men in military bands and artisan battalions. However, the Brussels Anti-Slavery Act, signed in July 1890, held the signatories, including the Ottoman Empire, accountable for the well-being of freed persons and lent support to the asylums established and run by missionaries. The act served to encourage the sultan's government to set up hostels in the peripheral port towns of Bengazi, Tripoli, Jidda, and Hudayda and in the core cities of Istanbul and Izmir.

In addition, the sultan launched a unique settlement program for liberated Africans in the province of Aydın, in the vicinity of Izmir.[50] The idea was to marry freed men and women to each other, create new village communities for them, and settle them as agricultural workers on state land. They were to be temporarily cared for in a state-run hostel,

48. Erdem, *Slavery*, 182.
49. Because Hakan Erdem and I have separately discussed this issue and given our broad agreement on its main features, all that needs to be done here is to briefly recap some of our main conclusions. See Toledano, *Slave Trade*, 241–245; Erdem, *Slavery*, 177–182.
50. Toledano, *Slave Trade*, 246–248.

then placed in their new villages, having been granted the necessary means to start a new life. Despite recurring funding problems, Erdem notes that in the early 1890s, at least some of these hostels and programs were up and running. He is more cautious when evaluating the success and efficacy of these, but mentions, significantly, that "in modern Turkey there are agricultural black communities only in the lands of the former Aydın *Vilayet,* in and around such towns as Bayındır, Tire, and Torbalı in the Little Menderes valley. The names of some of these black villages, such as Yeniçiftlik (New Farm), Yeniköy (New Village), and Hasköy (Royal Village), are certainly suggestive of the fact that they were purpose-built settlements for the freed blacks and that the scheme went ahead after all."[51]

At least in the capital and other major urban centers, women constituted the overwhelming majority of the enslaved Africans who were transported into the core areas of the Ottoman Empire in the nineteenth century. When freed, they were most commonly placed in domestic service. Arguably, in practice there was often little difference between their former status as slaves and their new one as freed because they were placed in households as live-in servants. But they did have a legal option to change employers without being considered in breach of the law, and if cognizant of their options, they were able to earn income, meager though it certainly was, and gradually save up for a future family. Some of the women also received professional training that enabled them to work in other jobs, as the following case illustrates.

In 1873, the local authorities in the province of Erzurum, in northeastern Anatolia, requested Istanbul to send a qualified midwife to help reduce the high rate of mother and infant mortality during childbirth.[52] The central government chose an African woman named Kamer, who had been trained at the imperial medical school in Istanbul and even had knowledge of French. This was a professional job, matching the woman's excellent qualifications, paying way above any amount a domestic African servant could ever hope to be earn. Kamer was a freed woman whom the Ottoman government had placed at the medical school to

51. Erdem, *Slavery,* 181.
52. BOA/İrade/Şura-yı Devlet/1216, *Mazbata,* 7.3.1873; confirmed by the Sultan, 12.3.1873.

resolve two problems at once. The first was the reluctance of Ottoman families to send their daughters to the Tanzimat-state schools, which from the 1840s produced the imperial elite professional corps of physicians, nurses, midwives, veterinarians, civil engineers, and various technology experts. For the same reason, Mehmet Ali Paşa, governor-general of Egypt (1805–1849), had to enroll several dozen freed African women in his newly established nursing school.[53] The second problem was, of course, the need to find employment for manumitted women. In this case at least, the story of Kamer was a great success, and an obviously gifted woman managed to acquire professional skills and find good employment in Ottoman society.

African men were perhaps the majority among the freed persons in the remote slaving provinces, such as those in North Africa and the Red Sea region. Erdem suggests that men were more easily detectable by the authorities because their bodies and faces were uncovered and because they worked outdoors, whereas gender segregation confined women to the home and the veil, thereby also concealing them from the police.[54] Some of the freed African men were placed in domestic service alongside the women, but they were also eligible for a variety of other jobs in the Ottoman economy. As early as 1865, we read, two enslaved men, ethnic origins unspecified, came into the possession of the Finance Ministry and had to be placed and cared for.[55] This happened after the death of a female slave dealer, Nazir Hatun, to whom they had belonged. Probably because she left no heirs, custody of the two was granted to the treasury, whose officials decided to place them in a vocational high school at Tophane, a quarter in Istanbul. Freed in the process, the two men were given a chance at skilled gainful employment and extended state patronage.

Among the placement options available to freed African men were the various vocational schools and different types of public works, such as mining and salt transportation, all involving what were undoubtedly physically hard jobs but also jobs that promised better than usual pay and freedom of movement within a given region and beyond. The Ottoman

53. ʿImad Ahmad Hilal, Ar-raqiq fi Misr fi-l-qarn at-tasiʿ ashar, Cairo: Al-ʿArabi, 1999: 212.
54. Erdem, Slavery, 171.
55. BOA/BEO/Mühacirin Komisyonu/vol. 758 (gelen)/# 126, Petition, 12.12.1865.

army seems to have offered attachment to freed African men more than other government organs did, providing sustenance, shelter, professional training, and a new identity. Drafting freed Africans into the army was the express wish of Sultan Abdülhamit II, repeated in various specific orders issued during the 1880s and 1890s.[56] For some reason, many of these men were placed in the various military bands, probably because they were deemed to have musical talents or because a band of black-skinned people performing in state ceremonials had visual impact. Other common placements for freed Africans were the several artisan battalions and naval crafts units, in which the men were taught technical skills and then deployed to service or combat units, such as artillery, transport, and encampment. Skills acquired in the military could also be used in civilian life after termination of service, potentially putting the men in higher-income brackets than were the ones employed in unskilled service jobs.

Nevertheless, the picture was by no means ideal. Despite the good intentions of many Ottoman officials and the vigorous efforts of British consuls, in such a vast empire, with so many diverse and conflicting interests, not all orders from Istanbul would be strictly adhered to. Even when the voice from the imperial palace and the main power centers in the capital was loud and clear, and not always was it so, compliance in remote entrepôts often lagged. Local governors-general and lesser office-holders had to balance the guidelines handed down from Istanbul against the pressures of local interest groups, many of which were composed of slaveholders or were sympathetic to the slaveholders' point of view. Even with British consular officers watching closely, the final outcome of that balancing act often left a great deal to be desired. Here, it seems, it was not the state that was put in the middle but rather the enslaved, who were stuck between conflicting forces, frequently paying with their freedom for the ambiguity in practice. Despite the undeniable accomplishments of the Anglo-Ottoman measures to suppress the traffic in Africans, it was inevitable that many of the enslaved who put their trust in the Tanzimat-state and its officials felt betrayed by both the Ottomans and the British.

Such frustrations were often voiced through correspondents of the Anti-Slavery Society (ASS), that highly influential abolitionist lobby in

56. Toledano, *Slave Trade*, 239–248; Erdem, *Slavery*, 178–179.

Britain which operated internationally and throughout the Ottoman Empire.[57] ASS correspondents, often clergymen and missionaries traveling through or serving in remote Ottoman provinces, would from time to time report to their headquarters in London about incidents in which stated policy was either ignored or flagrantly violated. In London, the ASS would complain to the Foreign Office or, on rare occasions, directly address the Ottoman government, including the sultan (for example, in 1867 and 1872). Whitehall would ask the relevant British representative to put the case before the concerned Ottoman government agency, whether at the center or in the provinces. This would trigger an inquest into the matter, and some sort of a response was rendered back to the ASS and often published in its journal, *The Anti-Slavery Reporter*. With such a cumbersome process, and with slow communication among all the links in the chain, things took a very long time to be sorted out. Still, in these ASS correspondents, British consuls, and well-intentioned Ottoman officials the enslaved did have committed advocates, and justice—slowly though it came—was not infrequently served.

The main and recurring complaints by the ASS and British consuls regarding the treatment of runaway slaves was that in certain areas, a revolving door policy was being practiced by the Ottomans, with British collusion. In January 1877, for example, the Reverend Waldmeier, an ASS correspondent in Mount Lebanon, complained that freedom-seeking enslaved persons "go to the consulates, who make representations to the Ottoman governors, who in turn promise to make sure justice is done to the slave if placed in the government's hands."[58] However, after these are turned in, he asserted, "they are given back to their masters or sold in another town." Two months later, the consul in Jidda reported to London that the practice there was to return absconding persons to the slaveholders "on promise of kinder treatment."[59] He added that he had been warned by the governor of Jidda that the population was angry because

---

57. On ASS activities in the Ottoman Empire, see Toledano, *Slave Trade*, 236–237, 268–272.
58. ASS, 18/C92/98a–99a, Rev. Waldmeier (Mount Lebanon) to Joseph Cooper (ASS), 1.1877.
59. FO/84/1482/206–8, Cons. Beyts (Jidda) to Foreign Sec. Derby, 25.3.1877.

the consulate was receiving absconders and that if the protestors resorted to violence, he would have little means to protect the Europeans.

The consul indeed caved in to the pressure, as did the local Ottoman governor, and it seems that the revolving door policy was in effect at least in Jidda, though probably also in other remote towns where the Ottoman state did not have sufficient manpower to enforce its emancipation policy. During the same year, an enslaved person sought refuge on board HMS *Fawn,* anchored at the port of Jidda, but was later turned over to the British consulate in that town.[60] The consulate handed him to the governor, who gave him back to his master. When the ASS complained to the Admiralty in London about the case, the navy conducted an inquiry and concluded that what had taken place was "normal practice." Enslaved people in the entire Red Sea region—and well beyond—knew that this was the situation, but they still preferred to turn to the British at sea or on shore and take their chances with them rather than continue to live under enslavement.

The same was true about the Ottoman authorities, more specifically the police and the courts, whom enslaved persons continued to approach in order to escape slavery. This was especially so in the capital and other core Ottoman cities, where the government could enforce its policies against the trade in and enslavement of Africans. It is interesting and telling that both governments, the Ottoman and the British, closed ranks in the last two decades of the nineteenth century, fending off allegations that the Tanzimat-state was conniving at the traffic in Africans. In February 1893, the British Foreign Office replied to an ASS official complaint that the Ottomans were not in full compliance with their commitments under existing treaties to suppress the trade in enslaved Africans.[61] In its response, the British government listed the measures undertaken by the Ottomans since 1889, including the establishment of hostels for freed persons, and asserted that the traffic into Tripoli and Bengazi had come to a complete stop. Ottoman measures were quite effective, the Foreign Office observed, adding that no general charge of Ottoman indifference could be sustained by the evidence.

60. FO/881/3184, correspondence, 1–3.1877.
61. Toledano, *Slave Trade,* 248.

The following story may serve to conclude our discussion of both the growing role played by the Tanzimat-state in slavery matters and its increased cooperation with the British. This case involves the Istanbul police, the British consulate, and a group of twenty-six enslaved Africans in the latter part of 1870.[62] It is significant because we here have the closest evidence available to us thus far of enslaved voices, but it is no less significant because it effectively reflects the Ottoman-British-African pattern of action that had evolved in the 1870s and gelled by the 1890s. The story also shows how, despite being at times let down by the Tanzimat-state and even by the British, the enslaved continued to cling to their hope of freedom. They refused to allow their expectations to be shattered by failure, perhaps because the alternative was to resign themselves to enslavement.

In August 1880, twenty-six enslaved Africans, one of them with her child, petitioned Consul-General Fawcett in Istanbul. The following text is an official translation of the original Ottoman Turkish (both are available):

> It is humbly submitted to Your Excellency that, as previously stated, the undersigned were slaves in the houses of different persons at Stambul, that 8 or 9 months ago we had recourse to Your Excellency that your influence might be used in obtaining our liberty, and that by your orders we were sent to the Ministry of Police, where we were completely neglected in the Mussafir Khane [Misafirhane], without daily rations and suffering great misery. We again have recourse to Your Excellency's compassion and request you to use your influence to save us from slavery and to obtain our liberation.

The petition is signed by the women and men, or, more precisely, their names are recorded and a mark resembling a tilde is placed above each name in lieu of a signature. Obviously, the petitioners did not write the text but approached a person with scribal capabilities who framed and wrote the petition for them. This does not indicate, however, that the

62. FO/195/1299, Cons. Fawcett (Istanbul) to Amb. Goschen (Istanbul), 8.9.1880, enclosing a petition, in original Turkish and English translation, of twenty-six African female slaves held at the police misafirhane, signed on 19/31.8.1880 (texts are marked X/N 00558). On this petition, see also Erdem, *Slavery*, 173.

FIGURE 3.4. Petition of enslaved Africans to Consul-General Fawcett

initiative was not their own. Rather, it is quite plausible that they were aware of the sequence of events described in the petition and of the machinations that put them where they were. That is, they did in fact escape individually to the British consulate eight or nine months prior to the date of the petition, seeking manumission, and they knew that the consulate had referred them to the police. Their expectation was that the police would emancipate them and place them in new jobs within a reasonable amount of time. Yet they were left at the hostel for much longer than expected and in abysmal conditions. We may also assume that they had made numerous applications to the police to expedite matters, but to no avail. The British consulate, where they had been referred to the police, was therefore a natural address for the petition.

By the 1880s, as the petition demonstrates, all parties concerned came to see a certain procedure as legitimate and acceptable:

Enslaved Africans could run away to the British consulate—a Turkish-speaking man named Marinitch was at hand there to assist them;
the Ottoman authorities knew this was taking place and cooperated with Marinitch by admitting absconders into the police hostel;

and the British consul would intercede with the police in order to secure manumission.

But this procedure also points to the fact that Ottoman policy regarding African absconders was not being smoothly applied, that the transition through the main hostel in Istanbul was hard on the absconders, and that placement in wage-paying jobs was not easy. In short, there was a system in place, but it was far from perfect, which should not surprise us, given that attitudes in Ottoman society were beginning to change in favor of abolition only in the late 1870s and that the ownership rights of slaveholders still enjoyed a high degree of legitimacy.

By the latter part of the nineteenth century, absconding was becoming a legitimate way of getting out of enslavement in Ottoman societies. The Tanzimat-state was increasingly siding with the enslaved and gradually abandoning its long-standing policy of supporting the slavers' property rights. As argued in this chapter, that was yet another instance of the state using its growing powers to benefit the weak in Ottoman societies rather than to more efficiently oppress the sultan's subjects.[63] When the slaver-enslaved relationship failed to live up to the expectations of the enslaved, when the bond that had been formed was seen by them as having been violated, they turned to the state to seek redress. It was then that the government discovered a new role for itself—that of temporary patron, or patron *locum tenens*—and this is how the enslaved came to view it.

The role played by the Tanzimat-state vis-à-vis the slaver-enslaved dyad resembles the role that developed in the Viceroyalty of Nueva Granada in Latin America beginning in the late eighteenth century. There, Renée Soulodre-La France identifies a "triangle" involving the slavers, the enslaved, and the Spanish Crown.[64] In an argument against Orlando Patterson's notion of "social death," she offers an alternative view of the way

63. Another example of such action is described and analyzed by Iris Agmon. The author treats the establishment by the Tanzimat-state of the Orphan Properties Authority and its various Orphan Funds from the 1850s onward for the protection of orphans and minors, in Iris Agmon, *Family and Court: Legal Culture and Modernity in Late Ottoman Palestine*, Syracuse: Syracuse University Press, 2005: Chapter 4.

64. Renée Soulodre-La France, "Socially Not So Dead! Slave Identities in Bourbon Nueva Granada," *Colonial Latin American Review*, 10/1 (June 2001): 90–92, 99.

enslaved persons dealt with their predicament. They were very much alive to their rights, limited as these certainly were, she says, and successfully manipulated the Crown's self-image as Christianizing and humanitarian. It was, as Anthony McFarlane noted in another case, flight *to* state justice rather than flight *from* state justice.[65] Enslaved persons approached the Crown to assert recognizable rights within the colonial system, thereby, argues Soulodre-La France, trying to "reclaim a space in colonial society" and make for themselves a social life rather than accept "social death." They forced the Spaniards to acknowledge their humanity, even when they resorted to "antisocial, criminal" action, and indeed they did both in the Ottoman Empire.

In the realm of the sultans, when the Tanzimat-state failed to deliver or, earlier, simply turned away the enslaved, some of them, certainly not all, resorted to other means in their attempts to change their predicament. Some of the enslaved persons who took more extreme actions did that without prior recourse to the state; they acted violently against the slavers upon the collapse of the relationship. As in other societies, some of these actions were criminalized by the state because the governing elite considered them threatening to the existing order. Admittedly, the enslaved Africans and Circassians who committed crimes did not always intend to achieve a specific goal, be it an end to enslavement or reattachment to a new slaver, though not a few certainly had thought through their actions. Some of the crimes were crimes of passion, of rage, or of survival—survival mainly in the emotional sense. The nature of the crimes committed, the circumstances in which they were perpetrated, and the possible motives behind them will be discussed in Chapter 4.

65. Anthony McFarlane, "Cimarrones and Palenques: Runaways and Resistance in Colonial Colombia," in Gad Heuman (ed.), *Out of the House of Bondage: Runaways, Resistance and Marronage in African and the New World*, London: Frank Cass, 1986: 131–151 (quoted in Soulodre-La France, "Socially Not so Dead!" 93).

CHAPTER FOUR

Opting for Crime in Order to Survive

THOUGH INITIALLY BASED on the Şeriat, Ottoman criminal law soon developed apart from Islamic principles and penalties.[1] From the 1840s onward, the Tanzimat-state codified existing legislation, developing an Ottoman-based, then a European-influenced, penal system through a combination of codification and case-law evolution. In 1845, the Council of Ministers endorsed the High Court's view that enslaved persons should be liable to the same penalties as the free subjects of the sultan. This changed the Şeriat-derived practice that slaveholders were responsible for punishing their slaves and brought the state into the slaver-enslaved relationship to protect the enslaved and reduce arbitrary punishment. Enacted by the Tanzimat-state and enforced by its agents, the law naturally came to be identified by the enslaved with the Ottoman state.

---

1. For early Ottoman criminal law, see Uriel Heyd, *Studies in Old Ottoman Criminal Law*, ed. V. L. Ménage, Oxford: Clarendon Press, 1973; Ehud R. Toledano, "The Legislative Process in the Ottoman Empire in the Early Tanzimat Period: A Footnote," *International Journal of Turkish Studies*, 11/2 (1980): 99–108. For developments during the Tanzimat *period,* see Ruth Austin Miller, *From Fikh to Fascism: The Turkish Republican Adoption of Mussolini's Criminal Code in the Context of Late Ottoman Legal Reform*, Ph.D. diss., Princeton University, 2003.

As the enslaved gradually began to consider the Tanzimat-state as protector of their right to freedom and as their guardian against abuse and exploitation by the slavers, the Ottoman government became a pseudo-patron; the enslaved, a sort of wards of the state. When the state was seen as failing to live up to its image as the defender of the enslaved, some of the enslaved resorted to actions against the sultan's government and against what was one of its most explicit representations—Ottoman law. From the perspective of the enslaved, the failure of the state may be seen as yet another betrayal of the trusted relationship with agents and officeholders of the Tanzimat-state which was gradually being forged, yet another failure of the surrogate bond of patronage which was so essential for them.

Not all actions that were criminalized by the Tanzimat-state would necessarily qualify as crimes in other societies and cultures, or at least they would not be treated with the same severity. This was especially relevant to enslaved persons, who were forcefully brought into the Ottoman Empire from very different cultural backgrounds, such as in various sub-Saharan African societies and the different societies of the Caucasus. For example, sexual crimes are notoriously culture-mediated, and norms of sexual conduct in Africa or the Caucasus were naturally different from Ottoman-Islamic norms. Control of the sexuality of young, unattached men and women varied, as did the regulation of sexual access to women; consequently, for instance, rape was defined differently and measured by differing yardsticks. Arson was seen by Ottoman law as an especially heinous crime, and convicted arsonists could face the death penalty. The family of a homicide victim could agree to commute the death penalty into financial compensation, to be paid by the murderer, after he or she had served a court-imposed prison term. Other cultures took a different approach to murderers.

But before we discuss these issues from the perspective of the enslaved, we need to distinguish between sheer criminal behavior by unfree persons and crimes committed by them as an act of social defiance or resistance. This distinction is hard to establish, since motivation must be teased out of uncooperative documents. One test that we can apply is whether the action taken by the enslaved person in a specific case was intended to yield a concrete result, that is, extricate him or her from slavery, improve his or her living standards, or open up options to move to a better place and more amenable circumstances. Sometimes, the intent

was foiled by the failure of the action itself or by the capture and punishment of the enslaved person. In many cases, we learn about those stories
precisely because they ended up in police and court records, whose au-
thors had little interest in the enslaved point of view. Still, despite these
difficulties, there is a great deal that we can find out about the life of
unfree people in Ottoman societies.

The following two examples—the first of a homicide, the second of
a theft, committed by a freed and by an enslaved person, respectively—
may illustrate the point that murder and theft per se cannot be automatically interpreted as indications of defiance; sometimes they are no more
than criminal actions. In 1849, a murder occurred in the chicken market
in Istanbul.[2] The victim was a prominent member of the elite, serving in
the imperial palace, Ayaşlı Ali Ağa; the perpetrator, a freedman named
Abdüllah. Abdüllah had been manumitted by another member of the
elite, Mustafa Ağa, whose son, Eşref Efendi, was the preacher at the
mosque in the Bab-ı Cisr quarter in the capital. We have no details about
the incident beyond the claim that Abdüllah drew out a "Circassian
knife," stabbed Ali Ağa, and seriously wounded him. Ali Ağa died, and
the case became a matter of homicide. The victim's heirs refused to pardon the murderer, and an order for Abdüllah's execution was submitted
to the sultan for confirmation. Such cases leave us little room for an
enslaved-driven interpretation, since the perpetrator was already freed,
and there is no information to link his act to any background motive related to his former servitude.

In February 1855, Ahmet Bey, a former director of the finance de-
partment in the port city of Varna on the Black Sea, petitioned the
grand vezir regarding a theft committed by one of his former slaves.[3]
The perpetrator in this case was Cevher, an enslaved African man who,
the bey claimed, had stolen from his house a few items and some cash
and then run away. Cevher was apprehended in the quarantine house
of a neighboring town and was held there "to no avail," as the petitioner argued. This meant that the stolen goods were not recovered
from him, nor was Cevher himself returned to Ahmet Bey—for the

---

2. BOA/Sadearet/Amedi Kalemi Evrakı/6/65, draft memo, 3.2.1849.
3. BOA/Umum Vilayat Evrakı/petition of Ahmet Bey, n.d., and draft memo from
the Grand Vezir's bureau, 20.2.1855.

slaveholder Cevher, too, had a price tag. The grand vezir was asked to order that Cevher be sent to Istanbul with police escort so that the stolen items, the cash, and the slave himself could be restored to their lawful proprietors and justice be served. And indeed, it was so ordered by the grand vezir's office. What, then, can be learned from this story? The case could have been based on charges trumped up by a slaver in order to expedite recovery of an enslaved absconder. Alternatively, the theft could have actually happened, but we have no evidence on which to develop an enslaved-driven interpretation that might enrich our understanding of this specific action nor of the lot of enslaved people in the Ottoman Empire in general. In some cases this is precisely where we must stop.

Other stories, however, reveal some aspect of the predicament in which enslaved persons found themselves in the various societies that flourished under Ottoman rule. Their crimes range from petty theft, grand larceny, sexual crimes, and arson to murder. They are further classified into individual and group actions. By applying our method of backing and filling, of applying historical imagination to gaps in the historical record, we can attempt to assess the variety of options available to the enslaved in each case, the presence or absence of choice, the significance of the action chosen by the alleged offenders, and the social meaning that the action did or did not have. What did a perpetrator of a crime expect to achieve at the point that he or she violated the laws that the Tanzimat-state enacted and enforced? In most of the cases discussed in this chapter, I assume an ability on the part of the protagonists to understand what was allowed and what was not allowed, and I believe that they had the capacity to distinguish right from wrong.[4]

THEFT

Theft is the most commonly encountered offense in Ottoman criminal records. The high value put on property rights in the Şeriat and in Ottoman law criminalized even petty theft and imposed severe punishments

4. In this I differ from ʿImad Ahmad Hilal, who, as will be mentioned further below, assigns much of the criminal conduct of enslaved persons to their limited intelligence, incapacity to understand the consequences of their actions, and even their lack of morality or virtue.

for committing such offenses.[5] Crimes ranged from pilfering to grand larceny and at times involved breaking and entering in order to steal the goods. Although enslaved persons were also caught stealing from neighbors' houses, their thefts were usually spurred by what may be called target opportunities—that is, free access to the targeted items was easy and unhampered. The slavers' property lay fully exposed before the eyes of enslaved domestic workers, and they possessed an intimate knowledge of the hiding places of valuables and the day-and-night routine of household members. For enslaved agricultural workers, the means of production in the fields, the barns, and the farmhouse were all easily accessible, and the cultivators' schedule well known. For the enslaved insider, then, there was an opportunity-rich environment offering constant temptation. If attachment achieved any form of emotional bonding between the enslaved and the slaver, the loyalty generated usually produced the necessary resistance to such temptation. Most enslaved persons did not steal from their holders; in fact, very few did, even if we allow for the majority of cases not being reported or even discovered.

When attachment was weak, usually when the enslaved were being abused and ill treated, the opportunity to pilfer could mature into actual deed. It was then that state-imposed impediments—the criminal code and law enforcement—erected another barrier to theft, perhaps the very last. Deprivation and resentment could induce enslaved persons to steal from slavers or their neighbors and relatives, to whose houses they sometimes gained access while accompanying their masters on visits or when sent there to fetch various items. The risk of being caught was high, however, since enslaved persons in the household were almost automatically

5. For the texts of the various Ottoman criminal codes during the Tanzimat period, see Ahmet Lûtfi, *Mirat-ı adalet*, İstanbul: Kitapçı Ohannes, 1304 [1886 or 1887]. For the main issues in the debate over the evolution of nineteenth-century Ottoman penal codes see Hıfzı Veldet, "Kanunlaştırma hareketleri ve Tanzimat," in *Tanzimat I: Yüzüncü yıldönümü münasebetiyle*, Ankara: Maarif Vekaleti, 1940: 139–209; Tahir Taner, "Tanzimat devrinde ceza hukuku," in ibid., 221–232; Gabriel Baer, "The *Tanzimat* in Egypt: The Penal Code," in Baer, *Studies in the Social History of Modern Egypt*, Chicago: University of Chicago Press, 1969: 109–132; Baer, "The Transition from Traditional to Western Criminal Law in Turkey and Egypt," *Studia Islamica*, 45 (1977): 139–158; Toledano, "Legislative Process."

the usual suspects, and it was not uncommon for them to be wrongly accused of theft. In addition, to be able to profit from stealing, the enslaved perpetrators had to find a safe way of turning the loot to cash; they needed accomplices who would receive the stolen goods and either sell them or exchange them on their behalf. Involving other people exposed the enslaved pilferers to further risks, at times leading to greater hazards than being caught and punished by slavers or authorities. However, before we proceed in that direction, we need to look at a theft case that served as a legal precedent for all crimes committed by persons held in bondage.

The Nizami High Court records contain a story about an unnamed African man who was identified as the slave of Mustafa Bey, the former deputy-governor of İstanköy, near Istanbul, and then one of the sultan's ushers with direct access to him.[6] Sometime in early June 1845, our protagonist stole from the bey's house the following items: several medals, gold and silver utensils, two books, 484.30 Kuruş in silver coins, and 3,148 Kuruş in gold coins. He ran away but, perhaps in regret for his theft or in hope of receiving shelter, presented himself at the house of a female relative of Osman Efendi. We do not know much about that woman—the thief might have known her as an acquaintance of his holder's family—but she soon called the police, who arrested the man on 11 June. The stolen items were recovered and returned to their owner, and the enslaved man was detained by the authorities. The High Court was asked to rule in the case, and on 23 July it sent a report to the grand vezir for approval. In the specific theft case, they convicted the accused and sent him to prison for one year. But the court's opinion had a far broader implication, setting a precedent and a change of policy for enslaved men and women in penal matters.

The High Court ruled that the law determined that punishment for theft committed by free persons was three months to three years of imprisonment with hard labor, depending on the value of the stolen property. The court noted that there was no provision in the law for enslaved offenders, although the Şeriat stipulated that the right to punish a slave belonged to the master. However, the ruling argued that it was the state's

6. BOA/İrade/Meclis-i Vala/1280/*Mazbata*, 23.7.1845, and the Grand Vezir's note to the Sultan, 5.8.1845.

duty to uphold and apply the Şeriat in an appropriate and just manner. Experience showed, the court continued, that some masters resorted to excessive measures when punishing their slaves, while others were too lenient and refrained from any punishment. Some masters would conceal the slave's criminal record in order to obtain a higher price when getting rid of the culprit by sale. Consequently, corruption was spreading in society, and the law was not being properly enforced. Society had to be protected from all criminals—both free and slave—the court concluded, and slaves had to be protected from excesses, which meant that the Penal Code should be equally applied to free and subjects. Both corporal and prison penalties were to be applied to both, and female and male convicts were to spend jail time in separate penitentiaries.

A brief qualification is in order here. The High Court was not entirely correct in its generalized statement about what the Şeriat stipulates regarding the liability of enslaved persons and slavers when a crime was committed by the former.[7] Two distinctions are made by Islamic criminal law: the first was on the issue of deliberate intent (Arabic, *amd*) by the offender; the other is between capital crimes (Arabic, *hadd*) and lesser transgressions (Arabic, *cinayat*). If an enslaved person committed an intended homicide, he or she was liable to the *lex talionis* (Arabic, *qisas*), and justice was administered by the kadi, not by the slaveholder. The Şeriat court was also where enslaved persons were tried when infringing any crime under the category of hadd. In crimes of the cinayat type, an enslaved offender was treated as the property of the slaveholder, and the slaveholder was liable for the damage caused by the slave, although such liability did not exceed the value of the slave. In cases other than murder when crimes were committed with intent, the slavers could, with certain restrictions, surrender the enslaved offender to the plaintiff or pay the imposed damages.

Still, the High Court's ruling left one crucial issue unresolved: Were enslaved convicts to return to their holders after they served their prison term? This issue was taken up by the Council of Ministers, to which the grand vezir referred the matter for endorsement of the entire legal precedent that the ruling set. After the ministers reviewed the High Court opinion and agreed with it, they ruled that enslaved persons who had

7. This is elaborated in Toledano, "Legislative Process," 104–106.

served time in jail should be returned to their holders. On 5 August 1845, the grand vezir and the sultan duly concurred, and the matter became Empire law. This decision signaled to the slavers that although the Tanzimat-state was going to take a more proactive role in the slaver-enslaved relationship, it was not turning its back on the principle of slavers' proprietary rights over the enslaved. This was gradually to change over the following decades, and the boundaries of that relationship were renegotiated and redefined.

But here, more than in the court's decision, we are interested in understanding the predicament of the unnamed man at the center of the story and the choices available to him. The intriguing point is the sudden change of heart that impelled him to abandon his original plan and turn himself in. The decision to steal and abscond might have had any of several motivations, and we have no way of knowing what the real one was. Still, the household he had served in belonged to a member of the imperial elite in the capital, with direct access to the sultan, which meant that it was a wealthy and well-connected household. Our unnamed man was probably one of a number of enslaved men and women serving at Mustafa Bey's household, and compared to other enslaved domestics, especially to other enslaved men in non-domestic service, his life should have been relatively comfortable. Unless he was somehow abused, there was little chance that the alternatives available to him on the outside as a freed servant could improve his lot. This realization might have sunk in and played a role in the decision he made to end the flight, turn himself in, and accept being punished for stealing. In this case, it seems, the issue of choosing freedom over slavery or choosing defiance in the face of harsh realities did not play a major role, if any.

This story highlights the point that theft by enslaved persons was more often than not associated with their absconding. We have already seen that it was common for slavers to charge absconders with petty theft.[8] This was done to counter the runaways' claim of abuse, cast doubt upon their credibility, and reinforce the demand to have them restored to the slavers. Pilfering within the household, it appears, was handled within the family, and the caught perpetrator was punished by the slaver, often by beating. The tendency was to keep the state out of the

8. See Chapter 2.

relationship by not complaining to the authorities, thereby also avoiding the possibility that the enslaved thief would be given an opportunity to charge ill-treatment by the slaver. But not all theft charges that were brought against absconders were trumped up. One could reasonably expect that when enslaved persons decided to run away, they would take some belongings from the household in order to exchange them for food, shelter, and other necessities until a new source of income or subsistence could be found. Indeed, to identify removable, valuable, or useful items before absconding seems to have been essential for a successful flight.

Again, theft in the context of absconding has to be seen in the broader social framework of what I have called attachment and reattachment. The interim between abandoning one attachment and forming another was crucial to runaway persons. During that period the enslaved were without a reliable source of subsistence, without the protection of a patron, left to fend for themselves. The longer the period, the greater the risk of being exploited and pushed to the margins of society, where their well-being, sometimes their very lives, were threatened. Runaways therefore relied on people they came to know outside their own household to facilitate their survival in that risky period. Crucial contacts in this respect were people who could help the absconder sell or exchange the stolen items on the market without betraying their source. This dependency exposed the absconders to abuse and exploitation, since their vulnerability was obvious to any person they approached. The following three cases, all coming from Ottoman Egypt, demonstrate the point.[9]

In October 1858, the Cairo High Court reviewed the case of Tharanja, an enslaved Ethiopian woman, held by a female auctioneer, from whom she stole a few clothes, some pieces of cloth, and an ornamented box. It was alleged that she had two accomplices, an Ethiopian woman named Zahra and her husband, intriguingly named Ahmad Agha (Turkish, Ahmet Ağa) Bonaparte and probably associated with the military. In this case, Tharanja did not run away with the stolen goods but passed them on to her neighbor accomplices. When the theft was discovered,

9. All three are cited in ʿImad Ahmad Hilal, *Ar-raqiq fi Misr fi-l-qarn at-tasiʿ ashar*, Cairo: Al-ʿArabi, 1999: 223–224. However, my interpretation and use of these cases is completely different from his.

Tharanja was picked up by the police. During the investigation she admitted that she had stolen the items, and following due process, she was sentenced to three years' imprisonment. The motive here seems to have been economic, and the accomplices were probably supposed to sell the stolen items and remunerate Tharanja in an agreed-upon manner. Not seeking to flee enslavement, she nevertheless realized the options available to her and chose to improve her financial situation through a planned theft. Unlike in the next two cases, her accomplices did not deceive her, and her misfortune was not attributed to them.

The next story features an enslaved African woman named Mabruka, the "blessed one," whose master was Ishaq Hanin, a Jewish resident of Cairo. In 1855, she stole a few golden pieces from the house of Hanin's relative. She then approached three men in order to sell the stolen jewelry, but we have no information as to whether she had known them before or had arranged to use their services prior to stealing the items in question. In any event, the three men took the goods, disposed of them on the market, and went one significant step further—they seized Mabruka and sold her to another man, named Salim al-Halabi. The High Court sentenced the three men to three years in prison, and Mabruka was sent to work in a government workshop for a year and a half. She was then to restored to Ishaq Hanin, but the governor-general of Egypt, Sait Paşa (1854–1863), changed the court's decision in this respect and ordered her to be exiled to her native Sudan. Sait Paşa's stated policy was to deport from Egypt all convicted offenders when they completed their term in jail. Probably inadvertently, this policy also penalized the slavers.

The last case in our Egyptian series led to even more tragic results. In 1865, in the Upper Egyptian town of Girga, an enslaved African woman named Halima stole some cash and a piece of jewelry from her master. She ran away and went to the house of a man she might have known earlier, probably seeking the man's help in liquidating the stolen goods. The would-be accomplice seized the stolen items and killed her. We do not know if the murderer had planned his actions in advance, if he had intended to deceive Halima, or if he had perhaps even incited her to steal and flee. The murder may or may not have been part of the plan, if there was one at all. What is certain, though, is that the killer realized that Halima was in a vulnerable position and took advantage of it. Whether the story would have developed the same way had the enslaved person been a man, especially a strong one capable of defending himself, is a good question. The answer is that enslaved females were, in general, more vulnerable than enslaved males: they were more exposed to sexual abuse, violence, and exploitation of their labor.

The problem of attachment and reattachment, and the vulnerability incurred between relationships, was not unique to enslaved absconders. It applied very much also to manumitted persons during their transition from slavery to freedom. We have already seen some of the difficulties faced by freed persons, especially if African and female. Here I need only mention that the loss of attachment due to manumission could drive freed people to break the law. Failure to form a new attachment meant the absence of patronage and protection, exposing the freed man or woman to want and destitution. This pushed some of them down into begging and homelessness; from there master the road to pilfering and petty theft was short. If over an extended period of time a freed person was unable to find a durable source of subsistence, criminalized behavior could become habitual, permanently relegating such a person to the margins of society. Only the strong and lucky could extricate themselves from that unhappy predicament. The following story—by no means unique nor exceptional—may serve to illustrate these points.

In 1859, a freed African man named Cafer was deported to the Bulgarian town of Varna.[10] We do not know why he was deported, but the punishment must have been linked to a crime he had committed, one not serious enough to warrant a jail sentence. Deportation of subjects belonging to the lower strata was usually intended to remove a problematic person from the environment where he or she was causing trouble. Loitering, prostitution, and witchcraft were the reasons most often cited for deportation; it seems likely that Cafer's misconduct was loitering, which was often seen by the authorities as conducive to pilfering and more substantial theft. One night he was apprehended in a coffeehouse while trying to sell a few items. The people in charge thought his actions suspicious. Upon being questioned, Cafer admitted that he had entered

10. BOA/Sedaret/Meclis-i Vala evrakı/144/63, the local council of Varna and the neighboring districts to the Grand Vezir, 23.2.1862, *Mazbata* of the Meclis-i Vala, 16.4.1862.

the house of Abdüllah Ağa, an officer in the local artillery force in Varna about an hour and a half after sunset, when the man and his family were visiting their next-door neighbors. Cafer walked into the house, opened the door to a bedroom, broke the lock of a chest, and took a silver-plated mirror, a shawl, fourteen head scarves, a few embroidered handkerchiefs, and fifteen Kuruş in cash.

Clearly, these items were not stolen for personal use but to be traded on the market for cash. After Cafer had been picked up, the stolen goods were returned to their owner, and Cafer was sentenced by the High Court in Istanbul to three years' imprisonment. Upon reflection, this is a story about failed reattachment: an enslaved African man was manumitted and left his master's household without receiving an alternative gainful job. Cafer had no way to feed himself, no clothes, and no shelter; he lost the patronage of his manumitter, which meant the loss of protection, social relations, the prospect of marriage, and his identity as a household member. Other freed Africans in that position were often targeted for reenslavement, but Cafer seems to have been strong enough to avoid that, although he still found himself pushed to the dangerous margins of society. Perhaps on his own or perhaps in a band with other unattached men like him, he was wandering about town. Such persons were now and then hired on a temporary basis to do a menial job, but in times of economic hardship and unemployment they were reduced first to begging and then to stealing. Though caught at least once and deported, Cafer seems to have been unable to extricate himself from the vicious circle of poverty and crime.

It appears that outside the protective cordon of enslaving patronage, Cafer could not muster even the most basic survival skills. He was unable, for instance, to hook up with a network of thieves and traders in stolen goods, which would have enabled him to safely get rid of the merchandise he had stolen. Instead, he had to approach potential buyers in an open coffeehouse, where he was easily caught. After he had served his term, the likelihood of reattachment was realistically reduced even further. The most accessible alternative would have been to join acquaintances from jail and pursue a life of crime and punishment, of misery and destitution. Occasionally such men could find temporary employment, but their chances of slipping back to life on the streets of Ottoman urban centers were high. The main mosque-complexes in cities and towns served as gathering places for homeless and hungry people, the down and out, where they could get food from soup kitchens, shelter in the courtyards, receive small donations from congregants, hang out aimlessly, hopelessly. The next two theft cases show that enslaved persons also engaged in large-scale embezzlement, though rarely, partly because they lacked access and opportunity. The first story is set in a different time and place than are most of the other cases discussed in this book, but it is cited here because of its special interest and relevance to our survey. The case was adjudicated by the Şeriat court in Ottoman Cyprus in mid-1594, and the main protagonist was a white female slave named Rahime bint Abdüllah.[11] Rahime's holder was a district governor on the island, and he obviously esteemed and trusted her, since she served as his treasurer or accountant. Rahime was even trusted with delivering four loads of jewels, goods, and cash, with the total value of 15,000 gold coins, from the district to the provincial treasury in Nicosia (called Lefkoşa by the Ottomans). After the death of her holder, Rahime schemed with one of the province's high financial officers, named Mustafa, to abscond together with the money. They were not found. Indicating the high degree of trust that an enslaved woman could attain in certain cases, this is not a story about resistance but rather about daring and agency.

The last case in this series returns us to the heart of the Tanzimat period. In late 1859, an enslaved Circassian man named Hürşid stole a suitcase containing a very large amount of money—37,500 Kuruş—and ran away to Trabzon, a port town and a seat of provincial government on the southeastern shores of the Black Sea.[12] It was alleged that Hürşid had an accomplice, and the police investigated suspicions that he had acted in collusion with a high-ranking official, İsmail Paşa, formerly in charge of the postal service in the province of Trabzon. Hürşid had daringly accomplished grand larceny. The suspected involvement of the

11. For the text of the court record, see Ronald C. Jennings, *Christians and Muslims in Ottoman Cyprus and the Mediterranean World, 1571–1640*, New York: New York University Press, 1993: 240–240. The case was reviewed by the Şeriat court in Nicosia in Şaban 1002, which falls between 22 April and 21 May 1594.

12. BOA/İrade/Meclis-i Vala/18530/the Grand Vezir to the Sultan, 2.10.1859, and the Sultan's response, 3.10.1859, and enclosures.

head of postal services might indicate that the heist was based on schedule and route intelligence in the possession of the accomplice, perhaps
the planner, İsmail Paşa. The records show that this interesting case
attracted much attention and required great input from the Ottoman
authorities and courts.

The point to notice in stories about the "stealing slave" is not so
much the legal situation as the social predicament. Far from pointing to
the sheer stupidity (Arabic, qillat ʿaql) of enslaved African women, as
ʿImad Ahmad Hilal suggests, their being "easily caught," if indeed they
were, must be attributed to their vulnerability and great exposure.[13] Enslaved persons who stole did so either to gain some pecuniary advantage
or to fund an escape plan. The idea that enslaved perpetrators should be
returned to their owners after serving their sentence reflects the Tanzimat-
state's realization that social attachment was ultimately the best guarantee
against recidivism. Unattached and vulnerable, the enslaved and the freed
were much more likely to resort to criminalized behavior, inflicting further damage upon society and themselves. Yet, again reflecting the ambivalence of state policy regarding slavery, returning criminals to their
owners was also a reaffirmation of the slavers' proprietary rights over the
enslaved.

SEXUAL CRIMES

The Ottoman state, like many other states before and since, criminalized
the area we may roughly call morality. Because morality is a culture-
mediated social notion, its definition—more on the periphery than at
the core—tends to vary from one culture to another, especially over time.
In almost all cases, the core concept consists of the control and manipulation of sexuality, most often of the sexuality of young and unattached
women and men. As in other Islamic societies before them, the Ottomans allowed men unfettered sexual access to their wives and their female slaves. Although homosexuality was proscribed, this notion of proprietary entitlement extended tacitly to allowing sexual access to enslaved
men, too. However, with enslaved men a modicum of consent seems to
have been required, since forceful resistance, which occasionally found
expression in court and police records, was met with understanding,

13. Hilal, Ar-raqiq, 223.

leading to lenient sentences.[14] Otherwise, forced sex between husband and wife or slaver and enslaved concubine did not come under the category of rape, which in any event mainly concerned forced sex with a virgin. Thus, in the attitude to forced sex, too, social norms in the Ottoman Empire were not that different from those in contemporary European societies.

Women were seen as property and as a source of potential shame if their behavior was not "virtuous." Enslaved men and women, especially if not of the kul/harem type, were also seen as property, but they lacked the potential to inflict shame on their owners. Thus, adultery was criminalized, but conjugal rape was not, nor was prostitution. The cultural interface between the enslaved person's origin and host cultures also generated conflicts between different behavioral norms, including sexual conduct. All these factors created a sexual twilight zone, with ill-defined boundaries, that invited abuse of the weak by the powerful. In our case, this opened the door to the exploitation of the enslaved, especially the women among them, by the slavers, especially the male slavers. Our analysis in this book is heavily predicated on a power-derived perspective, and it is clear that law and culture reflected social and gender power relations. Thus, sexuality became yet another contested territory in which enslaved women were victimized and deprived of their sexual autonomy, with the state backing the exploiters through criminal law.[15]

This interpretative approach substantively differs from views such as those taken by Hilal, whose extensive and highly informative work on slavery in nineteenth-century Egypt reflects traditional attitudes to "moral" or sexual crimes.[16] In essence, and without explicitly spelling it out, Hilal does not see a victim and a perpetrator in these situations but what seems to be "shared responsibility," though he, too, realizes that the parties were not equal. To him, the Şeriat and Ottoman law reflected some sort of "objective" value system that embodied "correct" notions of good and bad. Slaves, he observes, engaged in crimes of adultery, prostitution, and sexual deviancy because of "moral laxity," among other factors

14. See, for example, a case cited in Hilal, *Ar-raqiq*, 229.
15. On this, see also Madeline C. Zilfi, "Servants, Slaves, and the Domestic Order in the Ottoman Middle East," *Hawwa*, 2/1 (2004): 8–10.
16. See Hilal, *Ar-raqiq*, 226–229.

(to wit, his title of a subchapter, "*Jara'im az-zina wa-l-biga wa-sh-shudhudh*"). Enslaved Africans committed sexual crimes, he believes, in large measure because of their frivolity (*taysh*), their lightheadedness (*tahawwur*), and their lack of virtue (*'iffa*). Yes, he concedes reluctantly, some of the blame may devolve on the slaveholders (for not marrying them off soon) and the British (for insisting on manumission without ensuring subsistence and protection), but sexual crimes were essentially an issue of the slaves' flawed moral character.

Thus, blame and responsibility are divorced from power, and the powerless and the victims are held responsible for crimes committed against their bodies. The plausibility of resisting the aggression is ignored, and the victims become accountable for not displaying the virtues expected of free, empowered Ottoman subjects. Furthermore, the element of choice is not even considered, and the victims are blamed for violating moral norms without choosing to do so. Paradoxically, in some sexual crimes, notably prostitution, choice was involved to an extent and reflected a measure of empowerment of enslaved African women. But first let us consider a number of cases in which crossing the socially acceptable boundaries of sexual behavior occurred and in which the notion of a sexual-moral twilight zone is evident.

Although not quite within our time frame, the following—not fully explicit—story may shed some light on the ability of individuals to exploit the gray shades of personal status within slavery. The source is a summary, contained in the Ottoman archives, of several documents sent in 1776 to the central government by Abbas Ağa, the governor of Kütahya, a town in central Anatolia.[17] According to the report, around the year 1770 the slave dealer Ali Beççe sold an Istanbul woman named Safayı to Halil Ağa of the town of Elmalı, not far from Kütahya. After a long time, Safayı ran away to Kütahya, where she claimed to be free and the wife of Halil Ağa. Later she was said to have engaged in "vile acts" (*ef'al-ı şeni'a*), a description usually reserved to prostitution or pandering. In consequence, Safayı was banished from Kütahya: she ultimately returned to her original abode—Istanbul. There she resumed various acts of deception, with the aim of causing damage to people, and the matter came, yet again, to

17. BOA/Cevdet/Zaptiye/4327, *Hulase* of papers sent by Abbas Ağa, Mütesellim of Kütahya, 25 April 1776.

the attention of law-enforcement agents. As a result of the investigation, which included revisiting her past activities in the provinces, the complaints were judged to be false and orders were issued to ignore them.

It is reasonable to expect that the original documents sent by the governor revealed details of Safayı's fraudulent conduct and illegal activities. However, absent these, we can still glean something from the summaries provided by the police and court clerk. The offenses attributed to this allegedly enslaved woman were of two kinds: deliberate falsification and some unclear connection to prostitution. Her deliberate falsification had to do either with pretending to be a slave, hence colluding with the slave dealer and pocketing part of the money paid for her by the buyer Halil Ağa, or with her claim to be a free woman, which she asserted after she ran away from Elmalı to Kütahya. In either case, the case does show the relative ambiguity and fluidity of status and the choices available in this regard. That is, a free woman could pose as a slave, act to improve her financial condition through sale, and thereby also regain attachment to a household and social protection. At the same time, well before the changes introduced by the Tanzimat in the standing of runaway slaves, an enslaved woman could pose as free and begin a new life in a different town. This was probably a lot easier for a non-African person, whose skin color did not automatically require providing proof of freedom to be accepted by the rest of society as non-slave.

In any event, we are exploring here the twilight zone on the margins of society. In Kütahya, Safayı could only have a make-believe attachment, since in reality she had to make a living, which she tried to do through some manipulation of her sexuality, probably as a prostitute. Although such an activity was not criminalized by Ottoman law, it was nonetheless labeled by the authorities as "immoral" and seen as "dirty" by society. This conduct was serious enough to warrant her deportation, a common punishment for prostitutes and other women engaged in unacceptable practices. The latter category also included, for example, female slave dealers involved in pandering and *kolbaşıs*—freed African women who served as heads of welfare lodges—when they performed African rituals considered uncivilized.[18] Perhaps the best known case of such a deportation is the one attributed to Mehmet Ali Paşa, governor-general of Egypt

18. For an example of such cases, see Chapter 5.

from 1805 to 1849, who in 1834 banished from Cairo to Upper Egypt a large number of prostitutes. Some of these women returned to Cairo a few years later, though others remained in the provinces, like the famous Küçük Hanım (Little Lady), to whom Gustave Flaubert devoted a great deal of attention during his visit to Egypt in the 1850s.[19]

Another deportation story, albeit somewhat ambiguous, occurred in Istanbul in 1786.[20] On 17 June of that year, Ahmet Hasbi, the kadi of Bursa—a former Ottoman capital southeast of Istanbul—signed a legal notice reporting the arrival in the city of two unmarried female slave dealers, said to have their respective origins in Bursa and in Syria. The head of the slave dealers' guild and certain police officers alleged that the two had engaged in activities that contravened the acceptable norms of the trade as enshrined in the imperial edict and regulations governing the purchase and sale of slaves. The women were banished from Istanbul to provide an example to the rest and to protect the code of the slave dealers' guild, according to the order delivered to the kadi by a special courier of the Imperial Council. Although the kind of transgression attributed to the two was not spelled out in the kadi's memo, it seems safe to assume that it was of a sexual nature—that is, they exposed enslaved females to male clients under the guise of displaying them in a private house as if for sale. The punishment, the following story will show, did not end the practice, however.

With all its lack of sufficient specificity, the case of the two slave dealers is a good illustration of the ambiguity that surrounded activities in various slave markets which crossed the line between the legal sale of enslaved women—occasionally also of enslaved men—and prostitution. Although, as we saw, the government tried from time to time to intervene in order to reestablish that line through strict regulation of market operation, the task was difficult. At the early stage after being purchased, the enslaved were especially vulnerable and least aware of their standing

19. See Gustave Flaubert, *Voyage en Egypt: Édition integrale du manuscrit original*, établie et presentée par Pierre-Marc de Biasi, Paris: B. Grasset, 1991: 280–288, 362–363; for an English translation, see *Flaubert in Egypt, A Sensibility on Tour* (trans. and ed. Francis Steegmuller), Chicago: Academy Chicago Press, 1979: 113–123.
20. BOA/Cevdet/Zaptiye/4327.

vis-à-vis the slavers. In general, slave dealing attracted all sorts of persons, sometimes of the less honorable kind, who were seeking to prey on the weak, pander to an existing market for sexual services, and make a quick and easy profit even in violation of the law and the ethical code of the slave dealers' guild.

Indeed, slave markets were the place in which human beings were bought and sold. It was there that the most humiliating aspects of the trade were present, where the most debasing practices were manifested. This was partly so because one of the major mitigating elements of slavery—the bond between the enslaved person and the slaver—was absent. Most slave dealers did not bond with the enslaved persons they were handling, since in most cases the enslaved did not spend much time in their possession. When buyers were examining enslaved persons who were put on display in the market, they, too, did not have any special feelings for the men and women whom they inspected, touched, and discussed with the slave dealers. Hence, the exchange surrounding the purchase was often harsh and demeaning. But if properly regulated and supervised, it did not need to transgress the line separating sale from sexual abuse or pimping. The Istanbul market was the largest in the Empire, and as the following passage will show, the attempts in 1805 to re-regulate its activity in order to prevent such conduct are quite revealing.[21]

From time to time, as information about criminal activities, especially sex crimes, was reported to the police, the Ottoman authorities used to issue and reissue imperial edicts and regulations to clean up the market—the term used in the case discussed here is *tethir,* "purification." Thus, some forty years prior to its final closure, the Istanbul slave market came under scrutiny, and a joint action by the government and the slave dealers themselves to weed out the criminal elements was mounted. The several lengthy documents that treat this episode reveal the mechanisms that operated in the market. Some of the operators were the slave importers (*celebs*), who brought the enslaved to the market, usually from their countries of origin; the slave dealers of the market itself (*esircis*), who bought from the importers and sold the enslaved

21. The following paragraphs are based on documents in BOA/Cevdet/Zaptiye/465, dated April 1805.

persons to individual slavers; the assistants to the slave dealers (*yamaks*), who facilitated and handled sales for the slave dealers; the criers/brokers (*dellals*), who announced the arrival or availability of new enslaved persons for sale by a certain slave dealer, or who acted as intermediaries in sales; the boatmen (*kayıkcıs*), who brought the importers and the enslaved to the dock at Tophane, a quarter of Istanbul on the west bank of the Bosphorus; and the customs officials (*gümrükçüs*), who assessed and collected the duties imposed on each entering slave.

Running the Istanbul market in 1805 were the head of the slave dealers' guild (*kethüdâ*), his deputy and market regulating officer (*yiğitbaşı*), five senior slave dealers (*usta başıs*) elected by the members, and thirty-nine accredited dealers (*ustas*). But all these people seem to have been subjected to the military authority of the chief commander of the Janissary corps (*Yeniçeri Ağası*), to whom, too, the two imperial edicts (fermans) issued in this case were addressed. The market in Istanbul consisted of a large commercial building (*han*) containing fifty-four stores, or sale spaces. These were either owned or rented by the slave dealers, with the wealthier merchants normally owning their stores. At the time, forty-six of the stores in the market were occupied; eight lay vacant. Space and time boundaries delineated the slave market operation: the market had a gate that separated it from the outside world, and market rhythm was set according to the hours of daylight and nighttime. When strictly applied, the rules distinguished legitimate activities from illegitimate ones. That is, the market was open to trading only in the daytime and was closed to people at night. During the day, only authorized persons were allowed to buy and sell within market territory; others were barred. The Janissaries and the guilds had to verify that every legitimate trader was registered in the government records, along with his or her guarantor (*kefil*), the person vouching for the slave dealer's upright character and sound financial status.

As the police investigation report shows, these restrictions were not strictly observed, and violations resulted in "corrupt and immoral practices." Fraud, tax evasion, and price fixing do not concern us here, and we shall focus instead on sexual crimes, which were considered by the Ottoman authorities to affect public morality. For sex-related crimes to be committed it was essential to breach the boundaries of space and time. The slave dealers' guilds prided themselves, as declared in their petition, on the honesty and integrity of their members, on not allowing any disreputable persons (*erzal*) into the market or the trade. All market operators would leave the premises at dusk, taking their slaves home with them and returning them to the stores the following morning. The guildsmen's petition asserted that dubious persons were not allowed to loiter in the market after dark. Intermediaries were not permitted in unless attached to a bona fide dealer. Although women did not serve as accredited slave dealers, the guildsmen admitted that several women posed as dealers, took enslaved females into their homes, lured male buyers there, and committed "depraved deeds." In other words, those women pretended to be slave dealers but in fact provided sexual services, offering enslaved women as prostitutes.[22] Following investigation, guild officials asserted, these women were punished and removed from the market area.

The police report found some difference between declared intents and market realities. At night, they concluded, "shameful and abominable acts" (*fezahet ve mel'anet*) were being committed in the stores, meaning that these were being used for illicit sexual activities. Even during the day, unreliable persons gained access to the market and engaged in actions that could cause "great corruption." The authorities demanded that guild leaders and supervisors undertake much stricter measures to prevent these actions from happening. They were supposed to prevent well-identified unreliable individuals from owning or renting shops at the market, and no one was to be allowed to stay in the stores at night. Registration of all market operators and their guarantors was required. As in other law-enforcement and bureaucratic matters, rather than interfering directly with slave dealers, the government reempowered their leaders to act forcefully, promising to punish them severely if they were remiss in their duties.

Circumstances surrounding slave dealing were such that crossing those ill-lit boundaries between forced prostitution and the sale of humans continued to occur, especially where the volume of the trade was large, in the big cities of the Empire. It is hard to gauge the volume and frequency of forced prostitution, since much went undetected and unreported, hence also unrecorded.

22. Zilfi notes that this was a common accusation leveled at female slave dealers in the seventeenth and eighteenth centuries (Zilfi, "Servants and Slaves," 6).

Another case in point surfaced in Cairo in 1831, although there, it was the head of the slave dealers' guild who complained to the authorities.[23] He charged that a number of dealers rented houses in town and used them for pandering, offering their enslaved African women to clients. This, he argued, stemmed from a lack of proper supervision by the authorities, whose agent for precisely such purposes he was supposed to be. There can hardly be any doubt that these women, fresh from the trauma of kidnapping, sale, arduous journey, and market exposure, were forced into prostitution with no real option of resistance. Even the option of absconding was not readily available to them, since they had no knowledge of the environment into which they had been injected and were still unfamiliar with the options available to them. To even consider the plausibility of running away, an enslaved person had to have gone through much of the process of reattachment to a new Ottoman slaver, which was not the case with the African women held in bondage by the slave dealers who operated in markets such as those of Istanbul and Cairo.

We earlier considered the action taken by a certain number of enslaved African women who sought manumission from the Istanbul police or the British consulate in the capital.[24] The police alleged that some of the enslaved absconders chose to engage in prostitution and that thus it was essential to place them in safe jobs after being liberated. Absent a satisfactory reattachment to a patron household, these women found themselves pushed to the unsafe margins of society, forced to fend for themselves in a demeaning manner. The element of choice in these cases must be considered very limited. However, at least one case from late 1828–early 1829 Egypt indicates that some enslaved African women preferred prostitution to service in the governor-general's household. In a dispatch from the provincial Nizami court in Cairo to a senior law-enforcement officer in Alexandria, it was reported that a few African female slaves from among the "government slaves," the ones belonging to the extended household of the governing family, had absconded to Alexandria. There, the report added, they behaved like "street women" and engaged in prostitution.[25]

To contextualize and interpret this information, we need to refine the

23. Hilal, *Ar-raqiq*, 227.
24. See Chapter 3.
25. Document cited in Hilal, *Ar-raqiq*, 227.

notion of choice. It is clear that the enslaved African women who absconded to Alexandria realized that they had at least two alternatives, about which they believed they had sufficient information to make a choice. One was their attachment to the governing household, where they served in menial domestic jobs, often—the jobs available to women—the ones demanding the most physical strength and stamina. The other alternative was to abandon their position and seek their fortune on the outside, specifically in Alexandria, far away from Cairo. The women must have gathered some sort of information regarding conditions in Alexandria, including employment opportunities. Freedom from slavery was probably one difference between the two options, but the rest is speculative: it is possible that prostitution was an alternative they had heard of, but it is also possible that they found themselves engaged in it as a last resort when other jobs fell through. It is also possible that persons interested in employing those women as prostitutes lured them into absconding with false promises about attractive job opportunities that never existed. In any event, choice was exercised by these enslaved African women at least in running away from Cairo; and we cannot rule out the possibility that they might have knowingly chosen prostitution over slavery, though in all probability that choice was based on mistaken or deceptive information.

The Ottoman state, again like other Islamic and non-Islamic states, did not criminalize prostitution per se but accepted it and sought to regulate it. Prostitutes were registered by the police and organized in a guild, and they paid taxes. Condemned by the Şeriat, prostitution was nonetheless tolerated, and in Cairo the guilds of prostitutes were classified among the "cursed and impious" ones, along with the other "immoral occupations" that required police control. In May 1834, Mehmet Ali's Council of Ministers abolished the tax on prostitutes—not a negligible source of income to the government—and banned them from Cairo. The main concern here, Khaled Fahmy argues, was fear that prostitutes would introduce venereal diseases and alcohol abuse into army camps and barracks, affecting in turn the soldiers' discipline.[26] The Tanzimat-state and, earlier,

26. Information in this paragraph and the next is derived from the following studies: Gabriel Baer, *Egyptian Guilds in Modern Times,* Jerusalem: Israel Oriental Society, 1964: 13, 27n, 33n, 35, 85, 173; Ehud R. Toledano, *State and Society in Mid-Nineteenth-Century Egypt,* Cambridge: Cambridge University Press,

Mehmet Ali's Ottoman-Egyptian government, attempted to banish prostitution from the public gaze, in effect pushing it underground and further
exposing the women to exploitation by pimps and criminals. All this doubly applied to enslaved women who found themselves forced to work as
prostitutes; they had not even the meager protection that free prostitutes
had, since in many cases they were absconders and still being sought by
their former masters.

The traditional—one might say Islamic—approach to prostitution
as a social phenomenon places a large measure of the blame on the
prostitutes themselves. This approach is reflected by Hilal in discussing
mid-nineteenth-century Egypt when he argues that in any society that
practices slavery, enslaved women have a limited awareness of sexual
mores, that is, virtue and chastity.[27] Hilal reasons that this was because
they "changed hands," being sold by one slaver to another, which led directly to prostitution among enslaved African women. These women,
he adds, also catered to the needs of the French soldiers of Bonaparte's
expeditionary army in Egypt (1798-1801). Based on Edward Lane's observations, Hilal refers to enslaved African women forced into prostitution by female dancers and singers (*gawazi*), who operated in the twilight zone between public performance and sexual services. Such
female performers acted as pimps and pocketed a share of the money
received by the enslaved women they employed. Enslaved Africans
were also forced into prostitution, Hilal tells us, by some slave dealers
in Cairo and by slaveholding pimps in the Sudan. Still, quite astonish-
ingly, he insists that all this emanated mostly from the enslaved
women's lack of morality. He prefers this explanation even though the
prime factor behind slave prostitution in Ottoman societies was the ob-

---

1990: 237–239, 247; Khaled Fahmy, *All the Pasha's Men: Mehmed Ali, His
Army and the Making of Modern Egypt*, Cambridge: Cambridge University
Press, 1997: 228–231; Judith Tucker, *Women in Nineteenth-Century Egypt*.
Cambridge: Cambridge University Press, 1985: 134, 150–155; Edward W. Lane,
Account of the Manners and Customs of the Modern Egyptians, New York: Dover,
1973 (1st ed., London: C. Knight, 1836): 377–382. For information on prostitution in Ottoman Egypt, see also ʿImad Hilal, *Al-Bagaya fi Misr: Dirasa
tarikhiyya ijtimaʿiyya, 1834–1949*, Cairo: Al-ʿArabi li-n-nashr wa-t-tawziʿ, 2001.
27. Hilal, *Ar-raqiq*, 227–228.

vious powerlessness and social vulnerability of these women, as well as the men.

ARSON

The Ottoman state considered arson a heinous crime. Next to epidemics and earthquakes, fires had a devastating impact on Ottoman cities, gutting whole quarters in a short period of time, with enormous loss of, and damage to, property and great disruption to social and economic life. Especially in crowded, wood-built areas, fires wreaked havoc, and the number of casualties was also quite high. Unlike natural disasters, fires, like wars, were created by human beings, and blame for them could be reasonably assessed and assigned. Deliberately set fires were traceable to specific perpetrators who could then be brought to justice. To deter potential offenders, the Tanzimat-state criminal law imposed heavy penalties on convicted arsonists, including death.[28] Although municipal authorities throughout the Empire possessed fire-fighting units, there was little they could do with the technology of the day and the limited access they had to running water. Once ignited, a fire could seldom be contained, and rather than be extinguished through human effort, it more likely would die down for want of remaining material to burn. Symbolically, the sight of flames and smoke from a fire burning out of control stood for a temporary breakdown of order itself, of the way things were and should be. For the haves, it was the ruin of their property, their wealth, their privileged position in society; for the have-nots, it was perhaps revenge, maybe an act of God inflicted either to rectify the injustices of the world or to punish humans—rich and poor—for sinful behavior.

The enslaved were have-nots. But like the rest of the down-and-out, most of them never thought of torching their oppressors' property, though they might gloat if they saw it happening. For an enslaved person, as for other subjects of the sultan, to decide to set fire to private or public property was a huge step. We therefore encounter few cases of arson in the court and police records, but those we do have are of special interest. The two stories discussed below bring out a great deal of passion, perhaps the intense emotions that go so well with the compelling

---

28. For Ottoman criminal law on arson, see Lûtfi, *Mirat-ı adalet.*

sight of the flames devouring the source of a deep grievance, the locus of grave injustice and humiliation, or the symbol of the suffering.

The first story took place in early 1862 at a village near Varna, a Black Sea port town in today's Bulgaria.[29] The protagonists were an enslaved African man named Rihan, owned by Süleyman, and Mehmet, one of the villagers. Rihan and Mehmet together stole some beehives, but only Rihan was caught and marked for punishment. When they met later on, Mehmet made fun of Rihan for taking the fall alone when he had managed to escape unscathed. Hurt and humiliated, Rihan sought to settle the score by setting Mehmet's house on fire. The authorities considered the matter to be very serious and referred it to the provincial court at Varna, which imposed damages in favor of Mehmet. We do not know who paid the money, Rihan or his owner, Süleyman, but after payment had been made, the case was sent to the High Court in Istanbul. Treating arson as a very grave offense and hoping to deter potential offenders, the High Court ruled that Rihan should be put to death by crucifixion in public. The grand vezir endorsed the court's decision, but the sultan thought that the death penalty was unwarranted here and commuted the sentence to seven years in prison.

This rare case of an enslaved African arsonist does tell us something about the state of mind of a perpetrator. Rihan refused to let Mehmet's mockery go unanswered. We do not know the nature of Mehmet's teasing, but he could have snapped at Rihan something to the effect that the free and white accomplice was smart enough to avoid punishment, whereas the African slave was not. We do not know whether Rihan had previously or often been exposed to such comments, but we may safely assume that this kind of teasing was not new to him. We do know, however, that he was hurt enough to seek revenge, to plan ahead and carry out the arson. While to an extent premeditated, this was also a crime of passion conceived in a rage. Here we may also speculate that Sultan Abdülaziz perhaps understood all that, for there is a tremendous gap between his relatively lenient ruling and the extremely harsh sentence meted out by the High Court, especially since the sultan also had to over-

29. BOA/İrade/Meclis-i Vala/20924/*Mazbata* of the court in Varna, 22.1.1862, *Mazbata* of the Meclis-i Vala Muhakemat Dairesi, 24.2.1862, the Grand Vezir to the Sultan, 8.4.1862, and the Sultan's response, 9.4.1862.

rule the grand vezir, who had endorsed the court's verdict. The sultan's rejection of the grand vezir's recommended sentence is especially noteworthy in that Abdülaziz had been on the throne for barely a few months, and his grand vezir was none other than the determined and highly regarded Fuat Paşa, whom he had chosen earlier over the other great Tanzimat reformer, Ali Paşa.

Our second arson case is a love story gone very bad.[30] It takes us to a major Ottoman port city on the Mediterranean—Salonika, in today's Greece—and reveals yet another aspect of servitude in an elite household. The main character is Dilferah, a twenty-one-year-old enslaved African woman, who since 1857 had served at the household of Hatice Hanım and her husband, Mehmet Ağa. Mehmet Ağa was the Tobacco Customhouse director in Salonika, a fairly senior figure in the provincial administration. Another important participant in the drama was Ahmet, a nineteen-year-old free servant in the same household. By 1861, Ahmet and Dilferah had formed a relationship, and Ahmet promised Dilferah that he would marry her. To accomplish that, he intended either to purchase her freedom from the slaveholders, doing it the legal way, or to elope with her, illegally. Dilferah, who seems to have been the more pragmatic and assertive of the two and who seemingly preferred the legal path, asked Ahmet how he planned to get the money to buy her from Hatice and Mehmet.

The record does not provide Ahmet's answer to that crucial question, but it may be safely inferred from the events that followed later on. We next read that the mansion of Hatice Hanım and Mehmet Ağa was set on fire and heavily damaged in consequence. Dilferah and Ahmet were nowhere to be found, but later the police seized Dilferah at a house in town; there was no mention of Ahmet's being apprehended, just that he managed to escape through the Citadel gate. After a search of the burnt house, it was discovered that money was missing from a drawer in the harem. The police concluded that Dilferah was the arsonist and charged that she had conspired with Ahmet to steal the money, burn the

30. BOA/İrade/Meclis-i Vala/20803/Investigation report by the Salonika court, 4.9.1861, *Mazbata* of the Salonika court, 30.12.1861, *Mazbata* of the Meclis-i Vala, 2.2.1862, the Grand Vezir to the Sultan, 14.2.1862, and the Sultan's response, 15.2.1862.

house, and run away. It thus becomes clear that Ahmet had no legitimate way to come up with the amount needed to purchase Dilferah and
that the two decided to steal money from Hatice and Mehmet either for
the purchase of Dilferah or to fund their escape. It is likely, however, that
Dilferah did the actual stealing, since she had easy access to the harem,
where the money was kept, whereas Ahmet was barred from entering
that part of the house. She also knew the household routine and had
ample opportunity.

As in the arson story of Rihan, this case, too, reached the High
Court in the capital, which sentenced Dilferah to death, while Ahmet—
perhaps in absentia—received ten years' imprisonment. Unlike in Rihan's case, however, the sultan did confirm the death penalty and issued
a ferman to the governor-general of Salonika, Hüsnü Paşa, to carry out
the sentence. We do not know whether Dilferah was executed, although
this is more likely than not. The only way she could have avoided execution was for her mistress, Hatice Hanım, to forgive her and ask for the
sentence to be commuted. If this happened, and it did occasionally in
other cases, the notation of the procedure would normally be attached to
the case file; here there was no such attachment. Yet a researcher may
find the note someday in another box, in another file, in another register
perhaps, and if so, I shall be visibly relieved, for it is obvious that the sentence meted out to this enslaved woman in love was a cruel and unusual
punishment.

Once again we have come upon an enslaved person, the most un-
privileged of all, an African female slave, who refused to accept her
predicament and instead tried to do something about changing it. Dilferah, which—ironically—means in Turkish "heart's joy," did not want
to remain enslaved but had plans for her life that included marriage and
family. She did, however, come against a wall that must have seemed in-
surmountable. After four years of service, she could look forward to
manumission in no fewer than three years, perhaps six, and even that
was not certain. At twenty-one, she was of an age to have already borne
children, either to her master, as his concubine, or, if liberated, to a man
of her standing in society. Indeed, Dilferah found someone she liked
enough to want to marry and raise a family with, but circumstances prevented that option from being realized, although the man, Ahmet, was
willing. The wall she faced surrounded her mainly mentally. She chose

not to accept that reality, preferred to challenge it, cross the line, break the chains, violate the law, and steal the money she and Ahmet needed in order to elope.

The burning of the house is the hardest part to explain, as it does not make sense. The documents remain forever silent about that. Why did Dilferah torch the house? It was superfluous to the main purpose she and Ahmet had in mind, for they could have taken the money she stole from the harem drawer and run away immediately. In fact, burning the house was so counterproductive that it may have cost her her life. Even if Dilferah did not imagine that the court would impose the death penalty for arson, she must have known that what she did was a major offense and that if she was caught, the punishment would be heavy. Dilferah did not expect to get caught, but somehow this is not enough. We need something else to complete the story, to explain the woman's behavior in this tragic story.

The missing element can only be a matter of speculation, but one possibility is worth considering: rage, uncontrollable anger. The indignation could have been targeted at the masters of the house, who may have abused her in the past, who may have balked at her romance with Ahmet, if they knew about it, laughed at her plan to marry him. Or her anger might have been more generalized and directed at the "system," the realities of enslavement that brought her from her native land in Africa to a major Ottoman city and placed such overwhelming shackles on her freedom that she could not have the husband and children she dreamed of. Both motivations could apply, but if we exclude the possibility of a mere accident, her act of arson had to have been motivated by a great rage, one most likely resistant to any rationalized process of weighing cost and effect, action and consequences. To complete the circle, somehow it seems fitting that the passions of love and rage were vented in setting fire to the house she was leaving to begin a new life. Even if we leave motivation aside, symbolically the fire expunged the old humiliation and powerlessness of servitude, and perhaps a new life could grow from the ashes, as often happens in nature.

MURDER

Homicide is arguably the ultimate score-settling crime. It is the last resort of the powerless and the oppressed, hence, too, the most extreme form of revenge available to the enslaved against abusive slavers. Although it is possible to quantify murder and theft crimes committed in the Ottoman Empire during much of the Tanzimat, no study to date has utilized the available records for statistical purposes.[31] Until this is done, it is only possible to say that my clear *impression* is that homicide rates among enslaved persons in the Empire were not disproportionately high. Indeed, it seems that enslaved people rarely resorted to murder, preferring other modes of protest and resistance. Hilal believes that most murders committed by slaves were done at the behest of their masters, who used them to settle their own accounts and vendettas.[32] There is certainly some evidence of such manipulation, though it would not seem appropriate to overgeneralize from it.

Instead, let me point to the special situation of enslaved murderers, in which they were put by the retribution mechanism of Şeri criminal procedures. Homicide was seen as a sort of civil injury that had to be negotiated between the perpetrator and a victim's heirs.[33] While enabling the death sentence to be commuted if the victim's family pardoned the murderer, these procedures also made it possible for an enslaved convict to become a part of the retribution and the property of the victim's legal heirs. But the application of this concept had different personal implications according to the circumstances of each case. In the following pages, I begin with the least severe repercussions and move to the harsher ones. The first story we take up served to establish the legal precedent for the principle that enslaved persons were to be tried as free persons and punished by the state courts, not by to their masters. A few

31. The Ottoman archives contain an excellent series of registers recording all theft and homicide cases adjudicated by the High Court in Istanbul from 1847 to 1866: BOA/Ayniyat defterleri/Meclis-i Vala'dan katl ve sirkate dair, vols. 470–502.

32. Hilal, *Ar-raqiq*, 221–223. Here, again, I do not subscribe to his interpretation, which attributes slave-committed homicides to the slaves' frivolity (*taysh*), light-headedness (*tahawwur*), and inability to foresee the consequences of their actions (222).

33. For more on this, see Toledano, "Legislative Process," and the sources cited there. See also Madeline Zilfi, "Goods in the *Mahalle:* Distributional Encounters in Eighteenth-Century Istanbul," in Donald Quataert (ed.), *Consumption Studies and the History of the Ottoman Empire, 1550–1922: An Introduction,* Albany: State University of New York Press, 2000: 292, 308–309.

months after the courts and Council of Ministers set the precedent in the theft case above, the system reaffirmed that principle in the following murder case, which—intriguingly—still leaves a few questions unanswered.

An enslaved African woman named Nursiye bint Abdüllah belonged to the household of the late Moralı Molla Yakup Efendi in the town of Yenişehir-Fener, which is located within the district of Tırhala in today's Greece.[34] After the Molla's death, Nursiye was inherited in equal shares by his widow, Selime, and four minor children—the sons Ömer, Ebu Bekir, and Abdürresul and the daughter Ümmükülsüm. In the late afternoon on 12 November 1845, when her mistress was out of the house, the slave, Nursiye, took a rope, strangled the daughter, Ümmükülsüm, and dumped her body in the sewer. She was caught and arrested and pleaded guilty to murder and described exactly how she had killed the little girl. At first, the mother demanded that the death penalty be imposed, and a verdict to that effect was duly issued. But later, Selime revised her position, saying that she could not stand by that decision. In a petition submitted to the governor of the district, Selime explained that she had transferred her ownership share in Nursiye to her children, and now, acting as their legal guardian, she asked for the sentence to be commuted to a *diyet* track, meaning that the court would impose a prison term on the murderer, and the children would be entitled to financial reparations. She also requested that the governor reduce her liability to defray the cost of the Nursiye's imprisonment and allow Selime to sell the slave to a man named Hacı Akkavi.

The courts, the grand vezir, and the sultan accepted the mother's application and decided to sentence Nursiye to one year's imprisonment. After that year, she was to pass to the hands of Selime and her sons, and because the mother was the legal guardian of her minor children, she could then dispose of the murderer as she pleased. The jail maintenance costs for Nursiye were also reduced in order to the prevent further injustice to the grieving mother. The Penal Code stipu-

34. BOA/İrade/Meclis-i Vala/1457/İlam Şeri, 3.12.1845, *Mazbata* of the local court at Yenişehir-Fener, 7.12.1845, Petition to the Governor of Tırhala, n.d. (but must be late 1845), *Mazbata* of the Meclis-i Vala, 5.3.1846, the Grand Vezir to the Sultan, 15.3.1846, and the Sultan's response, 18.3.1846.

lated that murderers faced jail terms ranging from one to five years, and in this case, only the lowest penalty was imposed, which leaves us with more questions than answers. Nowhere are we given Nursiye's motive for killing the young child in her care, and the fact that a buyer for Nursiye was found suggests that there was nothing fundamentally wrong with her, such as a mental illness, or a pattern of bad temper, or habitual misconduct and insubordination. To boot, the price she fetched was quite reasonable. Also, Nursiye did not attempt to run away after the murder, nor did she deny the charge, both of which make it hard to argue that this was an act of defiance against enslavement as such. However, the leniency of the sentence is indeed curious and can perhaps be explained by the court's desire to hasten the payment of reparations to the mother and her children, which could only happen after Nursiye's release from prison. Thus, this case demonstrates that the courts had to apply slavery-specific considerations when trying enslaved murderers.

In the following story, the inherent inequality of free and enslaved before the law becomes even more apparent, again with regards to the painful aspect of reparations for murder. According to the Nizami High Court records, an enslaved man and his master, both from the district of Uşak in today's Albania, were tried in 1847 for a murder they had allegedly committed together.[35] Although no further details are provided, we are told that each one of them was equally sentenced to seven years in prison. Given the court's decision, one may legitimately ask whether the enslaved person did not have a diminished responsibility for the act. Moreover, here comes the major difference between the two convicts, which stresses the much greater difficulties that enslaved persons had to face in such circumstances. From the sentence delivered by the High Court in Istanbul, as from the record itself, it becomes clear that the legal heirs of the victim waved their right to demand the death penalty and agreed to receive financial reparations (diyet), sometimes dubbed blood money. The court decided that after the period of incarceration at the specified prison in the capital, the slave would be surrendered into the hands of the victim's three heirs, who were still minors at the time of the trial.

35. BOA/Ayniyat/vol. 470/p. 125, Meclis-i Vala to the tax office in the province of Kütahya, 24.10.1847.

The enslaved man would himself constitute the slaveholder's reparation for the murder of which both he and the slaveholder had been convicted.

Murder is certainly a heinous crime, and undoubtedly the young children of the victim who were thus orphaned must have suffered greatly in consequence. But what kind of life was in store for the enslaved co-murderer once he became the property of the three children—by then probably adults—whom he had orphaned? It is quite reasonable to assume that the target was picked by the master and that the initiative to commit the crime was his. We may certainly believe that the enslaved man acted under supervised instructions from his owner. Still, of the two, it was the enslaved who bore the brunt of the sentence. If he was lucky, the victim's heirs would sell him immediately and spare themselves the distress of seeing their parent's murderer daily in their midst. At worst, they would find out that a slave with such a criminal record would fetch a very low price, or not be salable at all, and decide to keep him. In that case, one can only imagine the kind of treatment he could expect to receive. But this story was not unique, as illustrated in our next story.

The main actors in this drama are Hürşit and Abdülhalim.[36] Hürşit was an enslaved man who was probably a Circassian. He lived in the household of Nefise Hanım and her husband, Ömer Bey, in the town of Trabzon, on the southeastern shore of the Black Sea. The second actor, Abdülhalim, was the son of Sepetçioğlu Hüseyin, and he lived in the same town. One day, in the middle of 1857, Hürşit intentionally stabbed Abdülhalim with a "Circassian knife" and killed him. The Trabzon court summoned the two parties: Hüseyin, the father of the victim, and Ömer Bey, who represented his wife, the mistress of the murderer. Hüseyin decided to forgo the death penalty and instead receive financial compensation for his murdered son. For his part, Ömer Bey agreed to surrender the murderer and pay an additional amount of money to settle the matter. At that point, a legal complication emerged, for the newly enacted penal legislation clashed with the Şeriat stipulation that had governed capital cases until the 1840s. Since the victim's father had released his son's murderer from the death penalty, the Tanzimat-state Penal Code required that the offender be given a prison term, to be determined by

36. BOA/Sadearet/Meclis-i Vala Evrakı/85/100, Meclis-i Vala to the Governor-General of Trabzon, draft memo, 4.6.1857.

the High Court regardless of the reparations agreed upon. Although the murderer himself was to constitute part of the blood money, he could not be transferred to Hüseyin before serving his time in jail term, thereby inflicting added injury upon the victim's family.

Thus, Hüseyin not only lost his son but was unable to recover the bulk of the reparations due to him for his tragic loss. He therefore approached the authorities and demanded justice, and the High Court in Istanbul recognized the merit of his grievance. However, the remedy provided was unsatisfactory, for the court decreed that Hürşit would first serve his seven-year term at the dockyard prison in Istanbul and would only then be surrendered to Hüseyin in Trabzon. Alternatively, the court could have assessed the market value of Hürşit and ordered the slaveholder to pay that amount to the father immediately, since payment of the reparations was usually due before the enslaved culprit was imprisoned.[37] Instead, the High Court chose to endorse the structure agreed upon at the local Şeriat court. This delay must have been costly for the victim's father, and we can assume that Hürşit's value at the end of his jail term was much lower than when he was seven years younger. We may also wonder what the father could do with the enslaved man once he got him, for a convicted murderer would probably not fetch a high price on the market, if he was salable at all. Keeping him on as a slave instead, would have been nearly impossible in human terms and could have led to further abuse and tragedy.

The mystery that surrounds some murders is never resolved, and murders committed by enslaved persons in the Ottoman Empire are no exception. At times, we may sense that a dramatic story is hiding behind the insufficient information provided in the records, but there is little that can be done to tease more from them. A case of this nature is the terrible murder that occurred in 1850 at the village of Yük, located in the subdistrict of Dırama in present-day Greece.[38] The victims were the two young daughters of a Yük resident named Hasan: the older girl, Fatime, and the younger, Havva. The murderer was identified as Abdüllah, an enslaved African man who belonged to İbrahim, another villager. We do not know how or why Abdüllah killed the two girls, nor whether this had

37. For this in Ottoman Egypt, see Hilal, *Ar-raqiq*, 222.
38. BOA/Sadearet/Amedi Kalemi Evrakı/16/79, draft memo, 7.2.1850.

anything to do with taking revenge on their father. No hint is given of an insanity plea, nor of the possibility that the crime had been committed at the instigation of Abdüllah's master, İbrahim, possibly as a result of a dispute he and Hasan might have had. Such extenuating circumstances would normally surface even in the brief draft summary of the case by the High Court in Istanbul, which we have. We are told, however, that the murderer was ordered to be sent to the capital for sentencing. This was necessary either to have Abdüllah executed if the death penalty was not exchanged for blood money or to determine his prison term.

Other homicide cases allowed for a certain measure of ambiguity, which could reduce the liability of the perpetrator. In the following case, an enslaved African man seems to have used just such an opportunity to improve his legal position. This story also points us to the broader array of social options available in any Ottoman household. In early 1855, a tanner named Şerif Ali, son of Hasan, was murdered in the city of Izmir.[39] His male African slave Sait was accused of the murder and brought before the local court. At first he confessed to the crime, but later he retracted his confession and claimed that his mistress, Şerif Ali's wife, had ordered him to kill her husband. Because he could not supply any evidence to back his assertion, Sait asked to swear that his claim was true, and the judge allowed him to do so. No further details are provided beyond noting that the court also interrogated the relatives of the victim, and it appears that they accepted Sait's claim. The governor-general of Izmir reviewed the procedures and passed the matter on to the High Court in Istanbul. The High Court pointed out that Sait's oath had been dubiously accepted even though his confession had not been coerced, nor did he claim it to have been thus obtained. Therefore, the matter was referred back to the Izmir court for further investigation, and the document we have is the draft request that was addressed to the governor-general of Izmir in order to clarify the discrepancy and then return the case to the High Court for sentencing.

The court's dilemma in this case highlights a broader issue within the predicament of slavery while also pointing out the social web of relationships involving free and enslaved family members. The dilemma is

39. BOA/Sadaret/Umum Vilayat Evrakı/181/6, Meclis-i Vala to the Governor-General of Izmir, draft memo, 4.2.1855.

the degree of choice the enslaved actually had, the scope of their agency and autonomy, and hence the effective extent of their legal responsibility. Caught between his master and mistress, what was Sait to do? Assuming he was not involved in the dispute, such as by having a sexual relationship with one of them, whether forced or consensual, could he resist an order from his mistress to kill his master? The fact that he ultimately did kill his master could imply that he was closer to his mistress or alienated from her husband, or both. Sait might have harbored ill feelings toward Şerif Ali because of abuse, neglect, or exploitation, or he might have been drawn to his mistress, either because he was romantically attracted or because she showed him consideration or kindness. If there was a plot to murder Şerif Ali, the motive could have been a promise by the victim's wife to let Sait take charge of the tannery or to split the money received from selling the business. In short, this story reveals yet again the complexity of relationships in slaveholding households, which—in addition to the expected human web of non-slave relationships—had to incorporate and deal with enslaved persons, individuals who were not fully autonomous, not fully capable of resistance or able to avoid being dominated and manipulated.

Another category of homicide cases consisted of murders committed by enslaved persons in what appears to have been self-defense. Such a murder befell the Sharifian family in the holy city of Mecca in 1853.[40] The main protagonists were an enslaved African man named Bakhit ibn Abdallah, and his master, Sharif Yahya, the son of the late Sharif of Mecca, who served as the sultan-appointed custodian of Islam's holiest site. On the night of 13 March 1853, while both were at home, Bakhit hit Sharif Yahya on the head with a mace and killed him. Testimony was given, and accepted by the court as credible, that on the morning following the night of the murder, Bakhit admitted to the killing, saying that his master wanted to beat him with the mace, so he seized it from him, hit him back, and caused his death. The witnesses were two free men who happened also to be members of the Sharifian family, and their testimony was required because in court Bakhit disavowed any connection

40. BOA/İrade/Meclis-i Vala/11030/İlam Şeri, 24.4.1853, Vali of Cidde to the
    Grand Vezir, 30.4.1853, Fetva Emini's note, 21.7.1853, *Mazbata*, 8.8.1853, the
    Grand Vezir to the Sultan, 21.8.1853, and the Sultan's response, 22.8.1853.

to the death of his master. The victim's legal heirs—his mother and his two minor sons, represented by their paternal uncle, Sharif Mahdi ibn Abi Talib—demanded that the murderer be executed and adamantly refused to pardon him in exchange for reparations. The case went all the way from the Şeriat court in Mecca to Istanbul, where it was discussed by the Nizami High Court and reviewed by the office of the Şeyhülislam. The case was also reviewed by the governor-general of Jidda, the grand vezir, and ultimately—the sultan. The final result was that the High Court sentenced Bakhit to ten years in prison, after which he was to be released.

Although Bakhit later retracted his statement, his claim that he acted in self-defense opens the door to an empowerment-driven explanation. The argument is reinforced by the sentence that the Istanbul High Court handed down; that is, it was not the death penalty expected under the Şeriat but the more lenient alternative. This is a clear indication that the court believed the witnesses who testified that Bakhit had admitted to the murder, but it signals in addition that the court believed his claim of self-defense. If Bakhit did defend himself as stated, he certainly demonstrated a great deal of courage, especially if we consider the prominence of the victim, who was not only the son of the highest-ranking Ottoman official in Arabia but also a member of the most prominent family in the Sunni Muslim tradition. An enslaved African man had to be brave to stand up to Sharif Yahya and refuse to take a beating from him. Even if we are willing to entertain an explanation entailing some sort of temporary insanity, the action itself has to be understood as reversing the "order of things" in Ottoman Meccan society. Even if we take the view that this was an act of desperation by an enslaved man who had been pushed to the limit, we still have to consider that he created an option of self-defense and perhaps one of retaliation that were not generally available for enslaved African men in mid-nineteenth-century Arabian society. Significantly, an insanity plea was never put forth in this case by any of the parties.

Although individual defiance admittedly appears to be more ambiguous in other cases, it must nonetheless be considered and explored. The following story brings us to the borderline situation of pent-up frustration that the sustained hardship of enslavement could produce. Enslaved persons who, for various reasons, could not find their place either within the household or outside in society at large resorted at times to violence, though rarely to the extreme act of homicide. According to the Ottoman High Court records, in late 1850 an enslaved African man named Mehmet bin Abdüllah murdered Mehmet Bey, who was the son of Hasan Bey, the tribal chief of Karakoca in the district of Biga.[41] The enslaved man belonged to the Albanian estate manager of the British consul in the Dardanelles, which is in itself curious. Given the high British sensitivity to matters of African slavery in the Ottoman Empire, the consul could have been expected to notice that his manager had a malcontent African slave in his household, but there is no evidence of that.

Still, no motive is given for this homicide, although a hint is provided in the petition of the victim's heirs, who demanded the execution of the murderer. The heirs—Mehmet Bey's widow, three sons, two daughters, and father—stated that the slave Mehmet was "insolent and nasty." They also said that the perpetrator came to the victim's garden at night, tried to steal his belongings, and deliberately killed him with his pistol, probably as Mehmet Bey tried to prevent the robbery. Admittedly, this evidence is still scanty, but two things can perhaps be inferred from the petition. One has to do with the enslaved man's reputation as an unpleasant person, which could indicate his being unruly or more generally insubordinate. The other element is that the action, as put forth by the state and the plaintiffs, was said to have been deliberate, not an accident occurring in the course of an attempted theft or robbery. If we add to these the fact that the victim was a member of a prominent family in the community, we might have a somewhat different story to tell, perhaps centered on an act of defiance by an enslaved African who was unhappy with his state in life and finally chose to unleash his built-up anger in a murderous act of rage and frustration.

The next two stories are reminiscent of an earlier case, recently published by Madeline Zilfi.[42] In July 1762, an enslaved Circassian girl was given to an Istanbul slave dealer for sale, but she soon displayed unruly behavior and incurred the ire of her handlers. When the slave dealer's wife reprimanded her, possibly using force to subdue the girl, the the girl grabbed a knife and stabbed the woman to death. She was detained and

41. BOA/İrade/Meclis-i Vala/6081, Correspondence involving the administrative and Şeriat courts, the Grand Vezir and the Sultan, 8.11.1850–15.1.1851.
42. Zilfi, "Goods in the *Mahalle*," 294–295.

ultimately sentenced to be publicly hanged in the slave market as a deter-
rent to other enslaved persons. The similar element in these stories is the
alleged "unruly conduct," which led the slavers to use force in order to
prevail. The other similarity is the violent and deadly reaction of the enslaved persons in question to the slavers' attempts to subdue them by
force. The occasional use of mild force seems to have been an integral
part of the slaver-enslaved relationship almost anywhere, and it is mostly
extreme cases of regular abuse by the slaver or habitual insubordination
by the enslaved that end up in court records and other contemporary
sources.

In yet another category of homicide cases, we are left to guess the motive and surrounding circumstances, especially when the notation in the
sources is extremely terse. An example of such a case appears in a register
of the Ottoman Refugees Commission at the end of 1863.[43] The register
states that three enslaved Circassian men killed their master, also a Circassian refugee, stole his belongings, and settled in the town of Köstence.
The authorities, it added, were conducting an inquiry regarding information about this incident, which had been recently reported. Here, though,
the sheer audacity of the perpetrators stands out, for it appears that they
did not try very hard to cover their tracks, but instead resurfaced in a
nearby town in the hope of escaping justice. They obviously did not much
fear the police or the courts, which might give us the false sense that under the Tanzimat-state rule of law, a person could expect to get away with
murder, whether he or she was free or enslaved. In fact, based on a fairly
broad sample of Ottoman court records, the impression is the opposite,
not only because of the low incidence of homicide cases we find but also
because law-enforcement agencies seem to have been effective in catch-
ing and punishing murderers.

The population expected the Ottoman state to provide security and
generate respect for law and order. Local authorities throughout the Empire were responsive to temporary increases in crime rates, as was the
central government in Istanbul. A typical example relates to the special
circumstances that often prevailed in the Hijaz, a religiously sensitive
area that was also historically exposed to tribal-pastoralist pressures on

43. BOA/BEO/Mühacirin Komisyonu/vol. 758 (gelen)/# 190, correspondence
    with the Kaymakam of Köstence, 12.1863–1.1864.

its urban centers and commercial networks. In December 1854, following a murder case in the holy city of Medina—in which, incidentally, an
enslaved Ethiopian man stabbed to death one of the residents of the
Holy Shrine (Arabic, *Haram*) area—the dignitaries of the city addressed
a strong petition to the High Court in Istanbul.[44] In the petition, the
Shaykh al-Haram, high officials, and prominent ulama of Medina demanded that the sultan recognize the current practice, which allowed
murderers to be executed by a local court verdict *without* awaiting sultanic approval.

The basic reasoning in the dignitaries' petition was predicated on
the threat to public order from a rising tide of homicide cases, which required that swift justice be administered in the province. The petitioners
argued that long delays were being created by the requirement that court
papers be forwarded to Istanbul for review and approval by the High
Court and the sultan. Owing to the prevalence of blood revenge customs
among local tribes, these delays invited a breakdown of civil order. The
imminent danger could be averted only if a convicted murderer was
quickly executed, thereby barring his family and kin from taking matters
into their own hands. Istanbul accepted the logic of the petitioners and
duly granted permission for the local court to complete the legal process
in the Hijaz itself and put to death convicted murderers in the province
without imperial approval.

OTHER CRIMINALIZED ACTS OF DEFIANCE

Beyond the major types of crimes—larceny, sex crimes, arson, and homicide—enslaved men and women in Ottoman society resorted to other
kinds of action that can be classified as acts of defiance and resistance.
Some of the stories discussed here are of necessity borderline cases, and
I make an effort to contextualize them socially and culturally. Generally
speaking, there are two kinds of action in this category—individual defiance and group defiance. In our corpus, an individual's act of defiance
was often a unique expression of anger, resistance, or protest. Group action was different in that it was an organized reaction to a particular situation that had developed in a given locale. Enslaved persons acted as a

44. BOA/İrade/Meclis-i Vala/13109/*Mazbata*, 6.2.1854, the Grand Vezir to the
Sultan, 11.2.1854, and the Sultan's response, 12.2.1854.

group usually when some form of leadership was present; acting in a group helped to amplify the protest and achieve redress for specific grievances.

Individual Defiance

In November 1866, a slave dealer named Ahmet transported three enslaved Circassian women on a boat that was carrying timber from Trabzon to Istanbul.[45] One of the three, Tuti, was on the deck when the captain told her to go down into the hold. She refused, he started beating her, and she threw herself into the water in anger, but she was later rescued and brought back on board. On arrival in Istanbul, the incident was reported to the police, and both the captain and Ahmet were taken into custody. The captain was released soon after without being charged, but the slave dealer was accused of throwing Tuti into the water and sentenced to five years in prison. Ahmet refused to accept the verdict; he must have complained about it to various people, stressing that his children were suffering want and deprivation as a result of his absence. His efforts were successful when, after he had spent fifteen months in jail, the imam of the Fatime Sultan mosque—probably moved to act by intermediaries—petitioned the authorities to reconsider the case and do justice by Ahmet. A High Court investigation found Ahmet's story to be true, meaning that he was not to blame for Tuti's jump into the sea in reaction to the captain's blows. The court recommended that he be released, and both the grand vezir and the sultan endorsed the decision.

Here we have a case of an enslaved woman, this time a Circassian, who was unwilling to put up with abuse and reacted in an extreme manner that was potentially harmful to herself. To fill the gaps in the story, we need to separate what the documents tell us from what they do not but may still be assumed—with varying degrees of confidence—to have occurred. The record describes the captain's actions: he ordered Tuti to go down to the hold, then he beat her. It also describes what Tuti did: she refused to go down and, when beaten, threw herself in the water. By

45. BOA/İrade/Meclis-i Vala/26185/Petition of the Imam of Fatime Sultan, 30.4.1867, report of the Prison Director, 10.7.1867, *Mazbata* of the Meclis-i Vala, 11.12.1867, the Grand Vezir to the Sultan, 12.1.1867, and the Sultan's response, 13.1.1867.

adding the phrase that she did that "in anger," the record describes her mood and indirectly imputes a motive to her action. We should now try to fill the gaps by first addressing Tuti's refusal to obey the captain's orders and go down to the hold. Here we can offer only a tentative motive for her action: since this was her initial act of defiance, it may have been triggered by some immediate circumstance, such as wanting to breathe fresh air; or, if she was having an argument with enslaved women down in the hold, she might not have wished to return there and be in their company. In any event, though both enslaved and a woman, Tuti did not find it unfathomable to disobey the powerful captain—who was free and male and the top authority on the boat.

Our next step is to understand Tuti's reaction when the captain used force in dealing with her insubordination. Instead of accepting the situation and surrendering to superior force, Tuti chose another way. By jumping into the water, putting herself in harm's way, she attempted to draw a certain line for the captain, and probably for the slave dealer—and perhaps also to offer an example to the other two enslaved women, who were undoubtedly aware of what was happening on the deck and watching attentively. In a way, she said to all these people: That's it, no more beating. I won't take any more. Of course, this could have been a moment of irrational behavior, an action taken at the height of emotion, in response to pain and humiliation, in a desperate search for a way out, which only the sea could offer. Thus again, I wish to argue that by exploring the available options, the dilemma at hand, and the choice made by the enslaved, we can see agency and resistance emerge out of misery and powerlessness. If in some cases, as in Tuti's, the interpretation offered here suggests just one of the options available, in other cases, such as the following story of Nevres, the empowering explanation is virtually inescapable.

Nevres was an enslaved African woman who for a long time served in the household of Zeki Paşa.[46] According to custom and human decency, the Paşa should have manumitted her, but in mid-1864 he chose instead to sell Nevres to a slave dealer named Mısırlı ("the Egyptian")

---

46. BOA/İrade/Meclis-i Vala/23102/*Mazbata* of Zaptiye Meclisi, 24.5.1864, *Mazbata* of Meclis-i Vala, 13.7.1864, the Grand Vezir to the Sultan, 21.7.1864, and the Sultan's response, 22.7.1864.

Hasan for 900 Kuruş, not a very high price. Her expectation of liberation shattered, Nevres became completely unruly, adamantly refusing either to remain in Hasan's custody or to be resold. She repeatedly ran away as soon as the police would return her to him, acting in a way the record describes as "obstinate in the most extreme degree and very unreasonable" (*derece-i nihayette huysuz ve söz anlamaz*). Since Hasan was an old man and could not control Nevres, the police explained, he put her legs in chains. When the case was being sorted out by the police, Nevres also accused Hasan of beating her, but only the chaining charge could be established. The police arrested Hasan and kept him in custody for three months to facilitate the investigation. Upon reviewing the police report, which called Zeki Paşa's resale of Nevres "a reprehensible act," the grand vezir's office decided to manumit the woman, who had already been kept for two months at the facility for runaway slaves. The police asked the High Court for a ruling regarding Hasan's detention, suggesting that Zeki Paşa should return the 900 Kuruş to the slave dealer, who was in great financial need. The court decided to release Hasan but ordered the imperial treasury, instead of Zeki Paşa, to pay him the 900 Kuruş.

Nevres's story is a clear case of defiance, as she forcefully asserted time and again her desire to be free. She rightly had expected that her longtime master, Zeki Paşa, to manumit her, and when he did not, she resorted to the only action available to her—resisting the slave dealer Hasan, who wanted to get rid of her by resale to yet another slaver. With her legs chained she could not run away, but word of her condition must have reached the police quickly, especially if she was being offered for sale in an accessible place or a semipublic facility used by traders, such as a marketplace or a lodge. Hasan may or may not have beaten Nevres, but she did charge him with that, probably knowing that it would enhance her case and get her freed more quickly. Chaining was against the law, and apparently the police strongly disapproved of it, which was enough for the Porte to have Nevres liberated by decree and put an end to her ordeal.

Granted, the stories of Tuti and Nevres required some patch-up work, some backing and filling, to deal with the gaps in the record and recover the circumstances surrounding these cases. Reconstruction makes it possible to imagine the state of mind of not only Tuti or Nevres but many other enslaved persons in Ottoman societies who were caught up in the stresses of daily life. Speculating in an informed way enables us to reasonably assess the choices available to people like Tuti and Nevres in urban households and villages across the Empire. Enslaved persons were often told to do things they did not want to do, but they were obliged to obey, which must have had an accumulated negative effect. Disobedience and insubordination—as displayed by Tuti and Nevres—were often met with physical coercion, and that could sometimes lead to desperate acts by the enslaved, or it could further embitter them. Significantly, in none of the cases discussed here were insanity or mental illness mentioned as a possible explanation for the actions taken by the enslaved persons in question. This helps underscore the rational element in their choices and to weave in the psychological component that is often needed in order to complete the explanation.

Group Defiance

Whereas individual acts of defiance require personal courage, group action necessitates organization, leadership, and goal-oriented, calculated risk taking. Large-scale group action would normally qualify as an uprising or a rebellion, but the Ottoman government labeled even considerable organized disturbances of the public order as revolt (isyan) only reluctantly because doing so would have required costly and difficult suppression by force. Instead, the Ottomans preferred to deal with the rebels, negotiate with them, constructively engage them, and, finally, co-opt them into the imperial system.[47] The approach was no different in the few cases in which the group that launched an organized protest was made up of enslaved persons, usually men, seeking to end their oppression and gain freedom. Group action by the enslaved could occur only where they were not isolated in households or working in small numbers for individual farmers in Egypt, for example; it could happen only where the enslaved worked in groups. In the Ottoman Empire, enslaved people who lived and worked in groups were only:

47. See, for example, Karen Barkey's account of the Ottoman approach to the Celali revolts in the seventeenth century, in Barkey, *Bandits and Bureaucrats: The Ottoman Route to State Centralization,* Ithaca, N.Y.: Cornell University Press, 1994.

- the enserfed-enslaved Circassian families that cultivated the agricultural estates of their feudal lords
- the enslaved Africans who worked on the large agricultural estates (*çiftliks*; Egyptian Arabic plural, *gafalik*) of Ottoman-Egyptian elite members
- the enslaved Africans who worked in small gangs for their nomad slavers in the Hijaz

We have already discussed the petition presented to the High Court in Istanbul by the Medina dignitaries in December 1853 following a murder case in that holy city in which an enslaved Ethiopian stabbed a man to death in the vicinity of the Holy Shrine. In this incident, the central government agreed to allow the execution of convicted murderers in the province of the Hijaz without recourse to Istanbul and sultanic approval. Interestingly, the dignitaries who signed the petition warned of "the danger that negative behavior and killing in this country could follow the disturbances [organized by] Bedouins and slaves (Arabic, *al-ʿurban wa-l-ʿabid*)." The mention of slaves in this context raises the specter of bands of runaway Africans acting as bandits and ready to defend their own group members—be they perpetrators of a crime or victims.

For our purposes here, this constitutes evidence indicating that in the Ottoman Hijaz at the time, there was some form of organized resistance by enslaved Africans who acted outside the realm of legality and posed a threat to law and order in the province. To avoid direct confrontation, defuse a potentially rebellious situation, and maintain control, the Ottoman government in the Hijaz deployed arrangements with Bedouin tribal chiefs. These included noninterference in internal tribal matters, of which master-slave relationships were an important component. Consequently, enslaved Africans held by tribespeople could rarely obtain freedom through the Ottoman court system, nor, because of lack of cooperation by the Ottoman authorities, could they do so through the British consulate in Jidda. The enslaved nonetheless continued to seek manumission by running to British naval vessels anchoring at the various Hijazi ports and occasionally also to the consulate. In addition, these people had the option of joining bands of African absconders who had to fend for themselves in that tough desert environment, preferring it to continued enslavement.

From the 1820s on, during consecutive reigns as governors-general of Ottoman Egypt, Mehmet Ali Paşa and his successors imported and employed on their large estates a large number of enslaved African men as agricultural laborers.[48] Many of their dependent grandees were also granted such estates, but they often remained absentee landlords, leaving the daily management of these farms to loyal foremen. Hilal notes that not a few of the foremen were enslaved Africans, who proved capable and loyal enough to supervise agricultural production for their masters. Interestingly, conditions on those farms were apparently conducive to empowerment of the enslaved workers, but especially for the estate managers who emerged from their midst. Some of the managers became virtually independent, acting as gang leaders and flagrantly violating the law of the land. They formed armed militias that turned the farms into extraterritorial zones where fugitives from neighboring villages who sought to evade conscription, corvée, or state prisons found safe haven.

Hafız Efendi, for example, employed a large number of enslaved Africans on his estate in the district of Minya, appointing as manager one of them a Sudanese named Bakhit.[49] Bakhit harbored corvée evaders and fugitives from justice, including murderers, and refused to turn them over to the authorities. In 1851, when one of the village headmen tried to retrieve some of the missing men who fell under his jurisdiction, Bakhit and another man attacked him; the other man, a known murderer, grabbed Bakhit's gun and shot the *shaykh* dead. The killer was later arrested, but Bakhit managed to escape; he was never apprehended. In another case, Abdi Şükrü Paşa, the director of the state school system under Abbas Paşa (governor-general, 1849–1854), appointed an enslaved African named Mabruk to manage his large estate in the district of Daqhaliyya, giving the man complete authority to run the estate. Mabruk employed in agriculture many fugitives from military service and the law, beating and humiliating village shaykhs who tried to recover these men. He even tied one of the shaykhs to a water wheel to make it go round

48. For a good account of this hitherto underestimated phenomenon, see Hilal, *Ar-raqiq*, 110–123.
49. Cases cited in this and the next two paragraphs are from Hilal, *Ar-raqiq*, 116–118.

instead of using an ox. Villages and towns in the entire area were intimidated by Mabruk and suffered under his notorious abuse of power.

At one point, a few of the village headmen complained to the authorities, and Mabruk was summoned to the district governorate and ordered to surrender the fugitives to the shaykhs. He agreed to do so, but when he was released, he reneged on his promise. Accompanied by some local policemen, two of the headmen went to the estate and demanded the return of their men. They were attacked by some three hundred enslaved African men and other fugitives, all armed with guns and sticks, and were nearly killed. Finally, in November 1854, the district governor issued an order to arrest Mabruk and return the fugitives to the shaykhs. A military force was sent to surround the farm, and Mabruk and the runaways were seized. Mabruk claimed that he had acted on the orders of his master, the estate owner, and was not responsible for any wrongdoing. The entire gang was "severely punished" by the governor, but the record does not state what the penalties were, nor what happened to Mabruk himself.

Two more examples come from Egypt and date back to the year 1858. The first is the story of Khayrallah, an enslaved African estate manager who created a small armed militia, or rather a gang of bullies, made up of enslaved African and Sudanese men. He used his slave militia to terrorize the population and beat up anyone in the region who dared oppose him. Khayrallah also forced the *fallahin* to work for him without wages, becoming a slave-turned-enslaver. The other story is about Bilal, an enslaved African who ran the Minya-district estate of Selim Paşa, the governor of Damietta. Given the considerable distance between the seaport province of Damietta, on the northeastern coast, and the Middle Egyptian estate the estate holder could not have exercised much supervision over his manager. Indeed, Bilal received, sheltered, and employed on the farm fugitives of all sorts without any interference. All this came to an end when he beat to death one of his protégés. For that he was tried and convicted, but he received only the lenient sentence of one year's imprisonment, after which he was deported to the Sudan in accordance with the governor-general's policy regarding convicted criminals.

Each such group action challenged the local regime by introducing vigilante law and order and was not quelled until the representatives of the provincial government in Cairo interceded. Paradoxically, group actions benefited the estate holders, who saw their yields increase in a period of labor shortages. These high-ranking officials were not quick to intervene to restore the authority of local shaykhs and give up illicitly obtained manpower. By their actions, the enslaved in fact *reversed* the power structure, themselves becoming the employers of free fugitives who were trading their labor in exchange for food, protection, and shelter. In the wild periphery, away from Cairo, the enslaved farm manager was king. This was possible only where the estate holder was absent and where groups of enslaved men were present; it did not occur on land that belonged to smallholders, who cultivated the fields side by side with the one or two enslaved Africans they could afford to purchase and retain.

A similar situation existed also on the medium-size and large agricultural estates in Anatolia and the Balkans that had been granted to Circassian refugee landlords. There, too, groups of enslaved persons living in families possessed the prerequisites for collective acts of defiance.[50] After Circassian serfs were brought into the Ottoman Empire by their asylum-seeking feudal lords during the late 1850s and early 1860s, these serfs-turned-slaves occasionally resorted to violence to achieve liberation and extricate themselves from the control of their beys. Faced with growing violence between the enslaved and the landlords, with both sides armed and ready to fight each other, the Ottoman government tried to defuse the tension by establishing a new policy. Accordingly, in 1867 it allowed state land cultivated by the enslaved to be used as payment to the slavers to secure, via an Islam-grounded manumission contract (mükatebe), the liberation of such enslaved agricultural families. This was a typically pragmatic Ottoman compromise between the demand of the enslaved to be manumitted by the Tanzimat-state without the consent of the slavers and the beys' adamant opposition to any interference in their proprietary rights over the enslaved.[51]

The three following cases of violent group resistance displayed by

50. For a general survey of slavery among the Circassians in the Ottoman Empire, both agricultural and domestic, and for traffic in enslaved Circassians, see Ehud R. Toledano, *Slavery and Abolition in the Ottoman Middle East,* Seattle: University of Washington Press, 1998: 81–111.
51. For more about government-sponsored mükatebe, see Toledano, *Slavery and Abolition,* 95–104.

enslaved Circassian agricultural workers provide a good idea of the nature and dynamics of these disputes. The first is an instance of a somewhat less organized action; the next two actions seem to be well targeted and more effective.

In mid-1862, a series of incidents was reported in a memo sent to the Refugees Commission in Istanbul from the district of Kütahya.[52] A group of enslaved Circassians who belonged to Hoca Mehmet Efendi of Eskişehir had resorted to unruly behavior and criminal conduct. These enslaved individuals were allegedly involved in murder, theft, and insubordination to the authorities. Although no further details are provided, this does not seem to be a case of sporadic criminal activity on the part of a few individuals; rather, it appears to have been an organized and well-led group action by enslaved persons who were all the legal property of one and the same man—Hoca Mehmet Efendi. He happened to be a respectable man of religion and possibly held office in the local government, as his title implies. The impression we get from the text is, however, that these group activities were rather defuse and lacked a clearly defined purpose.

In late 1866, violent clashes erupted in the village of Mandıra near the old Ottoman capital of Edirne, on the European side of the straits.[53] The enserfed Circassians involved in these altercations demanded to be released from bondage, but their beys refused. All the four hundred households that participated in the clashes were armed, and the policemen sent to the spot were denied entry into the village. The governor of Edirne dispatched a larger police force under the command of a major, and that unit managed to bring the situation under control. Since tensions were still running high and there was great concern that violence on a larger scale would erupt again, the governor applied to the grand vezir for permission to disarm the entire village. In the meantime, he sent a mediator to try and reconcile the feuding parties. Further evidence suggests, inconclusively, that some of the villagers of Mandıra, probably the enslaved among them and possibly the most militant, were deported, resettled in Anatolia (on the Asian side), and banned from ever again returning to Rumelia (on the European side).

52. BOA/BEO/Mühacirin Komisyonu/vol. 758–38:1/# 403, 5–6.1862.
53. Toledano, *Slavery and Abolition*, 95–96.

While these and similar incidents led to the mükatebe contract policy, the solution did not always work well, for it failed to settle across the board demands for manumission from many enslaved Circassian agricultural workers. For example, it was reported in August 1874 that a serious confrontation between workers and unresponsive slaveholders erupted in the area of Çorlu, not far from Istanbul.[54] A large group of enslaved persons demanded unconditional manumission, but the slaveholders agreed only to a mutually negotiated and contracted liberation according to the mükatebe policy and threatened to use arms to put down the insurrection. Here the government moved swiftly, sending a military force and four field guns to the area with an ultimatum to the Circassian slaveholders. The ultimatum reiterated the mükatebe policy but decreed that the enslaved group in question would be liberated through a process supervised by an ad hoc committee, which would assess the value of the slaves concerned and determine the compensation in land to be given to their beys. In the face of such a show of force, the slaveholders surrendered, and the enslaved were manumitted and transported out of the area by some 250 carriages, which in itself is indicative of the large scope of the insurrection.

Ninety of the militant slaveholders were arrested, and the liberated families were given land in other regions of the Empire, resettled, and provided with means of production to enable them to rebuild their lives. In this case, the government insisted on a telling principle: the Circassian agricultural workers who had been manumitted were resettled in scattered villages in the interior, but only one family was allowed to settle in any one village. This fact indicates that the authorities realized that the potential for group action existed only where a sufficient number of enslaved persons lived together and could effectively organize for joint action. Although the group of people discussed in our specific case had been liberated, they also had—as a group—acquired a bad reputation for having once been engaged in acts of defiance and insubordination. To eliminate the risk of a recurrence, these families were separated from each other and distributed to different villages, making renewed contact among them and the organization of a new plan of action impossible.

Having thus far considered the lot of the enslaved from violent removal and coerced interjection to renewed attachment and its precarious

54. Toledano, *Slavery and Abolition*, 100–101.

vagaries, it is time now to examine the last chapter in that story. We have followed the enslaved in those cases when their mutual but unequal relationships with slavers failed and they had to struggle for better arrangements, plead with the Tanzimat-state, or act against its representatives and symbols. But even when bonding was as satisfactory as it could be on both sides, many enslaved people, whether within families or not, looked for solace in practices familiar to them from their home countries in order to overcome their sense of isolation in an alien host society. Chapter 5 will show how familiar Zar-Bori healing rituals—along with other elements from faraway homelands—were deployed to tame the chaos of the new and to perhaps temper the fear of the incomprehensible in their new homes.

CHAPTER FIVE

Taming the Unknown with the Familiar

THE EASTERN MEDITERRANEAN represents one of the most fascinating and fertile grounds for studying cultural diversity, fusion, complexity, struggle, and coexistence. It was in Ottoman times, and still is today, one of the world's best laboratories for ethnic studies. The past and recent calamities of Middle Eastern ethnopolitics are only too familiar today, but there is also another side to them all, which calls for scholarly efforts that might, in the long run, defuse some of the intractable political quagmires that make life in this region so frustrating, so painful, but also so humanly engaging and absorbing.

The main phenomenon that will be explored here is what I call *Ottoman cultural creolization*. By this I mean the process by which enslaved Africans and Circassians retained ingredients of their origin-cultures, these ingredients were fused with local-culture components, and the resulting hybrid-type cultures were disseminated in Ottoman societies. Creolization has rightly been associated with resistance to incorporation, but as Paul Lovejoy points out, degrees of resistance should be distinguished within these processes: strong resistance creates what he calls "separate subcultures" that are "impervious to creolization," whereas the emergence of "creole cultures" implies a certain measure of assimilation, integration, and acceptance of the dominant culture.[1] In the Ottoman Empire, enslavement perforce produced cre-olized cultural reformulations rather than separate subcultures.[2] The process began when the captured and enslaved were in transit from their home to their destination, as Islam was imposed on them, initiat-ing a long cultural-religious journey. The journey continued in the Ot-toman households that absorbed the enslaved and integrated them into society with varying degrees of success.

The *seeming* sociopolitical silence of Africans and Circassians pointed to in previous chapters was marked by a *seeming* near-complete cultural absence. African languages and African lore are virtually ex-tinct from contemporary post-Ottoman eastern Mediterranean soci-eties. However, in various areas, mostly rural communities of Circas-sians have managed to keep their dialects alive and retain core elements of their culture.[3] More research will be required to unearth residues of African cultures in this region, while Circassian retentions from the Caucasian past are being revived owing to renewed contacts with

1. For a succinct treatment of on the terms "creole" and "creolization," see Paul E. Lovejoy, "Identifying Enslaved Africans in the African Diaspora," in Lovejoy (ed.), *Identity in the Shadow of Slavery*, London: Continuum, 2000 (especially 13–19). For the basic concept of creolization used here (with which Lovejoy dis-agrees), see Sidney W. Mintz and Richard Price, *An Anthropological Approach to the Afro-American Past: A Caribbean Perspective*, Philadelphia: Institute for the Study of Human Issues, 1976. The quotation from Lovejoy is in Paul E. Love-joy (ed.), *Slavery on the Frontiers of Islam*, Princeton, N.J.: Markus Wiener, 2004: 8.

2. For a generally similar view, see John Hunwick's recent work "The Religious Practices of Black Slaves in the Mediterranean Islamic World," in Lovejoy, *Slav-ery on Frontiers*, 167.

3. Some studies are Amjad Jaimoukha, *The Chechens: A Handbook*, London: Rout-ledge Curzon, 2005; Jaimoukha, *The Circassians:A Handbook*, Richmond, En-gland: Curzon, 2001; Jaimoukha (ed.), *Circassian Cuisine*, Amman, Jordan: San-jalay Press, 2003; Jaimoukha (ed.), *The Cycles of the Circassian Nart Epic: The Fountain-Head of Circassian Mythology*, Amman, Jordan: Sanjalay Press, 2000; Ziramikw Qardenghwsch', *Circassian Proverbs and Sayings* (trans. Amjad Jaimoukha), Amman, Jordan: Sanjalay Press, 2003; Seteney Khalid Shami, *Eth-nicity and Leadership: The Circassians in Jordan*, Ann Arbor, Mich.: University Microfilms International, 1985; and more recent edited collections. For an ex-ample of activities in this direction, see www.kafkas.org.tr.

post-Soviet homelands in the Caucasus. Some ongoing ethnographic projects in Turkey and Arab countries hold promise for the near future, though they are fraught with access and methodological difficulties. For the time being, scholars must contend themselves with tracing some of the salient residues through the evidence available for the late Ottoman and early post-Ottoman periods. Using these limited data here, I shall try to put the evidence in the appropriate methodological context, partly by drawing on research done in adjacent fields—notably anthropology, sociolinguistics, and cultural studies—with regard to similar issues. The picture that emerges is intricate and fascinating.

An important part of our discussion will address issues of belief and the spiritual world of African-Ottomans. These formed the backbone of the culture they brought along from their homelands. To enter, and comprehend the intricacies of, the world that the enslaved inhabited, we would be well advised to bear in mind I. M. Lewis's cautionary note about the dynamic and relative nature of a popular religion that includes beliefs in marginal spiritual forces. These forces, he writes, constitute "a spiritual reservoir (frequently updated) which can be drawn upon to respond to the experience of affliction and stress in ways which make this meaningful to the victims and their families. Only when people cease to believe in spirits does recourse to them become ineffective and, fundamentally, irrational and therefore a sign of detachment from reality."[4] It is nevertheless important to recognize that in Ottoman societies there existed varying degrees of belief in the supernatural and that even Islamic-Ottoman orthodoxy was ambivalent with regard to such beliefs.

Evidence from nineteenth-century Istanbul points to the existence of at least some form of organization involving freed and enslaved Africans. Such evidence, which comes mainly from travel accounts and contemporary informants, was studied and interpreted by Y. Hakan Erdem in his *Slavery in the Ottoman Empire and Its Demise, 1800-1909*. Erdem was

4. I. M. Lewis, "*Zar* in Context: The Past, the Present and the Future of an African Healing Cult," in I. M. Lewis, Ahmed Al-Safi, and Sayyid Hurreiz (eds.), *Women's Medicine: The Zar-Bori Cult in Africa and Beyond*, Edinburgh: Edinburgh University Press, 1991: 16.

interested in finding out how freed slaves were cared for by the government after manumission, and examined the various ways this was done. His work looks mostly at the organizational aspect and mentions the cultural significance only in passing. Erdem's summary of accounts by Z. Duckett Ferriman, Lucy Garnett, Richard Davey, Leyla Saz, George Young, Halide Edip, and Emine Foat Tugay yields an intriguing description of a loosely defined network of lodges located especially—though possibly not exclusively—in Istanbul. Each of these lodges was run by a female African freed slave, called a *kolbaşı* or sometimes a *godya/godiya*. Erdem aptly describes her functions as those of both "union leader and priestess of a religious cult." The deity worshipped by lodge members was variously called *Yavroubé* or *Yarrabox*, then rendered in a Turkicized form as *Yavru Bey*, meaning "infant lord."[5] Below I shall offer a revision of this interpretation.

The lodges were founded, according to Lucy Garnett, "for mutual defence and protection, not only against the tyranny of masters and mistresses, but against sickness and other accidents of life."[6] The kolbaşı, who served in her capacity for life, was charged with caring for sick and unemployed freed Africans and placing them in gainful jobs. At times, the kolbaşı would purchase the freedom of enslaved persons in special need of rescue. An Ottoman document cited by Erdem suggests that the organization was yet another instrument of government service and control, similar to guilds, Sufi orders, quarters, and other intermediary formations. As I have argued in this book, the Tanzimat-state sought not only to increase its control but also to limit abuse and protect the weak and needy in society. In the specific case mentioned by Erdem, a kolbaşı named Tunbuti was exiled from Istanbul to Bursa in late 1817 for having shown "negligence and laxitude in the duties assigned to her" and for "disobedience to the authorities."[7] The government required that kolbaşıs maintain precise records of where they placed freed slaves, to

5. Y. Hakan Erdem, *Slavery in the Ottoman Empire and Its Demise, 1800–1909*, Basingstoke, England: Macmillan in association with St. Antony's College, Oxford, 1996: 173–176. For a similar account of these Istanbul lodges (which ignores Erdem's work but adds some untapped sources), see Hunwick, "Religious Practices," 160–162.

6. Cited in Erdem, *Slavery*, 174.

7. Ibid., 176.

whom they married them, and whatever other details were required for ensuring the successful reattachment of freed slaves. As with other government-backed intermediaries, the kolbaşı was allowed to collect dues from freed Africans to fund her lodge and services.

Citing Garnett, Erdem says that cult rules excluded men from rituals, let alone from leadership, but that men still received aid from kolbaşıs if need was demonstrated.[8] But Pertev Boratav's account of similar practices in Izmir during a later period, possibly extending well past the formation of the Turkish Republic, speaks of the godyas themselves as being mostly African men, with one exceptional case of a white man, Mustafa Kalfa, who was recognized as a powerful godya. Male babas appear to have been the leaders of such associations in southern Iran. Contrary to this, Günver Güneş asserts that most godyas in Izmir—who numbered five to ten at the beginning of the twentieth century—were elderly females, adding that Africans never disobeyed their godyas, and treated them with the utmost respect.

It does seem that retained African cultural elements, including rituals and roles assigned to leading persons in those communities, evolved over time, with practice adjusting naturally to the changing social and economic conditions in different locales. In Izmir, leadership was founded on sustained personal contact with, training under, and formal confirmation by a well-recognized godya. Initiation rites included the use of incense, and members had to undergo an incense ritual every year, during which they gave the godyas a small donation for their work. Godyas could allegedly heal from possession and counter the effects of snake and insect poison with a special drink (şerbet).

Smaller indoor rituals were held regularly in the various lodges with

8. Information in this paragraph and the next is based on Erdem, *Slavery,* 174; Pertev N. Boratav, "The Negro in Turkish Folklore," *Journal of American Folklore,* 64/251 (January–March 1951): 83–88 (references here are to pp. 87–88); Taghi Modarressi, "The Zar Cult in South Iran," in Raymond Prince (ed.), *Trance and Possession States,* Montreal: R. M. Bucke Memorial Society, 1968: 149–155; and Günver Güneş, "Kölelikten Özgülüğe: İzmir'de Zenciler ve Zenci Folkloru," *Toplumsal Tarih,* 11/62 (February 1999): 6. For more about the phenomena of possession and trance in various cultures, see the essays in Prince's collection, and A. Kiev (ed.), *Magic, Faith and Healing: Studies in Primitive Psychiatry,* Northvale, N.J.: Jason Aronson, 1996.

the active participation of the members, led by the kolbaşı or godya. Without going into too much detail, let me note that in the Ottoman core regions, the ritual performed by African lodge members consisted of dances, gestures, music, loud vocal utterances, periodic use of incense, and object worship.[9] Dancing was normally done in a circle with one or two persons in the middle leading and stimulating the others. The instruments played included, according to Boratav, "guitars made of bottle gourds and having tiny rings attached to the strings and cymbals, which are decorated with rings at the corners." The instruments were probably made of materials that could be found in the new environment but followed the models seen and heard in their places of origin. While these rituals resemble scenes from Sufi *zikr* rituals, going into *individual* trance was a more common occurrence in the African synthesized version—so much so that the term *babalı* (trance) in Ottoman Turkish came to describe an enslaved African "having a nervous fit."[10] The central role of the kolbaşı/godya in taking a person out of trance indicates that spirit possession was a commonly identified phenomenon in the community.

African ritual included the annual outdoor festival as well as the indoor events. The festival occurred in such core Ottoman cities as Istanbul and Izmir but also in Tunis and Ulcinj, a port town near the Montenegrin-Albanian border.[11] In both Istanbul and Izmir it is reported to have taken place in the month of May. Africans assembled from all parts of town and presumably from the surrounding area to celebrate for several days, in public parks, their spiritual and communal bond. Elements of the rituals performed regularly in the privacy of the

9. Summed up in Erdem, *Slavery*, 175, and described in Boratav, "Negro," 87–88. This is also stated in a court record at BOA/Cev Dahiliye/92.

10. See *Redhouse Yeni Türkçe-İngilizce Sözlük*, Istanbul: Redhouse Yayınevi, 1974: 115. The Ottoman Redhouse edition of 1884 links such fits with obstinacy rather than trance, but the association is still quite clear: "baba—6. (with negroes) A kind of epileptic fit; hence also, a fit of dogged obstinacy" (J. W. Redhouse, *A Turkish and English Lexicon*, Constantinople: A. H. Boyajian, 1884: Part I, p. 314).

11. For Istanbul, see Erdem, *Slavery*, 175; for Izmir, see Günver Güneş, "Kölelikten Özgülüğe," 4–10 (the reference to 15 May is on p. 7). Note Boratav's claim that in Izmir the festival occurred in July or August (Boratav, "Negro," 88). For Tunis and Ulcinj, see further below.

lodges were introduced into the public sphere, though, at least in Istanbul, there was a tendency to keep the celebrations within the community by demarcating the areas in the parks as private to avoid getting outsiders involved and thereby exposing them to an unfamiliar culture. For Izmir, Boratav and Güneş provide a detailed account of what seems to have been an elaborate event that involved larger segments of the population, the majority of whom did not belong to the African community. The comparison between Istanbul and Izmir leaves the impression that the paucity of information on Africans in the imperial capital stems mostly from lack of sufficient research, rather than from a qualitative difference in organization and communal life between these two major Ottoman cities.

Güneş builds on Boratav's ethnographic work and significantly expands on it, so we now possess reliable information about the annual Calf Festival (*Dana Bayramı*) in Izmir.[12] According to these studies, preparations required several months and were conducted under the supervision of the godyas. The holiday lasted four weeks, but celebrations took place only from Thursday night through Friday evening each week. After the first three weeks, during which rituals were performed separately in two of the quarters inhabited by Africans (Tamaşalık and İkiçeşme), and after a door-to-door collection of donations accompanied by music and led by the godyas, the two communities and the rest of the African population came together in a joint finale. With the money they collected, the leaders purchased a handsome calf and in an elaborate ceremony adorned it with decorative wires, napkins, and coins, which they attached to its horns and other parts of the head and body. The calf was carried to an open space adjacent to one of the two African neighborhoods, where it was slaughtered by a godya in full ceremony, and participants dipped their fingers in its blood. After that, the calf was cooked in a large cauldron and placed in the middle of the square; there members were joined by nonmembers and outsiders to share in eating the cooked calf parts.

At that point, the entire quarter became a festival site, with people dancing and singing, listening to African bands, watching street

12. The following is based on Güneş, "Kölelikten Özgülüğe," 8–9; and Boratav, "Negro," 88.

performances, and, if they were young, courting each other in a free and joyous atmosphere. In the late nineteenth and early twentieth centuries, the number of people taking part in the Izmir Calf Festival was about four thousand to five thousand, but the celebrations touched a broader circle of between ten thousand and fifteen thousand men and women. Güneş describes the festival as a "crazy" (çılgın) event, highly popular with many of Izmir's young, having become a carnival that people awaited each year with great anticipation. Regardless of religious criticism or government rebuke—on account of its un-Islamic character—large numbers of young people were drawn to it.[13] The liberating sensation that the carnival offered was in a way reminiscent of the unshackling experience that Zar rituals afforded Africans in smaller groups, as we shall see. In 1895, the governor-general of Izmir, Hasan Fehmi Paşa, prohibited the Calf Festival from taking place, but after he left office, the prohibition was ignored, and the festival continued into the early years of the Republic.

For Istanbul, Erdem put together from various contemporary accounts some information about the dress used by the kolbaşıs and their congregations and about the decoration of the lodges. Here, too, it is obvious that cult practices were a syncretic mélange of many local African traditions, which have hitherto been described in an undifferentiated way as simply "African." As enslaved Africans died out or were manumitted, this creolized culture remained their offspring's native culture, which they continued to cherish for generations to come, even after they became Turks, Iranians, and Arabs by circumstance and choice. Archival sources and ethnographic work among the remaining communities hold promise for future research in this area. Because kolbaşıs were obligated by the government to record in detail the services they provided to both enslaved and freed Africans, such as in what employment they placed them, to whom they married them, and so forth, valuable information on the social and spiritual life of individual Africans and their communities in the Empire might still be discovered in various Ottoman registers and other types of state records.

Communities of African descent were present not only in cities like Istanbul and Izmir but also in rural settlements in the Aydın province, in western Anatolian towns such as Torbalı, Söke, Ödemiş, Tire, Akhisar,

13. Güneş, "Kölelikten Özgülüğe," 9.

and in the region of Antalya.[14] Promising anthropological research could be conducted there in the future. There can hardly be any doubt that creolized versions of African culture existed—and still exist—in various parts of the Middle East, as has been recently demonstrated in Behnaz A. Mirzai's study on Iran.[15] In her article, she lists the following areas of African retentions and carryovers in certain social and regional segments of Iranian society: female genital mutilation in Baluchistan; the chewing of black tobacco in the region of Bandar Abbas; the use of certain musical instruments and songs, which accounts for the formation of the musical tradition of Hurmuzgan and the entire coastal area of southern Iran; and the belief system and spiritual practices of southwestern Iran, where the impact of Zar is evident. Much of that cultural content came from the east African coast, especially from the cultures of the Swahili littoral, the Sudan, and Ethiopia. Undoubtedly, this syncretism imbued and enriched not only Iranian society but the entire Ottoman Middle East, where Africans were forcibly brought and where their labor was exploited for centuries.

THE CREOLIZATION OF ZAR IN OTTOMAN SOCIETIES

Neither Erdem nor Boratav nor Güneş, nor other writers on folk culture among enslaved Africans and their descendants, have linked the cult practices they identified in the Empire to Zar, a type of possession cult involving trance and healing rituals.[16] One of my main contentions in this chapter will be that what was observed and described in nineteenth-century Istanbul and twentieth-century Izmir are clear retentions of Zar practices, which are infused with Sufi rituals and other localized Islamic components. This mixed cultural baggage was brought to the core urban centers of the Ottoman Empire from its northeast African periphery by

14. Ibid. For African-Turks in the region of Antalya, a study by Esma Durugönül is now in progress.
15. Behnaz A. Mirzai, "African Presence in Iran: Identity and Its Reconstruction in the 19th and 20th Centuries," *Revue française d'histoire d'outre-mer* (*RFHOM*), 89/336–337 (2002): 240–243.
16. For its classification as a "possession cult," see Gerda Sengers, *Women and Demons: Cult Healing in Islamic Egypt*, Leiden: E. J. Brill, 2003: 89; definition as "healing ritual" is on 279. See also contributions to Lewis et al., *Women's Medicine*.

the enslaved, an important part of whose origin-cultures had been Zar in its various forms. In the core areas, as elsewhere within the Empire, cre-olization continued on the communal level, reproducing new forms of Ottomanized Zars. But not all African retentions were Zar-related, and we shall also explore other components, such as the public festivals.

While resolving all issues concerning retention and creolization of African cultures in the core regions of the Ottoman Empire, we can still take the scholarly work done thus far a few steps further by asking, How, and from where, were various components of African cultures, including Zar, introduced into the major Ottoman urban centers and peripheral rural settlements? How did these components fuse with locally based Islamic rituals and beliefs? What was the role of such elements in the social, cul-tural, economic, and spiritual life of African communities in the Empire?

To form a better idea of the nature of Zar, we need to venture into the Ottoman frontier regions in northeast Africa, particularly the Sudan and Ethiopia. This seems to be where the cult in its nineteenth-century form originated and whence it entered the Empire via Egypt, the Hijaz, and the Persian Gulf. Most of the research on Zar has been done by an-thropologists, who observed ceremonies and interviewed members dur-ing the past half-century, with previous attempts going back to the early years of the twentieth century. For our limited purposes, the most useful studies are three, all dealing with Egypt and the Sudan: a little known but highly valuable book by the Egyptian anthropologist Fatima al-Misri; a much-cited monograph by Janice Boddy; and a recently published translation of a book by the Dutch scholar Gerda Sengers.[17] Building on these works and on Ottoman sources, I shall attempt to trace the path the cult had traveled from its Africa into the heart of the Empire.

Perched on the southern frontiers of the Ottoman Empire, the Sudan was the gateway for African people, commodities, and cultural practices entering the sultan's domains in the nineteenth century. Its proximity to, and strong contacts with, Egypt—one of the richest and most impor-tant Ottoman provinces—made the Sudan a convenient conduit for

17. Fatima al-Misri, *Az-Zar: Dirasa nafsiyya wa-anthrupulujiyya*, Cairo: Al-Hay'a al-Misriyya al-ʿAmma li-l-Kitab, 1975; Janice Boddy, *Wombs and Alien Spirits: Women, Men, and the* Zar *Cult in Northern Sudan*, Madison: University of Wis-consin Press, 1989; Sengers, *Women and Demons*.

inseminating with new ideas and practices other parts of the Empire, particularly the imperial capital and other core urban centers. Both the Sudan and Ethiopia had been supplying enslaved Africans to the eastern Mediterranean before the nineteenth century, but the volume increased dramatically during the early decades of that century.[18] The end of the age of Ottoman conquests at the turn of the eighteenth century and the drying up of Balkan sources of unfree labor shifted the focus of slavers to the peripheral regions of the Sudan, Ethiopia, and sub-Saharan Africa. Despite slavers' attempts to wipe out the history and culture of the enslaved, the reacculturation process to which they were subjected was only partially successful. First-generation retentions were passed on to the Ottoman-born second generation, and despite dilution and mixture, some key components—the cult of Zar included—survived well into the twentieth century.

Broadly defined, Zar is "a type of spirit, the illness it can cause, and the ritual by which the illness is assuaged; more generally, the 'cult' that surrounds such spirits."[19] Janice Boddy, a leading scholar on Zar, whose definition this one is, adds that "for those who observe and interact with spirits, as for those who experience possession, the human world is the foundation upon which the spirit world rests; it is ultimately the latter's source of meaning." Boddy distinguishes between "belief" and "ritual," or the closely related and the reflective. Because in both ritual and belief, participants act out real-life situations, Zar serves as a *symbolic* medium for *concrete* social issues in *specific* communities of discourse. For the northern Sudanese village that Boddy studied—and, by extension, for other communities in similar situations—the issues were mostly gender based, but some were also class related. Because trance rituals are allegorical, they reflect complex social realities and provide a license to act out what is normally forbidden to participants by prescribed normative behavior.[20]

18. For details, see Ehud R. Toledano, *The Ottoman Slave Trade and Its Suppression, 1840–1890*, Princeton: Princeton University Press, 1982: 14–90.
19. Boddy, *Wombs*, xxi. The following quotation is from p. 4, and other observations are derived from pp. 3–10.
20. On this, see also S. Ammar, "Psychiatrie et traitement traditionels en Tunisie," *Psychologie Medicale*, 16/7 (1984); and Sophie Ferchiou, "The Possession Cults of Tunisia: A Religious System Functioning as a System of Reference and a Social Field for Reforming Actions," in Lewis et al., *Women's Medicine*, 216–217.

Zar rituals may and do vary from one locale to another, although the basic performance patterns and belief systems in which it is embedded are quite similar. The similarities enable us to determine that the cult rituals observed in Ottoman core areas in the nineteenth and twentieth centuries are indeed variants of Zar practices imported from sub-Saharan and northeast African cultures. Most differences between local versions—even within the Nile Valley, let alone farther away—consist of "outward expression," as Boddy aptly puts it, "in the minutiae of dress, comportment, language, dance step, drum rhythm, and basketry design, among others."[21] But beyond the similarities of structure and purpose, two features are worth noting when comparing the Egyptian-Sudanese variants with the Istanbul-Izmir ones. One is derived from gender and class, the other from a fusion of Zar beliefs and versions of local Islams. With both these features, the fact that within the Ottoman Empire, Zar-practicing communities were made up of enslaved or freed Africans is significant.

The main protagonists in Zar belief and ritual are:

- the possessed person, usually a woman
- the healer or leader of the ritual, also more often than not a woman
- the possessing spirit—more often male than female—who enters the body of the possessed and gains control over it
- the group that participates in the ritual
- the *physically absent* but psychologically present family and immediate social circle of the possessed person
- the outside community, whose *invisible presence* affects much of the content of the ritual

By adding at the end the two absent or invisible actors into the Zar scene, I have, in what follows, incorporated the results of the leading studies on Zar in the Egyptian-Sudanese context.[22]

Current scholarship on Zar seems to endorse the view that the healing

21. Boddy, *Wombs,* 10.
22. Mainly those studies are Boddy, *Wombs,* 4–10, 125–266; and Sengers, *Women and Demons,* 80–122 (for a critical survey of the literature, see pp. 59–80). Sengers cites Dervisch's study on Zar in former Zaire (85–88), which provides a similar interpretation.

rituals performed in Zar reflect both the social predicament of the possessed and the concerns of her community. Despite nuanced differences,
most writers also agree that the purpose of the healer's intervention is to
mediate between the spirit and the possessed person so that they can negotiate a peaceful coexistence of sorts, which would enable the possessed
to cope with problems in her daily life. Both Boddy and Sengers call the
healing process "pacification" to distinguish it from "exorcism," which is
intended to get rid of the possessing demon altogether.[23] At least for Sengers, this temporary nature of Zar healing is crucial, leading her to classify
it not as a transition or passage rite but rather as what she calls a maintenance ritual. Maintenance rituals, she explains, do not produce "long-term
change" but instead "lead to a temporary discharge of psychological
and/or social tension."[24]

By admitting the "imagined worlds" of family and community into
the interpretation of Zar, I would argue, the door is thrown wide open to
any and all social and cultural contents, which allows us to account for
locally based variants of Zar throughout the Ottoman and post-Ottoman
Middle East. It is through this door, too, that we can bring in the impact
of gender and class and account for the fusion of vernacular Islamic
practices with Zar rituals and beliefs. The Zar scholars whose works are
cited here agree that the overwhelming majority of Zar practitioners
were women, though belief in the existence of spirits was widespread
and crossed gender lines. Some believe that in Ottoman times, the cult
was popular mainly among urban and well-to-do women, and others observe that later it gained wide reception among the poor rather, both
rural and urban. In any event, Zar begs for a gender-based interpretation, as both Boddy and Sengers convincingly show.[25] The weakened
position of women vis-à-vis men in African societies led women to seek
unconventional modes of expression, whether to vent their frustration
and make a protest or to create a space of their own for spiritual gratification and empowerment.

In the excluded and protected space provided by Zar rituals, women

23. Boddy, *Wombs*, 131; Sengers, *Women and Demons*, 23, 65.
24. Sengers, *Women and Demons*, 121.
25. Boddy, *Wombs*, 4–5, 389–390 (q.v., "Gender"); Sengers, *Women and Demons*,
    65, 299 (q.v., "Gender").

allowed themselves behavior that was totally incommensurate with their normal conduct. Boddy lists the following as being the most salient features of irregular behavior by women in Zar rituals: "smoking, wanton dancing, flailing about, burping and hiccupping, drinking blood and alcohol, wearing male clothing, publicly threatening men with swords, speaking loudly, [and] lacking due regard for etiquette."[26] This license to break with norms is granted because the possessed women are not held accountable for the infringements they commit under the orders of the spirit that possesses them. Adorned by costumes and ornaments and immersed in music and incense, the place is readily recognizable to participants and observers as a separate space where a different, socially liberating set of rules applies. Through the medium of the healer/leader and the spirits, role reversal becomes possible and acceptable; it takes place in a theater-type event that ends when the lights go out and the curtain draws down. The ritual is supposed to affect life for the healed person, who now can better interact with the real (not the imagined) world and the people (not just the spirits) that inhabit it.

In the Ottoman Empire, including Egypt and the Sudan, real people were immersed in a belief system predicated upon local interpretations and adjustments of Islamic tenets and norms. For the imperial elite, the Ottoman-Local elites, and the larger societies in which they lived, an important component of these vernacular forms of Islam (sometimes called "islams")—as opposed to one, universal, essentialized Islam—was the spiritual-mystical-experiential space that the Sufi orders created. In city, town, and village alike, Sufism as practice and belief system formed the backbone of social life. It was for the overwhelming majority of the people their way of relating to, and understanding, Islam. Small wonder, then, that writers on Zar could not but address the similarities and differences between Zar rituals and Sufi *dhikr*s. (*Dhikr*, the literary Arabic term, was colloquially pronounced in Turkish as *zikr*.)

Boddy found that Zar rituals resemble the zikr among the Qadiriyya and Khatimiyya orders of the Sudan but that the zikr "lacks their cohesion and transcendent focus."[27] Behnaz Mirzai lists a number of cases

26. Boddy, *Wombs*, 131.
27. Ibid.

from Iran in which Zar and Sufi rituals were fused, in Baluchistan, for example, where the most common possessing spirit was known as *Gwat* and the songs performed to exorcize it were in praise of the founder of the Qadiriyya Sufi order and of a famous Iranian Sufi leader.[28] Gwati possession-healing was performed by enslaved Africans with song and music for a number of days and nights. Sengers points out the similar nature of the zikr among the Moroccan Hamadsha Sufis and the Egyptian Zar but emphatically places the zikr in a different category from Zar rituals.[29] John Hunwick and Ismael Montana stress the *Bori*-Sufi hybridity of various cults-cum-orders in North Africa, with the Tunisian Stambali and the Moroccan 'Isawiyya orders (Arabic, *turuq*) as the prime examples.[30] The Bori-zikr sessions of the Stambali completely integrated notions from both genres of music, for example, by introducing a "Bori section" (Arabic, *nawbat al-Bori*) as one of the musical phases in the zikr session.

Beyond the difference in style and tempo, Sengers argues—and even though some of her informants referred to Zar as *zikr harim* (women's zikr)—Sufi rituals are well grounded in Islamic tradition and fully imbued with references to God's names and the Prophet's spirit, whereas Zar is situated outside that domain. Although Sufi zikrs contain an element of healing and although trance is present, the main purpose is to attain a closer relationship with God through an Islamic framework. By comparison, Zar is all about possession, healing, and trance, with residual vernacular Islamic features that are not germane to the ritual itself. In my view, Zar existed and can exist without Islamic elements (as in non-Muslim societies), but there can be no Sufi zikr without the Islamic content. Whereas Zar-Bori leads to *individual* trance (mostly a women's *affliction*), zikr leads to *collective* trance (a higher *achievement*, mostly accomplished by men).[31] As a generalization,

28. Mirzai, "African Presence," 229–246 (*Gwati* rituals are treated on pp. 243–244).
29. Sengers, *Women and Demons*, 65, 102, 184–185, 252.
30. Hunwick, "Religious Practices," 159–160, 162–167 (Hunwick speculates that Stambali may be related to Stambuli, i.e., from Istanbul, on p. 159); Ismael Musa Montana, "Ahmad ibn al-Qadi al-Timbuktawi on the *Bori* Ceremonies of Tunis," in Lovejoy, *Slavery on Frontiers*, 185.
31. Lewis, "*Zar* in Context," 8 (the emphases and slight rewording are mine).

too, Zar and Bori are mainly possession cults, whereas zikr is primarily a trance ritual.[32] That said, our concern here is not to compare the two but to explore the evolving relationship between Zar-Bori and Sufi zikr as a process of cultural creolization.[33]

Fusion had already occurred in the peripheral regions of the Nile Valley whence the cult entered the Ottoman Empire, picking up on the way local materials and braiding them into the rudimentary structure of Zar. Peripheral forms from Sufi rituals met with Zar as enslaved Ethiopians and Sudanese were forcibly dragged into the Ottoman-Egyptian Sudan and then into Ottoman Egypt itself. The accretion probably began in the early 1820s, after Mehmet Ali Paşa (who ruled Ottoman Egypt from 1805 to 1849) conquered the Sudan and began to recruit enslaved men into his army.[34] By and large, scholars agree that as people and goods moved northward in the Nile Valley, the west African Bori mixed with the Ethiopian Zar to produce a hybrid possession-healing cult with a variety of beliefs, rituals, and practices. That merged type poured into the northern Sudan and Egypt and from there spread into the Ottoman domains of the Middle East, mostly with the enslaved Africans but also with pilgrims to Holy Cities in the Hijaz.[35] Variously referred to as either Zar or Bori and without much

32. For a global typology of trance and possession, see Erika Bourguignon, "World Distribution and Patterns of Possession States," in Prince (ed.), *Trance and Possession States*, 3–34 (especially 4–18). For the psychiatric diagnostic and therapy dimensions, see A. Kiev (ed.), *Magic, Faith and Healing: Studies in Primitive Psychiatry Today*, New York: Free Press; London: Collier-Macmillan, 1964 (a revised edition was published by Jason Aronson in 1996).

33. Let me here stress the importance of the edited collection Lewis et al., *Women's Medicine*. Many of the contributors discuss the variants produced by cultural syncretism, mainly in North Africa, the Sudan, and Egypt.

34. On Mehmet Ali's Sudanese campaign, see Khaled Fahmy, *All the Pasha's Men: Mehmed Ali, His Army and the Making of Modern Egypt*, Cambridge: Cambridge University Press, 1997: 38 ff.; Ehud R. Toledano, "Mehmed Ali Pasha," *Encyclopaedia of Islam*, 2nd ed., vol. 7, Leiden: E. J. Brill, 1991): 425; and ʿImad Ahmad Hilal, *Ar-raqiq fi Misr fi-l-qarn at-tasiʿ ashar*, Cairo: Al-ʿArabi, 1999: 35–37.

35. See mainly the contributions to Lewis et al., *Women's Medicine*, led by the editor himself in "*Zar* in Context," (on the Zar-Bori "merger," see p. 2; on dissemination, see pp. 3 and 14).

attention to difference, many observers preferred to write Zar-Bori and describe what they saw and understood. Although I shall try to be as accurate as possible, the categories and the terminology do tend often to overlap.

Fatima al-Misri, whose interesting study on Zar in Egypt seems to have been largely forgotten by more recent Zar researchers, convincingly argues that Zar was unknown in Egypt before the Ottoman-Egyptian occupation of the Sudan in the early 1820s.[36] None of the available ethnographic accounts of Egypt in the first half of the nineteenth century, she asserts, mention a Zar-resembling phenomenon. These accounts are the authoritative *Description de l'Egypte,* compiled by the French experts who accompanied Bonaparte in 1798–1801, William Lane's classic *Manners and Customs of the Modern Egyptians,* and the well-known report by Sir John Bowring. Because they are all famous for their attention to detail, the absence of Zar references in them leads al-Misri to conclude that Zar entered Egypt with the Sudanese soldiers and the other enslaved Africans who were dragged in via Ethiopia and the Nile Valley. Richard Natvig, who worked on the history of Zar in Egypt, also believes that the cult was introduced to Egypt in the first half of the nineteenth century and that its spread was linked to the slave trade into the Ottoman Empire and possibly also to the Amhara-Oromo struggle in Ethiopia.[37]

Thus, from the very start, Zar practice formed an integral part of the enslaved culture that came into contact with the vernacular forms of Islam practiced along the road into Ottoman territory. In the case of some Africans from the central Sudan, Bori—a spirit-possession cult of the *maguzawa,* which gave it non-Muslim Hausa origins—was resistant to integration, as Paul Lovejoy suggests. But in most other cases, as he himself recognizes, an elaborate and profound creolization took place in both North Africa and the Middle East under Ottoman rule. John Hunwick demonstrates how common the fusion of Zar and Bori rituals was with Sufi practices during the nineteenth century in both these regions, and Montana shows that such practices were deeply ingrained in Tunisian

36. Al-Misri, *Az-Zar.* The dating argument is made on pp. 26–30.
37. Richard Natvig, "Some Notes on the History of the *Zar* Cult in Egypt," in Lewis et al., *Women's Medicine,* 178–188.

society in the same period.[38] In fact, Bori interacted both with the many popular rural variants of Islamic praxis and, later, with the urban variants that were present in Ottoman-Local elite households. When enslaved Africans were sold into households at the core—in Istanbul, Izmir, Salonika, Aleppo, Damascus—Zar rituals were further exposed to elements from urban Ottoman-Islamic cultures. All this accounts for the versions of Zar that travelers and other observers reported from across the Empire.

Since Sufi practices were common in Ottoman societies, themes from all walks of life and different orders were also expressed in Zar rituals. Whereas orthodoxy was willing—with varying degrees of reluctance—to accept Sufism as a legitimate component of Islamic life, Zar was generally rejected and condemned as un-Islamic. The treatises compiled by the scholar-jurist Ahmad ibn al-Qadi al-Timbuktawi, who visited the Ottoman Regency of Tunis in 1808–9, support this point.[39] In these works, al-Timbuktawi railed against the retention of the Bori cult by enslaved Africans and its spread through Tunisian society. He charged that these practices were unbelief and heresy and called on the Bey of Tunis, Hamuda Paşa, to act strongly to eradicate them. The bey and the Tunisian ulama were then already coming under attack from Wahhabi puritanism owing to the popularity of Sufism and Maraboutism in the Regency, but here al-Timbuktawi did not share the criticism, positioning himself in the middle: while accepting Sufism as a legitimate part of proper Islamic belief and practice, he fiercely rejected Bori.

It is now quite clear that we need to adjust our analysis of Zar-Bori to gender and class differentiation, in part because these practices were generally regarded as the domain of uneducated and superstitious women.[40] Indeed, integration of women into Ottoman and post-Ottoman societies

38. Lovejoy's point is in Lovejoy, *Slavery on Frontiers*, 19–20; studies on North Africa fusions by Abdeljelil Temimi, E. Dermenghem, Keiko Takaki, and others are cited in ibid., 30 nn. 41 and 42. For Hunwick's observations, see Hunwick, "Religious Practices," 167. Montana's article is "Ahmad ibn al-Qadi al-Timbuktawi."

39. Points in this paragraph are based on Montana, "Ahmad ibn al-Qadi al-Timbuktawi," 173 ff., 186, 188–194.

40. Sengers, *Women and Demons*, 22, 65.

seems to have lagged behind that of men, at least in most cases for which we have reliable historical evidence. Zar was considerably more prevalent among enslaved African women than among the men, but this was not only because females were the overwhelming majority among the enslaved carried into the Ottoman Empire in the nineteenth century. I. M. Lewis aptly describes the common sociocultural factor in possession as "the experience of identity-threatening stress, exacerbated by conditions of confinement and exclusion."[41] Enslaved women fit the model. For them, as for other women in Ottoman societies, Zar-Bori offered an opportunity to break away from the confines of home and family, act out their pent-up desires, and get the attention they were being denied. Simultaneously, and perhaps paradoxically, Zar-Bori also enabled women "to adjust to and accept pressures in ways which do not radically challenge the existing, male-dominated order."

Whereas in general Sufi zikr, Quran healing, and other practices condoned by Islamic *doxy* were largely in men's domain, Zar-Bori, the women's source of comfort, was either opposed or just tolerated by Islamic-Ottoman orthodoxy. Without attempting to infer broader gender characteristics, it seems that men tended to prefer *exorcism* as a cure for possession; it deals with the problem in one step and with little expense or ceremony. On the other hand, women seemed inclined toward the more long-term, inconclusive, and open-ended healing of possession by *adorcism,* or pacification through cult payment to the spirits. Adorcism entailed an understanding that there were no drastic solutions to problems and that piecemeal management of them was perhaps more effective, if costly and elaborate.

It is not surprising that women who attended Zar rituals considered themselves to be "good Muslims," and given some of the content of these

41. Lewis, "*Zar* in Context," 10 (this paragraph and the next also include other observations by Lewis from pp. 1–16). In this context see also Joseph C. Miller, "Retention, Re-invention, and Remembering: Restoring Identities through Enslavement in Africa and under Slavery in Brazil," in José C. Curto and Paul E. Lovejoy (eds.), *Enslaving Connections: Changing Cultures of Africa and Brazil during the Era of Slavery,* Amherst, N.Y.: Prometheus/Humanity Books, 2003: 81–121; and James H. Sweet, *Recreating Africa: Culture, Kinship, and Religion in the African-Portuguese World, 1441–1770,* Chapel Hill: University of North Carolina Press, 2003.

events, this identification with Islam should not be dismissed lightly. An element of Islamic legitimacy was embodied in the person of the kudya, or godya, the Zar healing priestess.[42] In Egypt, these were pious women, often ones who had performed the pilgrimage to the holy sites of Islam in Mecca and Medina and bore the epithet "pilgrim" (Arabic, *hajja*). Kudyas were frequently of Sudanese or Ethiopian extraction; they dressed in white, appeared to be devoutly Muslim, and were well versed in popular-style religious talk. One of al-Misri's informants, a kudya named Hajja Sacada, was the sister of Hajj Muhanna, the shaykh of the Qadiriyya Sufi order. The two women were the best-known Zar practitioners in Egypt in the 1970s, and they used to communicate with Zar spirits by reciting verses in praise of the Prophet.

Not infrequently, participants cleaned themselves before Zar rituals as Muslims do before prayer (Arabic, *wudu'*). Following the initial stage of dancing and trance, the kudya would calm down the participants, then lead them in reciting the *Fatiha,* the opening chapter of the Quran. As the ritual progressed, the Fatiha was recited many times, on each occasion in honor of another Islamic personage, beginning with the Prophet and moving on to his family and various leading and local Sufi saints and other public figures. This infusion of Islamic elements into the Zar-Bori ritual is reminiscent of what Kathryn McKnight calls African-Catholic syncretism.[43] Referring to seventeenth-century Cartagena de Indias, she describes a common phenomenon of injecting prayer components into indigenous healing practices. Specifically, in the case of Mateo de Arará, brought before the Inquisition Tribunal in mid-century, the man was accused of performing a ritual considered diabolical. The action was well grounded in a shamanic African ritual intended to extract from a group of people a *yerbatero* (a person using herbs to cause harm). This was done by uttering words and manipulating a little broom, but during the ritual Mateo also invoked "the Virgin Mary, Our Lord Jesus Christ."

42. The following information is provided in al-Misri, *Az-Zar,* 48, 61, 65; and Hunwick, "Religious Practices," 166–167. For purification before prayer, see Modarressi, "Zar Cult," 153.
43. Kathryn Joy McKnight, "'*En su tierra lo aprendió*': An African Curandero's Defense before the Cartagena Inquisition," *Colonial Latin American Review,* 12/1 (June 2003), 79.

In the African-Ottoman Zar-Bori ritual, invocations of the Fatiha were followed by the singing and playing of musical instruments, to please and pacify the possessing spirits. These spirits were of several types and categories, but most of them were male. The most intriguing category for us here is the one that included contemporary figures such as various Ottoman officeholders—governors, ministers, men of religion.[44] In this category we also find a name that keeps coming up in reports about Zar rituals in both Istanbul and Izmir. Unable to contextualize that specific spirit, observers recorded its name in the corrupt form they heard it in, as Yavroubé, which Erdem took as a mispronunciation of the Turkish *Yavru Bey*, or "infant god."[45] I would argue that the name is much more likely to have been Yaver Bey, which is the title of a high-ranking Ottoman military officer, an aide-de-camp, pronounced in the Arabic dialects of Egypt and the Sudan as Yawer—or Yawra—Bey.[46]

In a song cited by al-Misri, the Ottoman military context is obvious, with Yaver Bey appearing in a military column, on horseback, surrounded by guards, wearing a fez, carrying a golden seal, and adorned with other paraphernalia.[47] Given the fact that from the early 1820s enslaved soldiers served in Mehmet Ali's army and that Africans continued to serve under Mehmet Ali's Ottoman-Egyptian heirs, it is only reasonable to expect such soldiers and their families to have incorporated into Zar rituals the dominant figure of their aide-de-camp. Another reminder of this reverberation of Ottoman military themes in Zar rituals comes from a Sudanese branch of the cult.[48] There, the leader of the ritual is a man called in Arabic the *sanjak* (Turkish, *sancak*), clearly an adoption of a senior Ottoman military rank that the enslaved and freed African soldiers came to know in the Ottoman-Egyptian armies of Mehmet Ali Paşa and his successors, into which they had been forcibly drafted in the nineteenth century. The sanjak in that cult was endowed with great

44. Sengers, *Women and Demons*, 69–71, 259–263.
45. Erdem, *Slavery*, 174–175.
46. This is, incidentally, also the name of the interim president of Iraq, Ghazi A. al-Yawer, which indicates the past association of his family with the Ottoman administration of Iraq.
47. The poem referred to is in al-Misri, *Az-Zar*, 261–262 (number 9).
48. Sengers, *Women and Demons*, 90 (citing Gabriele Böhringer-Thärigen's *Besessene Frauen: Der Zar-Kult von Omdurman* from 1996).

physical strength, which enabled him to overpower the bad spirits that caused grave illnesses. In Tunis, too, though less specifically perhaps, the spirit hierarchy reflected power relationships within the Ottoman governing elite of the province.[49]

An informant from northern Sudan reveals the fluidity and lack of specificity in the perception of spirits, to some extent also of Yaver Bey.[50] The possessed woman, Nura, says that Yaver Bey "makes people tired," and his father is Hakim Basha (Turkish, Hekim Paşa, or Hekim Başı), a doctor wearing or holding a stethoscope and wearing a fez. All these attributes keep Yaver safely within an Ottoman military context, possibly with the aide-de-camp supervising the soldiers as they were performing physically demanding drills, wearing them down so that some of them consequently could have required medical attention from the doctor, or Hakim Basha, for exhaustion and related afflictions. However, as the context of Ottoman officialdom comes into sharp relief, a new ambiguity is injected into the scene. This only enhances the mystique of Zar and reopens the question of Yaver Bey's true identity, if it is at all possible to establish the true identity of Zar spirits. Thus, Nura tells us that Yaver demands green clothes, like the Green Sultan, commenting that green is the color of Islam, then hedging: "But it is not clear whether this sultan has anything to do with Islam. Perhaps he is the equivalent of an Islamic saint." And, finally, blurring all boundaries, Nura ponders Yaver's demand for green clothes: "Perhaps he and the Green Sultan are one and the same."

Thus, the cult of Yaver Bey was carried over with the enslaved from the periphery of the Ottoman-Egyptian Sudan, through rural and urban Egypt, into the Ottoman heartland and core cities. There, the "Ottoman Zar" figure was even upgraded to a major Zar spirit, appearing in most accounts of African-Ottoman cult rituals. Not surprisingly, a grafted, creolized, localized-Ottomanized-Islamized Zar gained a foothold within Ottoman-imperial and Ottoman-Local households. Before we deal with the manifestations of this in core areas, we need to look for a moment into the impact Zar had along the route, in Ottoman Egypt and the circles

49. Montana, "Ahmad ibn al-Qadi al-Timbuktawi," 180.
50. Sengers, *Women and Demons*, 93–96 (specific reference to Yawra Bey is on pp. 94–95).

of the Ottoman-Egyptian elite. Al-Misri provides a fascinating example of a Zar ritual performed for one of Khedive Ismail's daughters.[51] The princess was old and dying, and when all doctors failed to cure her and conventional means were exhausted, her harem ladies prevailed upon her to try a Zar healing ritual. A team of three kudyas was summoned to the palace and for two weeks performed Zar rituals in the presence of household members only, with the active participation of the enslaved Africans among them. Although a male spirit was supposedly exorcised from the old princess's body, she continued to suffer, her health deteriorating even further until she succumbed to her illness and died.

This account shows how effectively creolized Zar was woven into Ottoman-Egyptian culture during the nineteenth century; despite physical and mental distances, cultural penetration did occur. The main vehicle was enslaved African women, who were being imported in growing numbers into Egypt and the rest of the Ottoman Empire from the Sudan and Ethiopia. In our case, boundaries of class, culture, and education were breached:

- The crossing of a *class boundary* is demonstrated by the kudyas' transition—by carriage—from the poorer part of Cairo where they resided to the palace, which was located in the affluent and more central part of the city.
- The breaching of a *cultural boundary* is shown by the note that was innocuously inserted into the text, indicating that the words the kudyas uttered during the ritual were spoken in Arabic but had to be translated into Turkish so that the princess would understand.
- The positioning of Zar as a *counterculture to modernity and European education* is pinpointed by the appearance of an educated relative of the princess, who was weeping helplessly because she was so outnumbered by those family members who insisted on the ritual continuing despite the deterioration in the princess' condition.

For the Ottoman-Egyptian elite, it appears, Zar became either a form of entertainment and a pastime or a resort for healing when all else failed.

Another Zar ritual story, also cited by al-Misri, takes place at the house of a less prominent family, but still one that had several enslaved

51. Al-Misri, *Az-Zar*, 57–58.

persons in its service.[52] Enslaved African women seem to have had a greater role in this event, for one of them came into the middle of the circle and—acting as a *possessing* spirit—aggressively exclaimed that she would not cook unless given a silver ladle, nor would she do the laundry if not provided with a silver mangle. Speaking for the Zar spirit, the enslaved woman further threatened that if not placated, she would blind the possessed lady of the house and not let her rise from the floor. The participants immediately began to plead with the enslaved person, kissing her hands and asking forgiveness, but she rejected them, becoming even more aggressive and antagonistic. The enslaved woman finally calmed down only when the kudya herself promised her that all she was asking for would be brought in for the next session the following week.

At that point in the story, the participant-informant turned to one of the other ladies and expressed her shock at the audacity of the enslaved woman, asking, "How come a slave can have such power [over other, free people]?" The question was met with surprise, and she was hushed for fear of infuriating the Zar spirits present, commonly referred to as "the masters" (Arabic, *al-asyad*).[53] Here we have a feature of Zar that was especially relevant to enslaved persons, in that it enabled temporary role-reversal. In that episode, the enslaved woman became a powerful slaver making demands on the ladies who belonged to the social circle of her mistress and on whom she would normally be attending. Now under the liberating rules of the Zar ritual, it was they who had to beseech her to be merciful, who had to cater to her whims. In that socially suspended space and for those brief moments in time, it was they who had to kiss her hands, beg her to accept their homage, and placate her in every possible way. Although the empowerment was certainly temporary, it nonetheless reminded slavers and enslaved alike that they were accountable to superior powers. Unlike God and the Prophet, "the masters" were less rational, much more capricious, and always lurking in the background, poised to possess the remiss.

The fusing of Zar practices, or what could perhaps be termed Zar

---

52. Ibid., 33–36 (conversation cited is on pp. 35–36).
53. Hunwick (citing René Brunel's *Essai sur la confrérie religieuse des 'Aîssâoûa au Maroc* [1926]) mentions *ajwad* (generous ones) as another epithet for them ("Religious Practices," 165).

cult formation, becomes more comprehensible if we follow it along the routes it traveled from source to target societies, adding to its development along a historical time line. Early twentieth-century accounts indicate that there existed in the Sudan two types of Zar cults: Zar-Bori, which was more akin to the Hausa possession cult of west Africa; and *Zar-tambura* (sometimes *tumbura*), which followed Zar as practiced in Ethiopia.[54] Zar-Bori was a women's cult, while Zar-tambura was a mixed one, like the tambura band that played in Zar rituals. With time, and as these cults made their way into Egypt, they appear to have combined into one, and both Sengers and al-Misri assert that there is no question of there having been more than one cult of Zar in twentieth-century Egypt.[55] Al-Misri calls the subbranches of Zar in Egypt "orders" (Arabic, *tara'iq;* singular, *tariqa*), applying the same term commonly used for Sufi orders. She mentions four such orders, which might have been separate cults that merged into one.

Further into the Ottoman heartlands, however, we can distinguish at least some retentions of earlier Zar cults, which in different cities did not merge into a single practice. For example, the state of trance was called *boru* in Izmir but *baba* in Istanbul,[56] which may indicate a case of reversal during fusion and localization, or creolization. Like in the Ethiopian Zar-tambura, the Izmir cult allowed men and women as both members and godyas (kolbaşıs), but it used the trance term from the Hausa Zar-Bori. In Istanbul, the evidence seems to indicate that only women could become cult members and godyas, just as in Zar-Bori, though the term used for trance, *baba,* is not found in the Sudanese-Egyptian sources. The closest we can get to the latter term is in Zar songs, where in some Sudanese and Upper-Egyptian texts there is an appeal to a spirit addressed as *baba.*[57] According to Sengers, however, the core practices of these cults are quite similar despite some organizational

54. For a historical account of the following, see Pamela Constantinides, "The History of Zar in the Sudan: Theories of Origin, Recorded Observation and Oral Tradition," in Lewis et al., *Women's Medicine,* 83–99 (especially 89 ff.); and Natvig, "Some Notes." See also sources cited in Sengers, *Women and Demons,* 89–90.

55. Sengers, *Women and Demons,* 90; al-Misri, *Az-Zar,* 66.

56. Güneş, "Kölelikten Özgülüğe," 6.

57. Al-Misri, *Az-Zar,* 260 (number 5, from Upper Egypt) and 262–263 (from the Sudan).

differences. Also, the demonology repertoire in Hausa Bori is more elaborate than the Ethiopian-Sudanese Zar observed in Ottoman and modern Egypt.[58]

Other African cultural elements seem to have been retained in both Zar rituals and public festivals as practiced in Istanbul and Izmir in the late nineteenth and early twentieth centuries in that important roles were assigned to blood, fire, music, and dance. Güneş accepts the view of earlier writers that the Calf Festival had its origins in the ancient civilizations of the Nile Valley, developing out of an ancient Egyptian annual sacrifice of a girl—adorned and then ceremoniously thrown into the river—to fend off drought and ensure a good harvest.[59] As human sacrifice became unacceptable in later times, this theory goes, the adorned calf replaced the girl, and the ceremony was passed on in many cultures across the continent of Africa. Whether true or not, the adorned calf invites a comparison with the story of the Golden Calf—familiar to Muslims, Christians, and Jews from the Bible and the Quran—although there, sacrifice was offered to the calf itself as a deity.

Though tracing the origins of these pagan practices is way beyond the scope and purpose of this book, we can hardly fail to notice the striking similarities that keep recurring in the rituals, often leading—or misleading—the observer to think that all of them have one basic pattern, that a specific model keeps resurfacing in different places at different times. For example, Speros Vryonis Jr. convincingly argues that underneath a thin layer of orthodoxy, both in the Christian Balkans and in Muslim Anatolia between the fourteenth and the sixteenth centuries, the "masses" of peasants and nomads were deeply attached to pagan forms of religion and spirituality.[60] "The tribal religious *baba*, usually in dervish form," he writes, "was in fact the old tribal shaman who communicated with the supernatural forces and constrained them." Is this, we may wonder, the predecessor of the baba in Zar rituals that conferred

---

58. Sengers, *Women and Demons*, 90.

59. Güneş, "Kölelikten Özgülüğe," 6–7.

60. Speros Vryonis Jr., "Religious Changes and Patterns in the Balkans, 14th–16th Centuries," in Henrik Birnbaum and Speros Vryonis Jr. (eds.), *Aspects of the Balkans: Continuity and Change*, The Hague: Mouton, 1972: 151–176 (the quotation is from 161).

on possessed African persons in Ottoman societies the term *babalı?* Likely, perhaps, but hard to establish historically. Were the African-Ottoman kolbaşıs heirs to the shamans and dervishes who roamed the plains of Asia Minor, not just to African predecessors? This is a fascinating conjecture but even harder to substantiate.

If we look for regional antecedents of the Calf Festival, we can find several such instances. Again, Vryonis strongly argues for continuation and retention in this, too.[61] "Propitiatory animal sacrifice (*thysia, kurban*)," he asserts, "is one of the remarkably stable factors in the folk religion of Greeks, Armenians, and Balkan Slavs, from antiquity until early modern times." Citing a sixteenth-century Croatian who lived as an enslaved man in the Ottoman Empire, Vryonis believes that the specific type of animal sacrifice practiced by Muslims in Anatolia was passed over from popular Christianity. In the ritual, the animal was cooked, rather than burnt, and its parts were divided among the poor, the neighbors, and the priest.

This may support the tentative suggestion that the Izmir Calf Festival had some regional antecedents. It appears at first glance that the festival, as it was still observed in Izmir well into the twentieth century, had a modern-ancient parallel in the Anastenarides, which was celebrated by Bulgars and Greeks in Thrace. Anastenarides took place in May, like the Izmir festival, and was "accompanied by animal sacrifice, dance-induced ecstasy, fire-walking (*pyrobasia*), and *oreibasia* (nocturnal wandering in the mountains)." Byzantine chronicles of the twelfth century describe these ceremonies, as do modern observers, and scholarly studies accept their pre-Christian, Dionysian character. So, was the Calf Festival an African retention, or did it have some link to ancient local traditions? Although further research is needed, I am inclined to think that the festival was originally an African tradition, because it was practiced and maintained by Africans, whereas others joined in only as spectators and noncore participants. The similarities with the Anastenarides would then have to be considered incidental, probably stemming from the common patterns of many ancient beliefs and rituals.

The annual Bori festival celebrated in Tunis may reinforce this

61. Information in this and the following paragraphs is based on ibid., 156–157, 174–175.

view.[62] Once a year, Bori adepts used to gather from all over the province in the month of Şaban (Arabic, Shaʿban) and perform a visitation and sacrifice combined with trance-healing Bori rituals. The time was picked according to the Muslim calendar to coincide with the Prophet's birthday and the period leading to Ramadan, the month of fasting; the May Calf Festival, in contrast, was apparently season determined. Enslaved and freed Africans in Tunis slaughtered a male goat instead of a calf, but with similar motions and procedures. In Tunis, the ceremony was further Islamized by the adoption of a local patron-saint, Sidi Saʿd, at whose tomb on the Mornag Plain the festivities were held. An evil spirit incarnating the patron and called Bu Saʿdiyya played an important role in the various rituals during the visitation (Arabic, *ziyara*). The repertoire of these annual events in Tunis, Izmir, Ulcinj, and probably in other places with a critical mass of African population displayed similar attractions, such as music and dance performances, including *capoeira*-style dance-fights, fire plays, and what Hunwick called saturnalia.[63] Thus, it seems that the immediate inspiration for these annual festivals came from Africa not only in Ottoman North Africa but also in the eastern Mediterranean, including Izmir.

Be that as it may, the issue of origin is less significant than the role of blood, which is part and parcel of any animal sacrifice. In both the private Zar ritual and the public African festival, spilling blood, drinking it, dipping fingers in it, or spreading it over body areas were—all or in part—an important component of the act.[64] In all interpretations of such rituals, blood symbolism is accorded a major place. Without elaborating the issue, we need, however, to note that a duality is posited between good/pure and bad/impure blood, as blood signifies femininity, fertility, life, but is also the carrier of demons into the body, hence out of it too.

---

62. For Tunis, see Montana, "Ahmad ibn al-Qadi al-Timbuktawi," 180 (drawn from Timbuktawi); and Hunwick, "Religious Practices," 159–160, 165–167 (based on studies by G. Zawadowski from 1943 and René Brunel from 1926). For the festivals of Ulcinj, see Alexander Lopashich, "A Negro Community in Yugoslavia," *Man*, 58 (1958): 169–173.

63. Joseph C. Miller thinks a comparison to *candomblé* is more appropriate than a comparison to capoeira (personal communication, March 2005).

64. See, for example, Sengers, *Women and Demons*, 111; Hunwick, "Religious Practices," 153 ff.

Like Jewish mysticism, Islamic occult traditions also acknowledge the existence of demons (*jinns* and *'ifrits*) and provide methods of exorcizing them. Thus, in Quran healing, drawing a drop of blood from a finger or a toe enables the jinn to get out of the body, and healers justify the practice on the basis of a hadith attributed to the Prophet Muhammad.[65]

Boddy suggests that spilling the blood of sacrificial animals during Zar rituals symbolizes both the Zar spirit and the patient and forms a necessary part of the healing process. Its effects are passed to the other participants, who not only touch and smear the blood over parts of their bodies but—despite religious prohibition—also take a sip of it.[66] Whereas the purpose of animal sacrifice, especially of chickens and roosters,[67] and blood touching in Zar rituals is to serve in healing the possessed individual, it seems that sacrifice and blood in public festivals have a collective function. Since on such public occasions no specific person was being targeted for healing, or so it appears, touching the blood of the slaughtered calf and distributing its cooked meat to the congregants serves a broader, communal purpose. Extrapolating from both the Zar ritual and the festival origin myth, that purpose seems to have been to provide a protective measure, renewable every year, against ills befalling the community, the town, the village.

Music and dance were also common to both the private Zar ritual and the public festival. Zar healing is produced through the resolution of a conflict within both body and mind, and for that resolution song and dance are the required vehicle.[68] Dance and song, writes Sengers, "transport the body beyond its own boundaries and living world," employing "rhythm, tempo, movement, intonation and melody" to "strengthen body and mind." But rather than dwell separately on the impact of music, words, dance, or incense, an understanding of the ritual can perhaps be gained by stressing their combined effect, the unity of the experience. Since possession takes over body, soul, and mind, a person can be

65. For a discussion of blood symbolism, see Boddy, *Wombs*, 61–70, 100–106, and Sengers, 165. For the practice of drawing blood to get rid of a demon, see Sengers, *Women and Demons*, 130, 153.
66. Boddy, *Wombs*, 333.
67. As noted in McKnight, "'*En su tierra lo aprendió*,'" 73 (citing several anthropological studies of West African cultures).
68. See, for example, Sengers, *Women and Demons*, 173.

healed only by addressing all aspects of the self. To pacify the spirit it is necessary to appeal to all senses and to "negotiate" a new modus vivendi between the possessor and the possessed, as between the possessed and the community in which he or she lives. But it is also necessary to look after the well-being of the community itself, as it seems to be the purpose of the public festivals.

Observers of the Izmir Calf Festival described the dances performed as being quite different from Turkish and Anatolian folk dancing, which suggests an African origin.[69] From a description of these performances, one cannot escape a comparison with capoeira dancing, brought from west Africa to Brazil and associated with the culture of enslaved Africans.[70] The dances observed in Izmir included dance-fighting with dancers aiming sticks and daggers at each other. Another observer describes fire tricks as forming part of the dance, with men bringing fire close to their lips and mouth and with dancers touching various body parts with hot bottles. A Turkish writer was impressed with the violent nature of these dances, likening them to the ʿAshura rituals among the Shica.

Thus far, we have examined and attempted to interpret the cultural components retained by enslaved Africans in the Ottoman Empire. But the picture will not be complete without looking at how these retentions were received by the various Ottoman societies into which the enslaved were absorbed. Despite Ottoman inclusiveness and relative tolerance of difference, enslaved Africans had to struggle to retain their cultural identity, to carve out their own African social and spiritual space, to constantly defend their space against hegemonic elite notions and an ambivalent Tanzimat-state.

69. For a synthesis of several accounts and the author's own impressions, see Güneş, "Kölelikten Özgülüğe," 8, 10, and 10 n. 43.
70. On capoeira, see Maya Talmon-Chvaicer, "The Criminalization of Capoeira in Nineteenth-Century Brazil," *Hispanic American Historical Review,* 82/3 (2002), 525–547; Talmon-Chvaicer, *The Complexity of Capoeira: The Reflection of Distinctive African Slave Cultures in Rio de Janeiro and Bahia,* Ph.D. diss., University of Haifa, 2000 (in Hebrew). The most current monograph on the topic is in Portuguese: Carlos Eugênio Líbano Soares, *A capoeira escrava e outras tradições rebeldes no Rio de Janeiro, 1808–1850,* Campinas: Editora da UNICAMP/CECULT, 2001 (for this reference I am indebted to Joseph C. Miller).

OTTOMAN ATTITUDES TOWARD AFRICAN RETENTIONS

African culture and other non-mainstream cultures in the Ottoman Empire were associated with marginal social groups. They ranked low on a status scale that in the nineteenth century accorded its top spot to the well-trained, well-off members of the Ottoman imperial and Ottoman-Local elites—the loyal servants of the sultan and the backbone of his Tanzimat-state. All the rest, the overwhelming majority of the population, were pegged on that scale in a descending order, with each group suffering from a certain deficiency as compared to the full-fledged Ottoman gentleman and lady. In the eyes of the elite, the marginalized and their culture did not measure up to Ottoman standards. Those people and cultures were uncouth, underdeveloped, not properly Islamic, primitive, and incomprehensibly bizarre. But they also held the attraction of the exotic; and at times, as with Zar and African public festivals, they were allowed to invade the realm of proper elite tastes. The tension at the sociocultural divide and the cross-fertilization that occurred at contact points will drive our exploration in the following pages.

Our sources tell us that the rituals performed by the kolbaşıs and their followers were considered impudent and rude (*biedebane*), much the way disapproval was cast upon the customs of the Circassians received as refugees in the Ottoman Empire after their expulsion from the Caucasus by the Russians.[71] In Ottoman documents from the Tanzimat period, references to Circassian culture include expressions such as "wild," "savage," "vile," and "uncivilized." A leading reformer, Ahmet Cevdet Paşa, stated that no manners known to the civilized world existed among the Circassians (*beynlerinde âdab ve rüsüm-i medeniye yoktur*). The sale of children—fairly common among heritably enslaved Circassian families—was described by officials as a "strange custom" (*adet-i garibe*). And Samipaşazade Sezai, a well-known Tanzimat-period writer, refers in his play, *Sergüzeşt*, to the same practice among Asian Muslim peoples as

71. Ehud R. Toledano, *Slavery and Abolition in the Ottoman Middle East*, Seattle: University of Washington Press, 1998: 105–106, 109, 125–126. For similar perceptions among *ilustrado* nationalists in the Philippines of the "uncivilized" within society and on its periphery, see Michael Salman, *The Embarrassment of Slavery: Controversies over Bondage and Nationalism in the American Colonial Philippines*, Manila: Ateneo de Manila University Press, 2001: 11.

"old Asian savagery" (*Asya vahşet-i kadimesi*). This core elite perception of marginalized groups also applied to the origin-cultures of most enslaved Africans, those in the sub-Saharan regions lying beyond the boundaries of the "well-protected domains," to quote the title of Selim Deringil's book.[72]

We can contextualize the phenomenon using the convenient framework recently provided by both Deringil and Ussama Makdisi, who, in two separate articles, interpret late Ottoman attitudes in light of post-colonial, subaltern writings.[73] We need not go into the theoretical intricacies—interesting in their own right— that undergird these two studies. Suffice it to say that Deringil situates this deprecating core elite attitude in the broader view of a "civilizing mission" that the Ottomans saw themselves launching as part of their Tanzimat and post-Tanzimat "project of modernity." Perched as they were between Orient and Occident, the Ottomans developed—fairly late, according to Deringil—their own brand of colonialism, which he terms "borrowed colonialism." Makdisi argues for a case of "Ottoman Orientalism"; that is, the manner in which the Ottomans constructed the Arab subject peoples resembled in large measure the way Europeans constructed Orientals, including, of course, the Ottomans. This dynamic process consisted of deploying representations of the Other that were at once resistant and empowering, inclusive and exclusive. Both Deringil and Makdisi seem to agree that Ottoman-Arab elites participated in this complex venture and that elites at both the core and the periphery excluded and marginalized weakened segments of Ottoman societies, making differentiations based on gender, ethnicity, or class.

If we take this analysis one step further, we may safely include enslaved Africans and Circassians in those marginalized sectors. In this case, we could say that the Ottoman elite, and concomitantly the Tanzimat-state, regarded both these groups, first, as geographically peripheralized and,

72. Selim Deringil, *Well-Protected Domains: Ideology and the Legitimation of Power in the Ottoman Empire, 1876–1909*, London: I. B. Tauris, 1998.
73. Selim Deringil, " 'They Live in a State of Nomadism and Savagery': The Late Ottoman Empire and the Post-Colonial Debate," *Comparative Studies in Society and History*, 45/2 (April 2003): 311–342; Ussama Makdisi, "Ottoman Orientalism," *American Historical Review*, 107/3 (June 2002): 768–796.

second, as internally marginalized. That is, when still inhabiting their native lands south of the Sahara, they were seen as uncivilized, and when forcibly dragged into the Ottoman Empire and enslaved, they were seen as marginal and hence excluded. Deringil cites a book entitled *The New Africa* (*Yeni Afrika*), which was written by Mehmed İzzed, an interpreter for the imperial palace, as an example of the "borrowed colonialism" he is imputing to the Ottoman imperial elite.[74] In it, İzzed refers to Africans as "savages and heretics [who] can only be saved by an invitation into the True Faith." As for the Circassians, here they fall under the category of nomads, whose savagery (*vahşet*) and ignorance (*cehalet*) arouse in the "modern mind" contempt and paternalism.[75] Attempts to civilize these people once enslaved and within Ottoman society were naturally required. These included conversion to Islam in the case of Africans and socialization into orthodox forms of Islam for Circassians and other people of the Caucasus.

A clear example of this borrowed colonialism is the attitude of the Ottoman elite toward the Calf Festival, the most public manifestation of African culture in a major Ottoman city. In May 1894, an article in the Izmir newspaper *Hizmet* ridiculed the preparations and organizers of the Calf Festival, saying:

> No matter how much the Calf Festival, special only to our city, has been criticized, this custom continues yet again. Despite everything that has been written about this *odd* and *ridiculous* tradition, there remains no other way but to smash the people's *ignorance* (*halkın cahilliği*). If we ask them, we shall get this answer: if the calf's blood is not spilt, then a headless African will come, will cause us trouble, and will bring disease to our city. Such stories are only to be loudly *laughed at*. Are baseless things such as these to be believed? . . . We cannot do anything but be sorry for this custom of Africans (*zenciler*), which is the result of *pure ignorance* . . . We cannot avoid being *amazed* and *pained* at the fact that four or five thousand of our *sober-minded* (*akıllı uslu*) white people (*beyaz ahalimiz*) take part in that Calf

74. Deringil, " 'They Live in a State of Nomadism,' " 312.
75. Ibid., 317.

Festival, which consists of four or five hundred persons getting together, and with four or five Ottoman liras (*mecidiye*) buying a calf, slaughtering and cooking it.[76]

This, and similar writings set up a dichotomy between *Self* and *Other* (the Ottoman Turkish in parentheses is not necessarily the precise translation of the English, but the adjectives used in this and other texts denote the qualities referred to):

WE	THEY
white Ottomans (*beyaz ahalimiz*)	Africans (*zenciler*)
civilized (*medeni*)	uncivilized (*vahşi*)
serious	funny (*tuhaf*)
educated	ignorant (*cahil*)
reasonable	ridiculous
sensible (*akıllı*)	odd (*garip*)
well-mannered (*edebane*)	ill-mannered (*biedebane*)

It is therefore so disappointing that some of "our people" are lured by "their" savagery (*vahşet*). The line is crossed not simply by accident, nor just once, but actually every year, and with such persistence that no persuasion or prohibition can stop it. The tremendous pull of a "wild festival" must have lain, then, in its liberating appeal, in the very fact that civilized society condemned and berated it. Not surprisingly, it was the young who were most drawn to the event, *en masse* ignoring the ire of their elders.

At least part of the objection to African rituals and festivals was based upon religious grounds, and the pagan practices were condemned as being contrary to Islamic doctrine, hence punishable by the authorities. African rituals were rightly identified as falling within the realm of belief, faith, and the spiritual, a space where Islam and Islamic practices claimed to have unrivalled supremacy. Among the poor and uneducated, where Islamic syncretism had predominated for centuries, the appearance of un-Islamic cults was seen as a challenge—especially since they

76. Güneş, "Kölelikten Özgülüğe," 9 (the emphases are mine).

became popular in urban and rural areas throughout the Empire, proving themselves resilient by merging with Sufi practices and by incorporating Islamic components of prayer and lore. This was sometimes seen as insidious infiltration aimed at de-Islamization, and action against such practices was demanded by local leaders, who succeeded in enlisting the support of orthodox ulema and conservative leaders in the upper echelons of government. From time to time, such elements managed to influence the authorities to act against those who led Zar rituals, namely the kolbaşıs and the *godyas*.

For example, kolbaşıs and some congregants were banished from Istanbul on at least four recorded occasions—in 1810, 1817, 1827, and 1839.[77] The 1817 case has already been mentioned as an example of punishment for being negligent of the government placement and registration requirements. The earliest (1810) and latest (1839) cases do not add much to the picture, but the 1827 banishment of seven kolbaşıs at once supplies interesting and useful information.

In 1810, the sultan himself issued and signed the edict (ferman) that banished Nakşı Hatun, a kolbaşı from Istanbul, to the island of Mytilene (Turkish, Midilli).[78] She was accused of "unacceptable activities," and the sultan addressed the order to his chief halberdier, or head of his personal bodyguard, and to the court registrar in Mytilene. The former was to supply the escort to the banished woman, and the latter was to receive her in his jurisdiction, report her arrival to the authorities in the capital, and make sure that she did not leave the island, with or without permission, unless authorized by the central government.

The 1839 account of the exile of two women from Istanbul to Bursa draws on a draft of an edict phrased as being in the sultan's own language and put to him for personal endorsement.[79] In the text, the sovereign addresses the court registrar in Bursa regarding a woman known by the title Paşa Hanım, which signifies respect, and a kolbaşı named Fatime.

77. The 1817 and 1827 cases are both cited by Erdem from archival sources (Erdem, *Slavery,* 176), but see the following passage for a more detailed discussion of the 1827 case, which was not accessible to Erdem in full when he was working at the BOA. The 1810 and 1839 cases have not been discussed before in published works.

78. BOA/Cevdet/Zaptiye/1131, 4 May 1810.

79. BOA/ Cevdet/Zaptiye/1194, 16 April 1839.

The two were accused of committing "noxious, impure deeds that are unacceptable . . . in my imperial capital," as the sultan puts it, meaning practices that contravened cultural norms and hence challenged the existing social order. The reference is to the Zar rituals in which the kolbaşı and her esteemed accomplice participated. The women were being exiled, the edict continues, both to punish them for their misconduct and to deter others from engaging in similar activities. The two were to be accompanied by an officer from the chief of staff's bureau, and, as usual in such cases, the registrar was warned not to allow them to leave Bursa, not to distance themselves by "even one step," without obtaining proper consent from Istanbul. An example of a court registrar's report is provided in the 1827 case of the seven banished kolbaşıs.

On 14 August 1827, the registrar of the Şeriat court in Varna—an Ottoman-Bulgarian port city on the Black Sea—recorded the arrival of seven kolbaşıs who had been exiled from Istanbul.[80] The seven African women, he wrote, were accused of conducting in their lodges, where they lived, what were called "African weddings." On those occasions, lodge members assembled, musical instruments were played, fire tricks were displayed, and other kinds of "abominations" and unacceptable actions were performed as part of a healing process for demon-possessed Africans. Echoing the expulsion edict, the report stated that the women were banished to Varna in order to save their communities from evil and harm. The seven, all mentioned by name and address, were collected from different quarters of the city, and the sultan's chief halberdier appointed one of his officers to accompany them from Istanbul to Varna. They were to remain under detention in Varna and not allowed "to take [even] one step" toward another location until a further edict was issued regarding their case.

All these edicts and reports, but especially the 1827 one, are indicative of the problem the authorities were faced with owing to the rituals conducted by the kolbaşıs in their capacity as cult leaders for their African congregants. All Africans had been converted to Islam upon entry into the Empire. Retention of their origin-culture elements was condemned as un-Islamic, though it was reluctantly tolerated. Occasionally, the discrepancy between principle and practice impelled the government

80. BOA/Cevdet/Zaptiye/Dahiliye/92, 14 August 1827.

to act against them, probably at the instigation and urging of more orthodox community leaders. There seems to have been less of an opposition to practicing adherents and more to persons in leadership roles.
There was a similar concern in Spanish-controlled Cartagena during the
seventeenth century, when persons in the leadership role of *mohán* were
targeted by the Inquisition Tribunal.[81] Amerindian moháns were teachers and leaders alleged to have had a pact with the devil in connection
with their healing functions. These leading folk healers (*curanderos*)
were strongly opposed by the Catholic Church in Latin America.

Given that in the Ottoman Empire, Zar rituals and African festivals
not only attracted Africans but also appealed to broader audiences, spiritual leaders such as kolbaşıs and godyas were probably seen by established Muslim leaders as potential competitors for the hearts and minds
of community members. The existence of that common market of ideas,
rituals, and practices suggests that the belief system of non-elite and
marginal groups was much more fluid than previously thought. That
colorful and dynamic cultural milieu contained a wide array of options, a
broad range of overlapping and syncretic practices, all having their local
advocates, teachers, and leaders. To attract potential followers, leaders
had to be creative and innovative, and because state-backed orthodoxy
often did not have the upper hand, its leaders needed to mobilize government support to impede the competition. Whereas this cultural milieu was mainly a non-elite space, it should be noted that Zar and other
non-Islamic practices appealed to members of elite circles as well. The
persistence of such practices also suggests that the level of cultural integration of Africans into Ottoman society, especially as regards spirituality and religion, was not as high as had been previously thought.[82]

We can learn a great deal from the four seemingly terse and factual
edicts and reports. All "condemnable acts" attributed to the kolbaşıs
are clearly part of the Zar ritual. The reference to possessed persons

81. McKnight, in " '*En su tierra lo aprendió,*' " 63, notes that out of four hundred
     cases brought before the Inquisition Tribunal between 1610 and 1660, 30 per-
     cent were about sorcery and witchcraft, 16 percent involved Africans, and
     11 percent dealt with enslaved persons.
82. Consider the implications of this to the "good treatment debate" discussed
     above.

(*babalı*) needs no further elaboration, whereas both the instrument music and the role of fire mentioned in them are associated with the healing process. The music played in Zar rituals consisted of constant rhythmic drumming, later replaced by one of two main types of bands, *Tambura* and *Abu Ghit,* or sometimes both, to match the nature of the possessing spirit in a particular case. *Tambura* and *Abu Ghit* are the band names commonly used in the Sudan, Egypt, and other Arab countries. But in Iran, especially in Khuzistan and Baluchistan, where Zar was common among the descendants of enslaved Africans, different names and varying types of instruments were and still are employed.[83] African-Iranians use, among other instruments, a larger drum—called *dohol* in Iran, *dammam* in Indian Gujarat—which produces the monotonic beats required for the kind of rhythm conducive to trance.

The kolbaşıs in our documents were also accused of "playing with fire" (*ateş oynamak*) in their rituals. In all likelihood, this refers to performances of the fire-eater type that took place in both the private, small-scale Zar rituals and the larger festivals of Istanbul and Izmir.[84] In private events, this would be performed by a single performer who specialized in the handling of what seemed to watchers to be balls of fire flying in and out of the man's mouth. In the larger public events, there would be many street performances, including fire-eating and capoeira-style fights.[85] Fire was also used for lighting incense, an element of major importance in Zar rituals, and for keeping the incense burning throughout the lengthy ceremonies, which was done by maintaining constantly lit fire lamps.

The mention of "African wedding" (*Arap düğünü*) in our deportation cases provides another link to Zar practices. The dictionary meaning of *düşün* indicates both marriage and circumcision ceremonies, or, more broadly, initiation rites. Sengers correctly observes that "the Zar mimics

---

83. Mirzai, "African Presence," 241–245. I have not found specific band names for the core areas of the Ottoman Empire.

84. See, for example, the "wedding" ceremony described in Sengers, *Women and Demons,* 91–98 (especially 92 and 98), 108. This and the following paragraphs draw on her work.

85. Or *candomblé* (see note 63 above).

the model of a general initiation rite" and is specifically constructed along the lines of a wedding ceremony:

- The possessed woman is the "bride" (Arabic, ʿarusa) of the possessing male spirit and is dressed accordingly.
- The same term is used for both marriage ceremonies (farah, in Egypt).
- A contract is arranged between the groom/demon-master and the bride/possessed-woman (Arabic and Egyptian, ʿaqd).
- Guests behave as they would in a wedding—light candles, form a formal procession (zaffa), dance to band music, and have a feast.

There is also a subtle play, not always explicit, on the sexual theme of penetration, as the demon enters the possessed bride. I would add that the presence of blood—albeit sacrificial—is suggestive of the loss of virginity. Finally, Sengers asserts that "the emphasis on the wedding motif in Zar symbolizes the social world of women in significant aspects; it is an important metaphor in their relationship with demons."[86] In yet another related twist we learn that in Ottoman North Africa, these "priestesses"—called there ʿarifa (plural, ʿaraʾif)—were not allowed to marry, because they were allowed to marry only spirits.[87]

To complete our discussion here, I need to point to a truly fascinating phenomenon: the morphing of the Zar ritual from possession healing into entertainment performance. Evidence from Iran and the Persian Gulf region indicates that elements of the Zar "wedding" seem to have been detached from their original ritual function and blended into these—and perhaps other—Middle Eastern local cultures. In a way, this is the flip side of African-Ottoman cultural creolization. Accordingly, some elements of Zar have been taken on and transplanted into the ceremony of real weddings. The use of drumming to summon participants, the playing of typically Zar band music, and the staging of dance and trance performances are all adopted as part of the entertainment program, while the performers themselves are members of local African communities. Having lost their original healing purpose, these features of Zar have come to serve another purpose, for a fee.

86. Ibid., 96.
87. Montana, "Ahmad ibn al-Qadi al-Timbuktawi," 181 (citing Timbuktawi).

In Iran and the Gulf area, the newly acquired function of the Zar ritual as amusement still retains its affinity to the marriage ceremony: Mirzai asserts that the ritual of *Liwa*, which includes the Zar elements listed above, is still being performed at weddings in southeastern Iran, Kharg, Sohar, Dubai, and Bahrain.[88] At the same time, Hunwick mentions that in Morocco, African bands made up of *Gnawa* (black, originally enslaved and freed) and some local people have become street performers, reenacting the music, dance, and trance elements of Bori rituals for donations.[89] They are also invited to private homes to purify them to eliminate evil spirits. In this, it appears, the cult has strayed even further away from healing and spiritual support to entertainment, from serving the needs of a community in distress to serving the needs of leisure for the public at large. Or perhaps, as Sayyid Hurreiz has put it, a ritual is becoming a folk drama.[90]

PATTERNS OF CULTURAL CREOLIZATION
IN THE OTTOMAN EMPIRE

Retention of origin-culture ingredients, their fusion with local-culture components, and the dissemination of hybrid versions within Ottoman societies are all part of what I call Ottoman cultural creolization. In this chapter I have discussed mostly African-Ottoman creolization processes, leaving for future research Circassian-Ottoman creolization and other ethnic Ottoman creolization processes. In principle, African-Ottoman creolization can be assumed to provide the model for other creolization processes, allowing for variants in content and historical circumstances. Here I shall touch upon aspects of creolization that are not exclusively African.

The admission of the notion that Zar is interpretable allegorically invites locating it within a *social* and *cultural* context. Thus, we may look for similarities between events and situations in the spirit world and those in real social life, with Zar functioning as "a mirror-image of daily life."[91] In

88. Mirzai, "African Presence," 244–245.
89. Hunwick, "Religious Practices," 165 (citing Brunel).
90. Sayyid Hurreiz, "*Zar* as Ritual Psychodrama: From Cult to Club," in Lewis et al., *Women's Medicine*, 147–155.
91. Sengers, *Women and Demons*, 89–90, agreeing with Cynthia Nelson (quotations in this paragraph are from pp. 89 and 185).

both, women—as the majority of believers—must "manipulate, plead, and calm," because they exist in a "dangerous world dominated by husband and spirits, both of whom constantly need to be kept happy." Possession is linked to many social woes, such as infertility, which is the chief concern in the Sudanese case, and, in other contexts, to sexuality, marriage, family relationships, children, and economic problems. To that, we may add a related, *political* interpretation: that Zar is "a form of antilanguage, subordinate discourse, or counterhegemonic process."[92] An ostensibly innocuous ritual became a powerful tool for entering the otherwise inaccessible world inhabited by Africans and the non-Africans who associated with them in Ottoman societies.

Since Africans in the Ottoman Empire were either enslaved or freed, or the offspring of enslaved and freed persons, we may gain access to their world by breaking the sociocultural code of their creolized Zar practices. Adjusting the observations made about Zar rituals in which the participants were free persons only enhances the importance of this tool with regard to the enslaved. It does not require a leap of faith to recognize the ritual's psychological healing purpose for individuals who had been brutally torn from family, community, and country and then enslaved, thrust into an alien society, and relegated to the lowest social rung. The initial severance from home and the crossing of nearly unbridgeable cultural boundaries were the most traumatic. Reattachment to, and bonding with, a new slaver, was enormously difficult, involving reeducation and reacculturation, which occurred mostly on the individual level. Even if successfully accomplished, as was often the case in Ottoman societies, the new attachment was never completely secure, nor could it be taken for granted, for the threat of resale was always lurking in the background.

But resale was not the only threat to the well-being and tranquility of the enslaved, although it was clearly the most frightening. Even the much-hoped-for manumission harbored the prospect of being cut loose, of losing yet again a hard-earned attachment, without the guarantee of a new attachment outside the realm of enslavement. Despite the Ottoman-recommended norm of manumission after seven to ten years of service, not a few enslaved persons accumulated a sad history of several severances and reattachments in their lifetime, with all the emotional and physical

92. Boddy, *Wombs*, 310.

wear-and-tear that these involved. In that stressful reality and psychocultural vacuum, the soothing role of origin-culture reenactment, most notably in Zar and Bori rituals, is obvious.[93] The rituals and public festivals not only provided African-Ottomans with a much-needed sense of community; they also served as a compensatory mechanism, a substitute for the loss of the original family, neighborhood, and village structures. Within this context, we may see the kolbaşı/godya both as a mother/father figure and as a leader who socially cemented the community.

It is not surprising that the kolbaşıs/godyas were venerated by members of their congregations, who did not hesitate to support them out of their meager, hard-earned resources. To enslaved and freed Africans who joined such cults, there was no substitute for the trust they placed in those leaders, nor for their total belief in their special powers. The relief that godyas provided from daily hardship, however temporary, enabled many of the members to carry on with their difficult lives. They looked forward to their regular meetings and to the specially scheduled events that were announced by the familiar drumming they could hear from afar. Festivals were also faithfully observed, for they offered joyful community activities and a public release from misery, and the kolbaşıs organized and led the way here, too.[94] Given the psychological and physical healing role played by Zar in many African origin-cultures, the stressful predicament of the enslaved, and the high percentage of women participants—women both were the overwhelming majority among the enslaved and were considered more susceptible to Zar—it is not surprising to find that the cult managed to survive all attempts by religious leaders and government officials to weed it out.

In this context of cultural retention and creolization, what was the mindset of enslaved Africans (and Circassians) in Ottoman societies? Reconstructing it is admittedly a risky business, but the hierarchy that emerges is likely to contain three discernable layers:

- The *most remote and powerful layer would be a deity*, either from an animist childhood experience (mediated by the kolbaşı/godya) or—if the

93. For a similar observation, see Hunwick, "Religious Practices," 149, who speaks about a "psychological trauma."
94. For the Izmir case as deliverance from a daily miserable existence, see Güneş, "Kölelikten Özgülüğe," 6.

individual is better integrated into society—from an Islamic notion of
a deity (mediated by the imams or Sufi shaykhs);
- The *closer and somewhat less powerful layer would be the state* (mediated
by its officeholders from the sultan down to the policemen at the
nearby precinct). Somewhere in that category, though separate from it,
would figure the *foreign powers* (mediated by their consuls, to whom
the enslaved could escape for help).
- The *closest layer, the one with power over their daily life, would be the
slavers* (unmediated).

Except for the enslaved-slaver relationship, the other affiliations
were *mediated:* in the spiritual relationship, the kolbaşıs and godyas
were the connecting link, whereas the power of the state was exercised
through its agents. One of the major processes identified in this book is
the interjection of the Tanzimat-state into the slaver-enslaved relationship. It served to mitigate the predicament of slavery and often protected
the enslaved against abuse and extreme exploitation. The role of state
agents and foreign consuls, both serving as mediators between the enslaved and the Tanzimat-state, was highly important. These agents interpreted and applied state policy regarding slavery and maintained the
face-to-face contact with the enslaved. The other mitigation of enslavement occurred through the retention of origin-culture components and
their creolization within the rich variety of locally articulated Ottoman
cultures. Here, too, the crucial importance of the mediators is apparent.
For the Africans, they were the ones to interpret the Zar world and make
sense of it to members of their community. Their role as healers reflects
both their actual function and its symbolic meaning.

It is fascinating that in the Zar concept the two types of mediation
were strongly intertwined: the *spiritual* mediation to a deity and the *tem-
poral* mediation to the state. This combined mediation brought both the
possessed and cult members into a heightened sense of relevance and
efficacy. Most susceptible to this double impact was the category that
contained spirits of senior Ottoman officeholders: the kolbaşı/godya mediated between the possessed and the spirit of, say, Yaver Bey, Hekim
Paşa (or Başı), a vezir, or even the sultan; but, at the same time, the spirits of Ottoman officeholders were themselves images of persons who
performed another kind of mediation, that is, between the enslaved—or

the free, for that matter—and the Tanzimat-state. This intertwining of the deity-spiritual mediation with the state-temporal mediation rendered both the deity and the state accessible, real, tangible to the possessed and the community of believers in which they lived. The generally perceived popularity of possession by the spirit of Yaver Bey in particular, but also by spirits representing other Ottoman officials, indicates that they probably offered greater release and gratification to those involved in the ritual, actively or passively, than did possession by other spirits. This gratification was achieved, I would like to argue, because through merging two mediating images, Yaver Bey and other officeholders came to embody *both* a deity and the state.

While the scope of retention and creolization, hitherto only partially recognized, casts a different light on the efficacy of resocialization and reacculturation of the enslaved in Ottoman societies, it does *not* indicate the complete failure of these processes. Rather, it weakens the argument for what I had called the good treatment of the enslaved. That is to say, integration of the enslaved into Ottoman societies did occur, and many of them managed to forge new attachments to family, household, and community. However, as could only be expected, there remained a significant residue of origin-culture ingredients in the minds of enslaved individuals, along with a strong, genuine need to give the origin-culture both personal and collective expression. That need was kept alive and replenished by the newly enslaved men and women who were being constantly forced into the Empire during much of the nineteenth century. But it was also being passed on to Ottoman-born generations and has been socially and culturally reproduced for the past century and a half.

Still, we have not witnessed a keen interest in the revival of African-Ottoman and creolized cultures, which can be partially explained by the depressed state of the potential constituencies that could claim and promote these cultures as their own heritage. On the other hand, and somewhat paradoxically, the indifference reflects the strong desire of successfully integrated Africans to fully assimilate into Turkish and Arab societies. This is also the main reason for the reluctance to deal with the burden and heritage of Ottoman enslavement,[95] although there are recent indications that this might be changing because outside attention

95. Toledano, *Slavery and Abolition*, Chapter 5.

has been drawn to the enslavement of Africans by Arabs and Ottomans.[96] By contrast, the crucial importance of an active political interest can be easily seen in the emergence of the various Creole movements in both the West Indies and the Indian Ocean islands during the second half of the twentieth century.[97] The case of Circassian-Ottoman culture, which has been partly retained in various, mostly rural diaspora communities, lies somewhere between the African-Ottoman and the Creole cases. These Circassians have retained language and certain elements of ethnicity but seem to have forgotten their enslaved past.

The Ottoman and Iranian cases of cultural creolization are certainly not unique. They are typical examples of the processes witnessed in other societies—Muslim and non-Muslim alike—where enslaved Africans were present. These have been studied in various places, such as Dominica, where various kinds of folk art performances and activities were carried over from west African traditions, forming part of that blended culture which Africans have preserved and transmitted down the generations in the new societies where they ended up living. Thus, African elements are discernible in dance, music, and theater performances in Creole societies in the West Indies and the Indian Ocean.[98] Although it is still possible to observe such phenomena in present-day social situations in those societies, for the Ottoman Empire we need to rely on historical accounts to reconstruct the processes encountered elsewhere and endow them with Ottoman specificity.

Lexifiers are languages from which creoles and pidgins derive most of their vocabulary. Creoles developed in settlement colonies, where contacts between the speakers (native or fluent) of the lexifiers were intense, unlike the superficial trade contacts that produced pidgin languages. "Creole populations," writes Salikoko Mufwene, "those born in the settlement colonies from at least one nonindigenous parent, preceded the

96. See the discussion of the changing research environment in Chapter 1.
97. Lambert-Félix Prudent and Ellen M. Schnepel, "Introduction," in Prudent and Schnepel (eds.), *Creole Movements in the Francophone Orbit*, Special issue of the *International Journal of the Sociology of Language*, Berlin: Mouton de Gruyter, 1993: 5–13; see also articles in the same issue by Robert Chaudenson and Vinesh Y. Hookoomsing.
98. Stephanie Stuart, "Dominican Patwa—Mother Tongue or Cultural Relic?" in Prudent and Schnepel, *Creole Movements*, 68–69.

emergence of creole vernaculars, in the homestead conditions in which non-Europeans were minorities and well integrated, though socially discriminated against."[99] Mufwene offers a more flexible, more historic, and less linguistically determined definition of creole than most scholars use, which allows for a broader cultural assessment of creolization, like mine in this chapter.[100] To extrapolate from his approach, the necessary conditions for creolization—of language but also by extension of culture—are substantial and sustained contact between speakers of African vernaculars and speakers of a lexifier, the lexifer speakers being the dominant social group. In our case, both Turkish and Arabic were the lexifiers within the Ottoman Empire. Turkish was the lexifier in Istanbul, in Anatolia, and among Ottoman-Local elites throughout the Empire; Arabic was the lexifier in the Middle East and North Africa; Ottoman Turkish was the lingua franca in the entire eastern Mediterranean area.

But, as Mufwene stresses throughout his work, the lexifiers were not standard but nonstandard varieties. According to what he calls the Founder Principle, the development of creoles depended to a large extent on the language spoken by the group of initial settlers in the colony. Since in the early stage of colonization in the seventeenth and eighteenth centuries, the settlers were mostly of European indentured servants and low-class employees of colonial companies, their nonstandard language acted as the formative lexifier in creole emergence once the African enslaved people began to arrive.[101] The enslaved Africans themselves came from a variety of regions within Africa, bringing with them a host of nonstandard African languages and a variety of dialects.[102] Paul Lovejoy talks about "overlapping diasporas" rather than one African diaspora in the Americas, and David Richardson points out that many Southern plantations included enslaved persons from diverse regions, often not sharing a common language, often unable to communicate among themselves without the mediation

99. Salikoko S. Mufwene, *The Ecology of Language Evolution,* Cambridge: Cambridge University Press, 2001: 9.
100. Ibid., 10–11.
101. Ibid., 29.
102. Ibid., 25–80.

of the owner and the owner's staff, who spoke a nonstandard dialect of American English.[103]

The Ottoman situation is both different and similar in some of its aspects. It is different because creolization here occurred within the host society, often in major urban elite households (*kapıs*), where standard Ottoman Turkish was the lingua franca. But this was mainly the case with the socialization and acculturation of what I call the kul/harem enslaved persons: the white females destined for reproduction and service in elite harems and the men recruited and trained to occupy administrative and military positions in the sultan's service. In urban elite households, men—and to a lesser extent some of the women—were taught the main canonical texts of Ottoman culture. In provincial elite households, where, from the late seventeenth century onward, members of Ottoman-Local elites spoke both standard Ottoman Turkish and at least one vernacular—an Arabic, Greek, or Slavic dialect—the enslaved kul/harem members of the household were exposed to this type of linguistic mélange.

Whether in Istanbul, the provincial capitals, or other cities, enslaved Africans encountered a simplified version of the lexifiers, since they were considered uneducated and were often but not always illiterate. Still, we may safely assume—until detailed linguistic studies show specifically—that enslaved Africans were exposed to a variety of regional, ethnic, and class dialects of both Turkish and Arabic. As on plantations in the Southern United States and the Caribbean, though on a much smaller scale, within Ottoman-Local elite households enslaved persons were spoken to various dialects—in Ottoman Turkish by the slavers and in an Arabic dialect by the free servants, who likely came from the province where the household was located. In addition, there is evidence that African languages survived the first generation of enslaved migrants and were creolized in the following generations.

103. Lovejoy, *Slavery on Frontiers*, 5; David Richardson (ed.), *Routes to Slavery: Direction, Ethnicity, and Mortality in the Transatlantic Slave Trade*, London: Frank Cass, 1997. See also Paul E. Lovejoy and David V. Trotman (eds.), *Trans-Atlantic Dimensions of Ethnicity in the African Diaspora*, London: Continuum, 2003; and Paul E. Lovejoy "Identifying Enslaved Africans in the African Diaspora," in Lovejoy (ed.), *Identity in the Shadow of Slavery*, London: Continuum, 2000 (Lovejoy notes that contributors to this collection dispute the assertion that all enslaved Africans shared a common heritage).

In some larger communities, such as Izmir, knowledge of the lexifier was not essential, and as late as the middle of the twentieth century, people there could speak only their African language. Güneş points out that when donations for the Calf Festival were being collected in Izmir's African neighborhoods, the godyas had to explain the point in Borno, Afini, and other African languages.[104] Sophie Ferchiou and Ismael Montana describe the fascinating social organization of the enslaved population in Ottoman Tunis.[105] These congregated according to the various African ethnicities of their homelands and adhered to different Bori shrines (*gida*) with different patron spirits. They spoke their native languages and maintained communities under the leadership of the Bori mediums (Arabic, *'ara'if*). Ferchiou further classifies the order-cults into three categories according to their position on the continuum from Sufism to Bori.

The following scenario is quite plausible. Imagine a batch of five enslaved African young women who were purchased by an agent for the household of an Ottoman high officeholder in mid-nineteenth-century Cairo. The five could have come from central Africa, the southern Sudan, the shores of the Red Sea, or from Ethiopia's ethnic regions, with each speaking a different African language. In the harem they would meet the mistress and the women of the harem, who would most likely have been Circassian or Georgian women enslaved at a young age. In their native homelands they spoke any one of the tribal dialects of the Caucasus, but after the years they spent in the new household, they were fully conversant with elite Ottoman Turkish. Our enslaved Africans would probably also meet at the mansion free Egyptian female and male servants, who spoke any one of the Egyptian Arabic dialects of Cairo and Upper or Lower Egypt. It was not unlikely that a Sudanese servant, speaking his own dialect, would also be in attendance. The linguistic *mix*—not to say hodgepodge—is not hypothetical; I describe the actual and most likely environment into which enslaved Africans were thrust. Ottoman societies truly offered an elaborate and intricate cultural laboratory in the long nineteenth century.

104. Güneş, "Kölelikten Özgülüğe," 7.
105. Ferchiou, "Possession Cults," 210; Montana, "Ahmad ibn al-Qadi al-
    Timbuktawi," 179 ff.

The spread of Arabic into the African continent—on the eastern shores, along the Mediterranean littoral, and in sub-Saharan regions—was a centuries-old phenomenon. Arabic accompanied the Arab invasions and the traffic in enslaved persons. This has led some linguists to argue that in the context of creolizaton Arabic has to be treated as an African language. What is certain, though, is that the interaction between Arabic—in both its standard-written and nonstandard varieties—and various African languages and dialects produced new Arabic-influenced languages that today some consider to be new African languages.[106] The enslaved Africans who were being forced into the Ottoman Empire during the eighteenth and nineteenth centuries also reached Arabic-speaking regions, where they were employed in a wide array of jobs. Thus, if purchased by elite households, they had to cope with a mixture of standard and nonstandard variants of Turkish and Arabic, but the more interesting phenomenon is that they might have encountered the original dialects by which their pidgin/creolized language was lexified. Many of them, especially men, were purchased by Bedouins in the Hijaz or by Egyptian *fallahin* in Lower and Upper Egypt, especially during the cotton boom of the 1860s. The dialects in which these slavers addressed the enslaved were, in the Hijaz, a Bedouin Arabic dialect or, in Egypt, any of the Delta or Sacidi (Upper) Arabic dialects.

One of the classic cases of Arabic creolization occurred in the Ottoman-Egyptian Sudan during the nineteenth century. While northern Sudan was fully Arabicized, the south remained relatively unaffected for a long time by either Arabic or Islam. The process of enslavement in the southern Sudan, which was carried out with a large presence of slave-trader encampments in the region, exposed the native population to Arabic as a contact language and produced what have been termed Arabic pidgins or creoles. Juba Arabic became the lingua franca of the entire region and later traveled with its speakers when they moved to what are now Chad, Uganda, and Kenya after the contraction of Ottoman-Egyptian rule. These former slaves and militiamen moved out of the Sudan to find new employment in neighboring Kenya and Uganda, where the creole

106. Mufwene, *Ecology,* 182–184, relying on work by Alamin and Ali Mazrui in 1998.

they spoke became the native tongue of their descendants, especially in urban areas.[107]

Unfortunately, very little research, perhaps none, has been conducted into the languages and dialects spoken by descendants of Africans in Turkey or the Arab Middle East and North Africa. Indeed, few communities of Africans have survived in the region. This puts the entire line of inquiry well into the category of endangered languages, ones that through evolution have become extinct.[108] "Languages do not die suddenly nor on their own," writes Mufwene. "They typically die because their speakers choose to speak other languages. The effect of such shifts is that those languages which are spoken less often fall into attrition and/or are no longer transmitted to other potential speakers, especially the younger generation. That is, the population of speakers is no longer self-reproductive . . . the current generation of speakers becomes smaller and smaller, and eventually there may be no more speakers of some languages."[109] This is what happened to African languages in the Americas and the Indian Ocean, Mufwene concludes, and I will add, that this is precisely what happened to African languages in the Ottoman Empire as well.

Circassian dialects did manage to survive to the present day in various communities in Turkey and Jordan and in two villages in Israel. These refugee communities were settled by the Ottomans in the 1860s after the expulsion of Circassians from the Russian-held Caucasus. About 10 percent of the refugees are believed to have been enslaved agricultural laborers who entered the Empire with their landlord-patrons. Classified by Ottoman law as slaves, they remained attached to their landlords, who were assigned land and means of production and settled in village communities in frontier and sensitive regions. The families of enslaved agricultural workers were gradually manumitted during the last two decades of the nineteenth century with the support and financial asistance of the Tanzimat-state.[110]

Although the lingua franca of these Circassians is now either Turkish, Arabic, or Hebrew, the fact that they remained in Circassian communities

107. Ibid., 177, following studies by Jonathan Owens and Catherine Miller.
108. Ibid., 191, 199–200.
109. Ibid., 199.
110. Toledano, *Slavery and Abolition,* Chapter 3.

rather than scattered in society at large probably accounts for their ability to retain creolized versions of their original cultures and dialects. In one of the two Israeli villages, Rihaniyya, there is a cultural-historical museum, and original festivities are still being observed by the community. Since the early 1990s, after the collapse of the Soviet Union, contacts between the community and their Caucasian homeland were reestablished. Circassian cultural retentions were assisted by the fact that the refugees were settled in new villages—mostly along the Ottoman frontiers. This made it possible for their languages and cultures to survive throughout the Ottoman and post-Ottoman Middle East, especially in today's Turkey. Their situation was contrary to the situation of enslaved Africans both in the Americas and in the Ottoman Empire, who were not ethnoliguistically segregated according to their ancestral African communities, which led to the endangerment of their languages.

But partial segregation, which Mufwene considers a desirable privilege, is only one precondition for ethnolinguistic and cultural survival. The other precondition, perhaps the flip side of segregation, was integration into the dominant socioeconomic group. Economic integration of enslaved Africans in the Americas also helped to bring about the endangerment of their native African languages, which did not survive in the plantation colonies. As a rule, Mufwene asserts, "languages other than the lexifier survived longer when speakers of the same language were not absorbed by the speakers of the lexifier."[111] In reality, enslaved Africans and Circassians were rapidly absorbed into Ottoman societies, especially in urban domestic settings, where most of the enslaved Africans lived and whither many free and freed Circassians migrated. This meant that the lexifier, whether Turkish or Arabic, also effectively extinguished the languages and cultures that the enslaved brought with them into the Empire.

Future research on cultural processes in the eastern Mediterranean during the Ottoman period should concentrate on examining two historical processes: the process of absorption and integration of enslaved Africans and Circassians into Ottoman societices, and the gradual disappearance of their unique cultures. Both processes seem to be still ongoing and dynamic.

111. Mufwene, Ecology, 200.

Concluding Remarks

INTEREST IN THE STUDY of enslavement is undergoing one of its cyclical surges. Here, instead of adding another brick of information to the growing edifice of scholarship in the field, a worthy venture in its own right, I revisited and reinterpreted the history of enslavement in the Ottoman Empire during the long nineteenth century. By putting the slaver-enslaved relationship at the center of the interpretation of enslavement, I hoped that new light might be shed also on the study of enslavement outside the Ottoman Empire, mainly but not only in other Islamic societies. The stress on responsible—at times even compassionate—patronage was one of the main features of enslavement in the Muslim world. It can also be the key to understanding other, less endearing aspects of the slaver-enslaved relationship and can reconstitute the enslaved as a full person in a complex web of human entanglements. Full personhood is, of course, essential to understanding any social predicament.

Although some fascinating views on the concept of enslavement are currently being developed, by John Edward Philips, among others, this book is not about the reconceptualization of slavery.[1] It might in passing

1. John Edward Philips, "Slavery as a Human Institution," paper presented at the "Slavery, Islam, and Diaspora" conference at York University, Toronto, Canada, 23 October 2003.

help to amend some of the conceptual flaws with regard to enslavement in Islamic societies as expressed, for example, in Alain Testart's recent and ambitious attempt to construct a universal model.[2] A major endeavor in that global comparative direction has been undertaken by Joseph C. Miller, whose encyclopedic knowledge and analytic skills will surely provide a more convincing interpretive framework than that offered by Testart. If my book is not about the conceptualization of slavery, nor about the slave trade, the numbers, prices, routes, or services extracted from the enslaved, what is it about? It is all about people, their actions, their feelings.

But it is not just about any people, nor any Ottoman subjects; it is about the plight and experience, the toils and the joys, the suffering and the solace that made up the lives of the sultan's enslaved subjects. Although far removed from the life experiences of most readers, the world of the enslaved can become, through documents by and about them, somewhat more tangible to us, somewhat closer to our perception than it has been before. Brutally snatched from their various homelands in Africa, young women and men, many of them children, were thrust into a society whose language, clothes, customs, and beliefs were totally alien to most of them. Kidnapped or sold by relatives, other boys and girls were taken from their homes in the Caucasus and traded in the big cities of the Empire to reach the households of Ottoman grandees. Africans and Circassians also cultivated fields in Egypt, the Sudan, Anatolia, and the eastern Balkans, and African men worked in mines and dived for pearls in Arabia. Yet they still carved out a space of their own, lived their lives as other humans did around them, grew up, formed families, had children, reached old age.

The main point put forth in this book is that the key to understanding enslavement on the individual level is to view it as an instance of a patronage relationship. To better comprehend enslavement, we must examine it as a web of relationships. For enslavement to exist, we need to have a slaver and an enslaved person. We also need a society that regards enslavement as an acceptable form of human relationship, a natural part of the way things are and ought to be. To invoke a well-known classification,

2. Alain Testart, *L'esclave, la dette et le pouvoir: Etudes de sociologie comparative*, Paris: Edition Errance, 2001: e.g., 23 ff.

the members of such a society roughly correspond to perpetrators, victims, and (acquiescing) onlookers. Only a significant change in that correspondence would likely produce a challenge to the system in the shape of antislavery ideologies, which might lead to abolitionism. By looking at individual relationships and the web they created within society, we can appreciate enslavement as both a personal and a group experience. Only thus can the agency attributed here to the enslaved be properly evaluated and their relationship with the slavers be seen as more than just an oppressed-oppressor dyad, although it certainly was that too.

In this context I stressed the importance of *attachment* as a major element of enslavement in Ottoman societies. Referring to the basic cultural notion of the patron-client school of Philippine studies, Michael Salman writes that "people desire to be included and empowered—one might say bonded—through kinship, reciprocal exchanges, and other forms of mutual obligation."[3] People fear being "shut out of such networks," which might jeopardize their ability to secure a position within the social hierarchy. This was doubly so with regard to the enslaved, given their loss of kinship attachment and the brutal severing of cultural and social ties to their homeland. The fear of losing a hard-earned reattachment to the slaver-patron played a major role in shaping the bank of options available to the enslaved in their new environment. It inevitably constrained their choice of action, as when considering the consequences of insubordination, absconding, or challenging norms of conduct. When the enslaved did resort to actions of this type, we need to bring agency into our interpretation of their behavior and evaluate the extent to which their behavior represented defiance and a strong desire to break the bonds of servitude.

The emphasis throughout the book has been on the struggle of the enslaved to maintain their dignity within what was essentially a predicament of indignity. Chapter 1 outlines the main features of the slaver-enslaved relationship and stresses the importance of bonding, whereas Chapters 2, 3, and 4 look at what happened when the relationship collapsed; they examine the consequences of betrayed bonds. More specifically, Chapter 2 discusses the dilemmas of those among the enslaved

3. Michael Salman, *The Embarrassment of Slavery: Controversies over Bondage and Nationalism in the American Colonial Philippines*, Manila: Ateneo de Manila University Press, 2001: 6.

who chose to abscond when they felt betrayed, and argues that in many cases leaving was a clear rejection of enslavement, not just rejection of a specific slaver-enslaved relationship.

In Chapter 3, the enslaved turn to the Tanzimat-state for help: they seek manumission and at least temporary patronage when their relationships with slavers fail. For some of the enslaved who could neither have their grievances redressed by the state nor see an opportunity to mend their broken bonds with slavers, going against the law became an option; the circumstances in which they committed various crimes are examined in Chapter 4. But even when the slaver-enslaved relationship worked well, many of the enslaved felt a need to embrace familiar practices in order to cope with social alienation. Chapter 5 explores the fascinating phenomena of cultural retention as an integral part of the experience of enslavement in the Ottoman Empire. All these themes have to be seen as facets of the approach that places the enslaved at the center of the narrative.

However, by stressing the complex nature of enslavement as a social phenomenon, I have run the risk of downplaying its harshness for the enslaved. This becomes almost inevitable when I argue that even under the most extreme form of domination, which enslavement indeed was, a measure of give-and-take, often a large measure, had to be employed to enable the slaver-enslaved relationship to function effectively. The opposite approach, what Michael Salman calls "the reification of slavery"— which in the Philippines and elsewhere was necessary to make abolition possible—is equally problematic. "Complex and invasive human relationships," he writes, "had to be reduced and refigured as things apart from a normative world of humane existence so that they could be carved like cancers out of a social body in which they were thoroughly enmeshed."[4] But "humanizing" enslavement, which is essential for understanding its emergence and perseverance as a universal social phenomenon, should not make us lose sight of the enormous human cost that resulted from its existence.

We must therefore realize that within enslavement, power and powerlessness were never the crude attributes that they might seem at superficial or "reified" glance. Rather, they both coexisted in myriads of life

4. Ibid., 268–269.

situations, often changing and constantly restricting and mitigating each other. The slavers were not all-powerful, nor were the enslaved completely powerless; and those power relations could change over time, just as other types of human relations periodically or occasionally do. We must constantly bear in mind the dynamics of life and avoid a rigid model of unchanging categories. Personality and circumstances created an array of complex relationships within households and harems, as in the fields, in pearl-diving dhows, and in whatever other places enslaved people were living and working. How the enslaved positioned themselves within these relationships and among other slaves and how they viewed these relationships has been the main concern of this book. Whereas I did try to bring out the dyadic aspect of the relationships between enslaved and slavers, the collective nature of the spiritual communities formed by enslaved and freed persons also played an important role in the lives the enslaved.

The retention of African cultural components in the host societies was the other phenomenon that combined need and challenge in the context of Ottoman enslavement. "Religious cults and sects," writes Milton Yinger, "have at least the potentiality of helping to carry their members over into a new life."[5] "In situations that demand rapid change, including a drastic reorganization of personality," these can serve a "bridging function." Richard Natvig further believes that the Zar offered precisely that bridging function to the enslaved Africans carried into Ottoman territories. These women and men were suffering from demoralization and disease, and it was only natural that healing cults such as Zar and Bori would become a main source of comfort and support for them. Because such cult rituals were criticized by orthodox clerics and occasionally the Ottoman authorities, I have suggested here that their retention by Africans can also be seen as indicative of agency and defiance. Clearly, more work needs to be done on this not only in the African-Ottoman context but also with regard to diasporas of other formerly enslaved people, especially the Circassians.

5. Cited in Richard Natvig, "Some Notes on the History of the *Zar* Cult in Egypt," in I. M. Lewis, Ahmed Al-Safi and Sayyid Hurreiz (eds.), *Women's Medicine: The* Zar-Bori *Cult in Africa and Beyond*, Edinburgh: Edinburgh University Press, 1991: 181.

Another major theme in this book is the role of the Tanzimat-state in shaping the individual's experience of enslavement in the Ottoman Empire. In recent years the trend has been to portray states and empires in the long nineteenth century as the ever-centralizing, oppressing tool of the elites. Contrary to that, the case of Ottoman enslavement provides here sufficient evidence to argue that the state's growing interference in the slaver-enslaved relationship in fact benefited and protected the weaker partner in the relationship. The Tanzimat-state, I have tried to show, increasingly abandoned its traditional support of the slavers' ownership rights and gradually began to favor manumission claims put forth by the enslaved. The Ottoman government fully realized that freed persons were vulnerable and in need of protection, that is, placement in new jobs, reattachment, and patronage. Indeed, it was as protector and provider that the enslaved came to view the state; this was what they expected of it, this was what they held it up to.

There can hardly be any doubt that court records are the main key to the lives of the enslaved, perhaps the closest we shall ever get to hearing and imagining their voices. While extensively relying on court records for the reconstruction of voice and action, I have been keenly aware all along of the need to treat these sources carefully and with critical eyes. Nonetheless, it is in the courts that the life dramas of the enslaved unfolded. These stories are not imagined by skilled writers nor invented by gifted playwrights. They are real, and even if we cannot be completely sure of all the facts, we are here treading on solid ground. Even if the cases we read about in Ottoman court files are not fully representative of broader realities, they convey a sense of reality that unmistakably coheres with the information we are able to gather from a diverse list of other sources. By allowing a more flexible notion of criminalization, which is sociohistorically contextualized, we can extend the validity of the observations made here to a segment of the population well beyond the confines of the penal system.

Neither slavery as an institution, nor the slave trade, nor even slaves as a social category has been the focus of my endeavors here. Rather, the enslaved woman and the enslaved man, their personal experience of enslavement, and the way they dealt with their predicament have lain at the heart of this book. New and somewhat older approaches in social anthropology and cultural studies have made this shift in emphasis possible.

Also enabling has been the changing research environment, which demands a greater stress on the human aspects of social history than on its structural aspects. The sources were there all along, but only a fresh examination of them could yield new results and open new vistas. If the court system invites an analogy with the theater, then the main protagonists I wanted to put on the stage here are the enslaved men and women, young and old, African and Circassian, strong and weak, brave and timid, daring and conforming. Their lives deserve our attention, their suffering our compassion, their humanity our respect, and their defiance our admiration. By showing their strong humanity, but without intending to glorify them, I sense that they have emerged as the true heroes of this book.

BIBLIOGRAPHY

ARCHIVAL SOURCES

Prime Ministry's Archives, Istanbul, Başbakanlık Osmanlı Arşivi, or BOA [Republic of Turkey]
The series used are listed below. In references the series title is preceded by BOA.
Ayniyat defterleri/Meclis-i Vala'dan katl ve sirkate dair, vols. 470–502
   (1847–1866)
Cevdet/Dahiliye
Cevdet/Zaptiye
İrade/Dahiliye
İrade/Hariciye
İrade/Şura-yı Devlet
Meclis-i Vükela Mazbata ve İrade Dosyaları (Cabinet Papers)
Bab-ı Alı Evrak Odası (BEO)/Mühacirin Komisyonu (Refugees Commission)
Sadearet/Amedi Kalemi Evrakı
Sadearet/Umum Vilayat Evrakı
Yıldız Collection/Meclis-i Tanzimat defterleri (and other subsections)

Istanbul University Library
İstanbul Üniversitesi Kütüphanesi/Mss #T1072, Arifi Beyin Cidde Vali Kay-
   makamlığında bulunduğu zamana ait muhaberat-i resmiye mecmuası,
   9.1887–2.1890

Foreign Office (FO), Public Record Office, London, United Kingdom
The following series were used. In references the series is preceded by FO.
195
198/82/X/M 00518

541
881

The British Library, London, United Kingdom
Add MSS/Hekekyan Papers

Anti-Slavery Society (ASS), Rhodes House Library, Oxford, United Kingdom
"Anti-Slavery Society" is often preceded by "The British" or "International."

BOOKS AND ARTICLES

Abou-El-Haj, Rifaat Ali. *Formation of the Modern State: The Ottoman Empire, Six-teenth to Eighteenth Centuries*. Albany: State University of New York Press, 1991.

Agmon, Iris. *The Family in Court: Legal Culture and Modernity in Late Ottoman Palestine*. Syracuse, N.Y.: Syracuse University Press, 2005.

Austen, Ralph. "The Mediterranean Islamic Slave Trade Out of Africa: A Tentative Census." *Slavery and Abolition*, 13/1 (1992): 214–248.

——. "The 19th Century Islamic Slave Trade from East Africa (Swahili and Red Sea Coasts): A Tentative Census." In William Gervase Clarence-Smith (ed.), *The Economics of the Indian Ocean Slave Trade in the Nineteenth Century*. Special issue of *Slavery and Abolition*, 9/3 (1988): 21–44.

Ayyıldız, Erol, and Osman Çetin. "Slavery and Islamization of Slaves in Ottoman Society according to Canonical Registers of Bursa between the Fifteenth and Eighteenth Centuries." Unpublished report on work in progress, 1996.

Baer, Gabriel. *Egyptian Guilds in Modern Times*. Jerusalem: Israel Oriental Society, 1964.

——. "Slavery and Its Abolition." In Baer, *Studies in the Social History of Modern Egypt*. Chicago: University of Chicago Press, 1969, pp. 161–189.

——. "The *Tanzimat* in Egypt: The Penal Code." In Baer, *Studies in the Social History of Modern Egypt*. Chicago: University of Chicago Press, 1969, pp. 109–132.

——. "The Transition from Traditional to Western Criminal Law in Turkey and Egypt." *Studia Islamica*, 45 (1977): 139–158.

Barkey, Karen. *Bandits and Bureaucrats: The Ottoman Route to State Centralization*. Ithaca, N.Y.: Cornell University Press, 1994.

Boddy, Janice. *Wombs and Alien Spirits: Women, Men, and the Zar Cult in Northern Sudan*. Madison: University of Wisconsin Press, 1989.

Bourguignon, Erika. "World Distribution and Patterns of Possession States." In Raymond Prince (ed.), *Trance and Possession States*. Proceedings [of the] Second Annual Conference, R. M. Bucke Memorial Society, Montreal, 4–6 March 1966. [Montreal: R. M. Bucke Memorial Society, 1968], pp. 3–34.

Brunschvig, R. "ʿAbd." In *Encyclopaedia of Islam*. 2nd ed. Leiden: E. J. Brill, 1960, vol. 2, p. 24 ff.

Cohen, Robin. "Diasporas and the Nation-State: From Victims to Challengers." *International Affairs*, 72 (1996): 507–520.

——. *Global Diasporas: An Introduction*. Seattle: University of Washington Press, 1997.

Constantinides, Pamela. "The History of *Zar* in the Sudan: Theories of Origin, Recorded Observation and Oral Tradition." In Lewis, Al-Safi, and Hurreiz, *Women's Medicine*, 83–99.

Davis, David Brion. "Looking at Slavery from Broader Perspectives." The 2001 American Historical Review Forum. *American Historical Review*, 105/2 (2001): 452–484 (including contributions by Peter Kolchin and Stanley Engerman).

Deringil, Selim. " 'They Live in a State of Nomadism and Savagery': The Late Ottoman Empire and the Post-Colonial Debate." *Comparative Studies in Society and History*, 45/2 (April 2003): 311–342.

——. *The Well-Protected Domains: Ideology and the Legitimation of Power in the Ottoman Empire, 1876–1909*. London: I. B. Tauris, 1998.

Doumani, Beshara (ed.). *Family History in the Middle East Household, Property, and Gender*. Albany: State University of New York Press, 2003.

Duben, Alan, and Cem Behar. *Istanbul Households: Marriage, Family, and Fertility, 1880–1940*. Cambridge: Cambridge University Press, 1991.

Durugönül, Esma. "The Invisibility of Turks of African Origin and the Construction of Turkish Cultural Identity: The Need for a New Historiography." *Journal of Black Studies*, 33/3 (January 2003): 281–294.

Eickelman, Dale F. *The Middle East and Central Asia—An Anthropological Approach*. 3rd ed. Upper Saddle River, N.J.: Prentice-Hall, 1998.

Erdem, Y. Hakan. *Slavery in the Ottoman Empire and Its Demise, 1800–1909*. London: Macmillan, 1996.

Ertuğ, Hasan Ferit. "Musahib-i Sani-i Hazret-i Şehr-Yari Nadir Ağa'nın Hatıratı-I." *Toplumsal Tarih*, 49 (October 1998): 7–15.

Fahmy, Khaled. *All the Pasha's Men: Mehmed Ali, His Army and the Making of Modern Egypt*. Cambridge: Cambridge University Press, 1997.

Faroqhi, Suraiya. "The Ruling Elite between Politics and 'the Economy.' " In Halil Inalcik and Donald Quataert (eds.), *An Economic and Social History of the Ottoman Empire, 1300–1914*. Cambridge: Cambridge University Press, 1994, pp. 545–575.

——. *Stories of Ottoman Men and Women*, Istanbul: Eren, 2002

Ferchiou, Sophie. "The Possession Cults of Tunisia: A Religious System Functioning as a System of Reference and a Social Field for Reforming Actions." In Lewis, Al-Safi, and Hurreiz, *Women's Medicine*.

Findley, Carter V. *Bureaucratic Reform in the Ottoman Empire*. Princeton, N.J.: Princeton University Press, 1980.

——. *Ottoman Civil Officialdom: A Social History*. Princeton, N.J.: Princeton University Press, 1989.

Fisher, Alan. "Chattel Slavery in the Ottoman Empire: Some Preliminary Considerations." In John Ralph Willis (ed.). *Slaves and Slavery in Muslim Africa*. London: Frank Cass, 1985.

Flaubert, Gustave. *Voyage en Egypt : Édition integrale du manuscrit original*. Ed. Pierre-Marc de Biasi. Paris: B. Grasset, 1991. For an English translation, see

Flaubert in Egypt, a Sensibility on Tour. Trans. and ed. Francis Steegmuller. Chicago: Academy Chicago Press, 1979.

Geertz, Clifford. *Works and Lives: The Anthropologist as Author.* Stanford, CA: Stanford University Press, 1988.

Ghazzal, Zouhair. "Discursive Formations and the Gap between Theory and Practice in Ottoman Shariʿa Law." Paper submitted to the Second Joseph Schacht Conference on Theory and Practice in Islamic Law, Granada, December 1997.

Güneş, Günver. "Kölelikten Özgürlüğe: İzmir'de Zenciler ve Zenci Folkloru." *Toplumsal Tarih,* 11/62 (February 1999): 4–10.

Hathaway, Jane. *The Politics of Households in Ottoman Egypt: The Rise of the Qazdaglis.* Cambridge: Cambridge University Press, 1997.

———. *A Tale of Two Factions: Myth, Memory, and Identity in Ottoman Egypt and Yemen.* Albany: State University of New York, 2003.

Heyd, Uriel. *Studies in Old Ottoman Criminal Law.* Ed. V. L. Ménage. Oxford: Clarendon Press, 1973.

Hilal, ʿImad Ahmad. *Al-Bagaya fi Misr: Dirasa tarikhiyya ijtimaʿiyya, 1834–1949.* Cairo: Al- ʿArabi li-n-nashr wa-t-tawaziʿ, 2001.

———. *Ar-raqiq fi Misr fi-l-qarn at-tasiʿ ashar.* Cairo: Al-ʿArabi, 1999.

Hogendorn, Jan S. "The Location of the 'Manufacture' of Eunuchs." In Miura Toru and John Edward Philips (eds.), *Slave Elites in the Middle East: A Comparative Study.* London: Kegan Paul International, 2000, pp. 41–68.

Hunter, F. Robert. *Egypt under the Khedives, 1805–1879.* Pittsburgh: University of Pittsburgh Press, 1984.

Hunwick, John. "Black Africans in the Mediterranean World: Introduction to a Neglected Aspect of the African Diaspora." In Elizabeth Savage (ed.), *The Human Commodity: Perspectives on the Trans-Saharan Slave Trade.* London: Frank Cass, 1992, pp. 5–38.

———. "Islamic Law and Polemics over Race and Slavery in North and West Africa (16th–19th Century)." In Shaun E. Marmon (ed.), *Slavery in the Islamic Middle East.* Princeton, N.J.: Markus Wiener, 1999, pp. 43–68.

———. "The Religious Practices of Black Slaves in the Mediterranean Islamic World." In Paul E. Lovejoy (ed.), *Slavery on the Frontiers of Islam.* Princeton, N.J.: Markus Wiener, 2004, pp. 149–172.

Hurreiz, Sayyid. "*Zar* as Ritual Psychodrama: From Cult to Club." In Lewis, Al-Safi, and Hurreiz, *Women's Medicine,* 147–155.

Islamoğlu, Huri, and Çağlar Keyder. "Agenda for Ottoman History." In Huri Islamoğlu-Inan (ed.), *The Ottoman Empire and the World Economy.* Cambridge: Cambridge University Press, 1987, pp. 42–62.

Jennings, Ronald. "Black Slaves and Free Slaves in Ottoman Cyprus, 1590–1640." *Journal of the Economic and Social History of the Orient (JESHO),* 30/3 (1987): 286–302.

———. *Christians and Muslims in Ottoman Cyprus and the Mediterranean World, 1571–1640.* New York: New York University Press, 1993.

Kiev, Ari (ed.). *Magic, Faith and Healing: Studies in Primitive Psychiatry.* Northvale, N.J.: Jason Aronson, 1996.

Kunt, Metin. *All the Sultan's Servants: The Transformation of Ottoman Provincial Government, 1550–1650.* New York: Columbia University Press, 1983.

Lee, Everett S. "A Theory of Migration." *Demography,* 3/1 (1966): 47–57.

Lewis, I. M. "*Zar* in Context: The Past, the Present and the Future of an African Healing Cult." In Lewis, Al-Safi, and Hurreiz, 1–16.

Lewis, I. M., Ahmed Al-Safi, and Sayyid Hurreiz (eds.). *Women's Medicine: The Zar-Bori Cult in Africa and Beyond.* Edinburgh: Edinburgh University Press, 1991.

Lopashich, Alexander. "A Negro Community in Yugoslavia." *Man,* 58 (1958): 169–173.

Lovejoy, Paul E. "Commercial Sectors in the Economy of the Nineteenth-Century Central Sudan: The Trans-Saharan Trade and the Desert-Side Salt Trade." *African Economic History,* 13 (1984): 87–95.

——. "Identifying Enslaved Africans in the African Diaspora." In Lovejoy (ed.), *Identity in the Shadow of Slavery.* London: Continuum, 2000.

——, (ed.). *Slavery on the Frontiers of Islam.* Princeton, N.J.: Markus Wiener, 2004, chap. 1.

——, (ed.). *Transformations in Slavery: A History of Slavery in Africa.* Cambridge: Cambridge University Press, 2000.

Lovejoy, Paul E., and David V. Trotman (eds.). *Trans-Atlantic Dimensions of Ethnicity in the African Diaspora.* London: Continuum, 2003.

Lûtfi, Ahmet. *Mirat-ı adalet.* Istanbul, İstanbul:Kitapçı Ohannes, 1304 [1886 or 1887]

Makdisi, Ussama. "Ottoman. Orientalism." *American Historical Review,* 107/3 (June 2002): 768–796.

Martal, Abdullah. "Afrika'dan İzmir'e: Izmir'de Bir Köle Misafirhanesi." *Kebikeç,* 10 (2000): 171–186.

McKnight, Kathryn Joy. "'*En su tierra lo aprendió*': An African Curandero's Defense before the Cartagena Inquisition." *Colonial Latin American Review,* 12/1 (June 2003): 63–85.

Miller, Joseph C. "Retention, Re-invention, and Remembering: Restoring Identities through Enslavement in Africa and under Slavery in Brazil." In José C. Curto and Paul E. Lovejoy (eds), *Enslaving Connections: Changing Cultures of Africa and Brazil during the Era of Slavery.* Amherst, N.Y.: Prometheus/Humanity Books, 2003, pp. 81–121.

——(ed.). *Slavery and Slaving in World History: A Bibliography.* 2 vols. Armonk, N.Y.: M. E. Sharpe, 1999.

Miller, Ruth Austin. *From Fikh to Fascism: The Turkish Republican Adoption of Mussolini's Criminal Code in the Context of Late Ottoman Legal Reform.* Unpublished Ph.D. dissertation, Princeton University, June 2003.

Mirzai, Behnaz A. "African Presence in Iran: Identity and Its Reconstruction in the 19th and 20th Centuries." *Revue française d'histoire d'outre-mer* (*RFHOM*), 89/336–337 (2002): 229–246.

Al-Misri, Fatima. *Az-Zar: Dirasa nafsiyya wa-anthrupolujiyya.* Cairo: Al-Hay'a al-Misriyya al-ʿAmma li-l-Kitab, 1975.

Mitchell, Timothy. *Colonizing Egypt.* Cambridge: Cambridge University Press, 1988.

Modarressi, Taghi. "The Zar Cult in South Iran." In Raymond Prince (ed.), *Trance and Possession States*. Proceedings [of the] Second Annual Conference, R. M. Bucke Memorial Society, Montreal, 4–6 March 1966l: [Montreal: R. M. Bucke Memorial Society, 1968], pp. 149–155.

Montana, Ismael Musa. "Ahmad ibn al-Qadi al-Timbuktawi on the *Bori* Ceremonies of Tunis." In Lovejoy, *Slavery on Frontiers*, 173–198.

Mufwene, Salikoko S. *The Ecology of Language Evolution*. Cambridge: Cambridge University Press, 2001.

Natvig, Richard. "Some Notes on the History of the *Zar* Cult in Egypt." In Lewis, Al-Safi, and Hurreiz, *Women's Medicine*: 178–188.

Owen, Roger. *The Middle East and the World Economy, 1800–1914*. Rev. ed. London: I. B. Tauris, 1993. See esp. "Introduction: The Middle East Economy in the Period of So-Called 'Decline,' 1500–1800," 1–23.

Özel, Oktay. "Population Changes in Ottoman Anatolia during the 16th and 17th Centuries: The 'Demographic Crisis' Reconsidered." *International Journal of Middle East Studies (IJMES)*, 36/2 (May 2004): 183–205.

Parlatır, İsmail. *Tanzimat edebiyatında kölelik*. Ankara: Türk Tarih Kurumu Basımevi, 1987.

Patterson, Orlando. *Slavery and Social Death*. Cambridge: Harvard University Press, 1982.

Peirce, Leslie. *Morality Tales: Law and Gender in the Ottoman Court of Aintab*. Berkeley: University of California Press, 2003.

Philips, John Edward. "Slavery as a Human Institution." A paper presented at the Slavery, Islam, and Diaspora conference, York University, Toronto, 23 October 2003.

Price, Richard. "Invitation to Historians: Practices of Historical Narrative." *Rethinking History*, 5:3 (2001): 357–365. The paper was originally delivered in Boston, 4 January 2001.

——. "The Miracle of Creolization: A Retrospective." *New West Indian Guide*, 75 (2001): 35–64.

——. "Paramaribo, 1710: Violence and Hope in a Space of Death." *CommonPlace: The Interactive Journal of Early American Life*, 3/4 (July 2003). http:// commonplace.dreamhost.com//vol-03/no-04/paramaribo/index.shtml

Prudent, Lambert-Félix, and Ellen M. Schnepel. "Introduction." In Prudent and Schnepel (eds.), *Creole Movements in the Francophone Orbit*. Special issue of the *International Journal of the Sociology of Language*, 102 (1993): 5–13.

Resmi, Ahmet Efendi. *Hamîletü'l-Kübera*. Ed. Ahmet Nezihi Turan. Istanbul: Kitabevi, 2000.

Richardson, David (ed.). *Routes to Slavery: Direction, Ethnicity, and Mortality in the Transatlantic Slave Trade*. London: Frank Cass, 1997.

Rick, Thomas M. "Slaves and Slave Traders in the Persian Gulf, 18th and 19th Centuries: An Assessment." In William Gervase Clarence-Smith (ed.),. *The Economics of the Indian Ocean Slave Trade in the Nineteenth Century*. Special issue of *Slavery and Abolition*, 9/3 (1988): 60–70.

Robertson, Claire C., and Martin A. Klein (eds.). *Women and Medicine in Africa.* Madison: University of Wisconsin Press, 1983.

Sagaster, Börte. *"Herren" und "Sklaven": Der Wandel im Sklavenbild türkischer Literaten in der Spätzeit des Osmanischen Reiches.* Wiesbaden: Harrasowitz, 1997.

Salama, Ovadia. "Avadim be-va'alutam shel Yehudim ve Notsrim bi-Yerushalayim ha-Othmanit" (Slaves held by Jews and Christians in Ottoman Jerusalem). *Katedra,* 49 (September 1988): 64–75 (in Hebrew).

Salman, Michael. *The Embarrassment of Slavery: Controversies over Bondage and Nationalism in the American Colonial Philippines.* Manila: Ateneo de Manila University Press, 2001.

Seng, Yvonne. "A Liminal State: Slavery in Sixteenth-Century Istanbul." In Shaun E. Marmon (ed.), *Slavery in the Islamic Middle East.* Princeton, N.J.: Markus Wiener, 1999, pp. 25–42.

Sengers, Gerda. *Women and Demons: Cult Healing in Islamic Egypt.* Leiden: E. J. Brill, 2003.

Şeni, Nora. "Fashion and Women's Clothing in the Satirical Press of Istanbul at the End of the 19th Century." In S. Tekeli (ed.), *Women in Modern Turkish Society.* London: Zed Books, 1994, pp. 25–45.

———. "Ville Ottomane et représentation du Corps Féminin." *Les Temps Modernes* (July–August 1984): 66–95.

Shaham, Ron. "Masters, Their Freed Slaves, and the *Waqf* in Egypt (Eighteenth–Twentieth Centuries)." *Journal of the Economic and Social History of the Orient (JESHO),* 43/2 (2000): 162–188.

Soulodre-La France, Renée. "Socially Not So Dead! Slave Identities in Bourbon Nueva Granada." *Colonial Latin American Review,* 10/1 (June 2001): 87–103.

Spaulding, Jay. "Slavery, Land Tenure, and Social Class in the Northern Turkish Sudan." *International Journal of African Historical Studies,* 15/1 (1982): 1–20.

Stouffer, Samuel A. "Intervening Opportunities and Competing Migrants." *Journal of Regional Studies,* 2 (1960): 1–26.

Stuart, Stephanie. "Dominican Patwa—Mother Tongue or Cultural Relic?" In Lambert-Félix Prudent and Ellen M. Schnepel (eds.), *Creole Movements in the Francophone Orbit.* Special issue of the *International Journal of the Sociology of Language,* 102 (1993): 57–72.

Sweet, James H. *Recreating Africa: Culture, Kinship, and Religion in the African-Portuguese World, 1441–1770.* Chapel Hill: University of North Carolina Press, 2003.

Taner, Tahir. "Tanzimat devrinde ceza hukuku." In *Tanzimat I: Yüzüncü yıldönümü münasebetiyle.* Ankara: Maarif Vekaleti, 1940, pp. 221–232.

Testart, Alain. *L'esclave, la dette et le pouvoir: Études de sociologie comparative.* Paris: Édition Errance, 2001.

Toledano, Ehud R. "The Concept of Slavery in Ottoman and Other Muslim Societies: Dichotomy or Continuum?" In Miura Toru and John Edward Philips (eds.), *Slave Elites in the Middle East and Africa: A Comparative Study.* London: Kegan Paul International, 2000, pp. 159–176.

———. "The Emergence of Ottoman-Local Elites (1700–1800): A Framework for Research." In I. Pappé and M. Ma'oz (eds.), *Middle Eastern Politics and Ideas: A History from Within*. London: Tauris Academic Studies, 1997, pp. 145–162.

———. "The Legislative Process in the Ottoman Empire in the Early *Tanzimat* Period: A Footnote." *International Journal of Turkish Studies*, 11/2 (1980): 99–108.

———. "Mehmed Ali Pasha." In *Encyclopaedia of Islam*. 2nd ed. Leiden: E. J. Brill, 1991, vol. 7, pp. 423–431.

———. *Slavery and Abolition in the Ottoman Middle East*. Seattle: University of Washington Press, 1998.

Troutt Powell, Eve M. "Will That Subaltern Ever Speak? Finding African Slaves in the Historiography of the Middle East." In Israel Gershoni, Amy Singer, and Y. Hakan Erdem (eds.), *Middle East Historiographies Narrating the Twentieth Century*. Seattle: University of Washington Press, 2006.

Tucker, Judith. *Women in Nineteenth-Century Egypt*. Cambridge: Cambridge University Press, 1985.

Veldet, Hıfzı. "Kanunlaştırma hareketleri ve Tanzimat." In *Tanzimat I: Yüzüncü yıldönümü münasebetiyle*. Ankara: Maarif Vekaleti, 1940, pp. 139–209.

Vertovec, Steven. "Three Meanings of 'Diaspora,' Exemplified among South Asian Religions." *Diaspora*, 6/3 (Winter 1997): 277–299.

Vryonis, Speros, Jr. "Religious Changes and Patterns in the Balkans, 14th–16th Centuries." In Henrik Birnbaum and Speros Vyronis, Jr. (eds.), *Aspects of the Balkans: Continuity and Change*. The Hague: Mouton, 1972, pp. 151–176.

Yalman, Ahmed Emin. *Yakın tarihte gördüklerim ve geçirdiklerim*. Vol. 1, *1888–1918*. Istanbul: Yenilik Basımevi, 1970, pp. 13–14.

Yazbak, Mahmoud. *Haifa in the Late Ottoman Period, 1864–1914: A Muslim Town in Transition*. Leiden: E. J. Brill, 1998.

Ze'evi, Dror. *An Ottoman Century: The District of Jerusalem in the 1600s*. Albany: State University of New York Press, 1996.

———. "The Use of Ottoman Shari'a Court Records as a Source for Middle Eastern Social History: A Reappraisal." *Islamic Law and Society*, 5/1 (1998): 35–56.

Zelinsky, Wilbur. "Coping with the Migration Turnaround: The Theoretical Challenge." *International Regional Science Review*, 2/2 (1977): 175–178.

———. "The Demographic Transition: Changing Patterns of Migration." In P. Morrison (ed.), *Population Science in the Service of Mankind*. Liège: International Union for the Scientific Study of Population, 1979, pp. 165–188.

———. "The Impasse in Migration Theory: A Sketch Map for Potential Escapees." In Peter A. Morrison (ed.), *Population Movements: Their Forms and Functions in Urbanization and Development*. Brussels: Ordina, 1983, pp. 21–49.

Zilfi, Madeline C. "Goods in the *Mahalle*: Distributional Encounters in Eighteenth-Century Istanbul." In Donald Quataert (ed.), *Consumption Studies and the History of the Ottoman Empire, 1550–1922: An Introduction*. Albany: State University of New York Press, 2000, pp. 289–311.

———. "Servants, Slaves, and the Domestic Order in the Ottoman Middle East." *Hawwa*, 2/1 (2004): 1–33.